Personal Relationships

For Eva

Personal Relationships

Love, Identity, and Morality

Hugh LaFollette

BLACKWELL
Oxford UK & Cambridge USA

Copyright © Hugh LaFollette, 1996

The right of Hugh LaFollette to be identified as author of this work has been asserted in accordance with the Copyright, Designs and Patents Act 1988.

First published 1996
2 4 6 8 10 9 7 5 3 1

Blackwell Publishers Inc.
238 Main Street
Cambridge, Massachusetts 02142, USA

Blackwell Publishers Ltd
108 Cowley Road
Oxford OX4 1JF
UK

Library of Congress Cataloging-in-Publication Data

LaFollette, Hugh, 1948–
Personal relationships : love, identity, and morality / Hugh LaFollette.
p. cm.
Includes bibliographical references and index.
ISBN 0-631-19684-6 (hbk. : acid-free paper). – ISBN 0-631-19685-4
(pbk. : acid-free paper)
1. Interpersonal relations. I. Title.
HM132.L25 1996
158′.2–dc20   95–6420
                                                      CIP

British Library Cataloguing in Publication Data

A CIP catalogue record for this book is available from the British Library.

Typeset in 11 on 13pt Bembo
by Best-set Typesetter Ltd., Hong Kong

This book is printed on acid-free paper

Contents

Preface

To live is to have personal relationships. We all have parents; most of us have friends and siblings; some are married and have children. Most of us think these relationships are extremely valuable, although they occasionally result in frustration, anger, or pain. Many of us spend considerable time with our families and exert substantial physical and psychological energy thinking and worrying about friendship, love, and marriage.

However, we needn't be wise men or soothsayers to recognize that despite our best efforts, close personal relationships are often difficult to establish and arduous to maintain. Many of our personal relationships are not especially close: we don't revel in the company of friends and family; we don't talk with them about what is important; we don't sensitively listen to their problems, observations, or speculations; we don't make serious efforts to promote their interests. Moreover, many of our relationships are transitory: if our friends criticize us, cease to be fun or funny, or start to get on our nerves, we may withdraw temporarily or forever.

True intimacy – that is a relationship of a different color. Most of us find it exacting to create and sustain intimate relationships where we share our lives, thoughts, fears, and aspirations. Some (many?) married couples never achieve intimacy. Those who do may have difficulty sustaining it. A cursory glance at the divorce rates should give the most optimistic among us cause for concern, especially when we realize that a not insignificant portion of those couples who remain married are not fully intimate either.

These problems are not confined to romantic relationships. Many of us have watched our friends transmute into mere acquaintances, distant strangers, or even bitter enemies. If friends strongly disagree about matters which are deeply important to each, then the demise of the friendship is not surprising. In other cases, though, our friendships deteriorate because neither of us is willing or able to do what we need do to sustain them. Why is it difficult to create and sustain personal relationships? Presumably we yearn for intimacy. And, at first glance, it does not seem as if it should be especially difficult to be friends, lovers, or to have a family. Something is awry. If friendship and love are as valuable as we think, and intimate relationships are relatively easy to form and retain, then why are they so imperiled? Several reasons come to mind.

Perhaps personal relationships are valuable, but not in the ways or for the reasons most of us suppose. For instance, I think personal relationships are valuable because they make us better people, not because they make us feel good. If so, those who enter relationships to feel good will likely fail to gain what intimacy can best provide; consequently, they have little interest in maintaining them.

Perhaps they are valuable but are more taxing to initiate and maintain than we first thought. Hence, many of us are unwilling to invest our time and energy in them. Like those of us too lazy or undisciplined to take care of our health, we may lack the discipline and drive to sustain our relationships.

Perhaps personal relationships are valuable and we want to make them work, but we just don't know how. That is, we may misunderstand human nature, and thus conceive of ourselves and relationships in ways which militate against or undermine intimacy. Or, as is typically the case with complex issues, the explanation is likely some combination of these and other influences.

Given our interest in personal relationships you would think we would want to know why close relationships are imperiled. To some extent we do: large numbers of us purchase pop psychology books on love, friendship, and marriage; many of us discuss (complain about?) our interpersonal problems; some seek professional counselling. This indicates a general willingness to think about and work on our relationships. Unfortunately, our beliefs about and images of ourselves and personal relationships are a malformed amalgam forged from fairy tales, television counsellors, and soap operas. These create expectations which are neither achievable nor ultimately desirable. We can escape their sway only by supplanting them with a better understanding of persons and personal relationships.

As it turns out, many of our flawed images of persons and relationships spring, at least in part, from some widespread philosophical views of persons, relationships, and morality – views which have become embedded in our culture. Many of us were taught, for example, that (1) persons and personal relationships are relatively static; (2) that each person knows herself better than others know her; and closely related, (3) that each of us is, at core, identified with our minds. Many of us were also taught that (4) there is no connection between being moral and being a good friend; some of us were even taught that morality and personal relationships conflict. I think each of these views is mistaken. In this book I will expose the weaknesses of these views and go some distance toward giving a more accurate account of the self, personal relationships, the nature of morality, and the interplay of morality and personal relationships.

So as not to mislead the reader, let me make it clear at the outset that this is a philosophy book. It is not an academic version of *How to Win Friends*... or of *Zen and the Art of Personal Maintenance*. I pose philosophical questions and I discuss them philosophically. But it is philosophical in the broadest sense: I take the common understanding of personal relationships seriously; I make numerous references to social science research; and I try to show the relevance of the philosophical arguments to practical concerns.

There are numerous issues here ripe for philosophical picking. Yet until recently relatively few philosophers have labored in these fertile fields. Even now some philosophers consider these issues as lying, at best, on the borders of philosophy. However, I will argue that careful reflection on personal relationships can illuminate traditional philosophical problems in ethics, epistemology, and metaphysics, most especially: the nature of the emotions, the self, and the relation between morality and self-interest.

To provide the reader with some flavor of this book, I will illustrate how mistaken images of the self can cloud our understanding of personal relationships, by briefly discussing the ways many people describe, talk, and think about the demise of personal relationships. Although this example will be less than convincing to some, it is plausible even in truncated form. Those presently unconvinced will, I hope, be persuaded by the end of part I.

When Relationships Fail

When long-term relationships languish or fail people frequently ask "What happened?" Our reasons for inquiring diverge widely. We may wish to know how we can restore an imperiled but worthwhile relationship. Perhaps we wish to identify the problem so that we don't duplicate it in our other relationships. Or we may simply be nosey, wanting to engage in the latest round of juicy gossip.

Whatever the reason, most of us think this is a question worth asking, a question for which there is often a clear answer. Doubtless there are significant questions we can ask when a seemingly meaningful relationship falters (e.g. "How, if at all, could they have interacted more satisfactorily?", "Are there lessons we can learn from the demise of this relationships?" etc.). If these are the questions our interlocutor wants answered, fine. Unfortunately, the question, as typically understood, implies dubious assumptions which reflect and promote a mistaken and detrimental view of persons and personal relationships.

Consider other circumstances where we might sensibly ask "What happened to the . . . ?" You return from vacation to discover your house is in shambles. You naturally want to know what happened. Or if I discover my office desk in splinters, I would ask "What happened?" (while muttering the standard repertoire of obscenities).

When we ask what happened to our house or desk, we want to identify the external force(s) which damaged them. After all, houses and desks are enduring objects: they persist through time unless modified by external forces. By the same token, when most people ask "What happened to the relationship?", they want to know, at least in part, what force(s) intervened to damage or destroy it. They thereby show a *tendency* to conceive of personal relationships as static entities – like houses and furniture – which continue to exist unless some external force changes or destroys them.

This exemplifies our tendency to nominalize verbs, adjectives, or adverbs – and then treat these nominalizations as if they were standard nouns. English is a flexible, creative language which permits us to reconstruct most words in nominative form. We originally speak of beautiful objects or beautiful people and subsequently speak of "beauty". There is nothing wrong with talking about beauty as long as we remember that it is a feature of things and not some entity separable from those things. Similarly, there is nothing wrong with using the noun "laughter" as long as we remember that laughing is a way cognitively sophisticated creatures behave; it is not some entity those creatures possess.

However, we often forget these nominative forms are grammatical conveniences. Since we were taught in elementary school that nouns refer to objects, we start thinking of these nominalizations as if they were standard nouns. The results are sometimes innocuous, but in other cases quite dangerous. Nowhere is this mistake more likely or more detrimental than in our talk about personal relationships.

We begin by talking about two people loving or relating to one another, thereby indicating that relating is dynamic: something people *do*. That is as it should be: relating is active, not passive. We later come to speak derivatively of these people as having a *relationship*. That suggests that relationships are static, enduring objects like cars, VCRs, or computers – objects we have, objects we possess.

Of course most people would deny that they think relationships are static. But our language belies that claim. More importantly, so does our behavior. Regardless of what we might say, most of us have some propensity to think relationships will dissolve only if there are intervening causes: sickness, economic problems, sexual maladies, infidelity, etc. When a relationship ends, both participants and outside observers are wont to identify some problem, some intervening force, which caused the relationship's demise. They do not conclude as they should, that likely the best explanation is the simplest: the relationship ended because the partners no longer relate.

Dynamic systems, by their very nature, tend to cease unless they are constantly energized. Babies can die from traumatic injury – or from the absence of nourishment. Trees can die from lightening – or from the lack of water. Radios cease to play music if the amplifier malfunctions – or if there is no radio signal. Likewise for personal relationships. They are not enduring entities which persist barring external interference. Rather they survive only if something is done to sustain them, only if the two parties continually relate in meaningful ways.

Perceiving relationships as enduring objects rather than dynamic activities leads to trouble. We protect enduring objects by shielding them from corrosive external forces: we erect fences around our houses; we lock our doors. By the same token, we are likely to believe we can sustain relationships simply by protecting them from detrimental outside influences. We shield our spouses from attractive members of the opposite sex; we protect ourselves from financial ruin. But we may forget to relate.

Thus, our efforts at maintaining the relationship are often misdirected. We do what we should not, and fail to do what we should. If we fear "the other man" or "the other woman," we may demand that our partners not spend time with attractive members of the opposite sex – especially not in private. If we worry about financial security, we may work extra hours to boost our income. These efforts may protect the relationship from these particular external forces. But at a cost. If I try to protect my wife from attractive males, I may thereby eliminate a potential friend – for her, for me, and for us as a couple. If I work extra hours to attain financial security, I likely deprive us of valuable time together. Efforts to protect our relationship from financial insecurity or infidelity take time and energy; these efforts may well divert our attention from each other and from our mutual interests and projects. Consequently, we should not be surprised if our relationships founder, or continue in less than satisfactory ways. Yet, when they do fail, we frantically search for the cause: another person, a problem at work, financial troubles, etc. If we find a simple cause we are satisfied; if we cannot, we conclude the cause is one we cannot identify. We refuse to recognize the dynamic nature of personal relationships and what that implies. We pay for our ignorance. If we are under the influence of this model of relationships, we are unlikely to do what we need to maintain a strong and viable pattern of relating.

The Issues

As the succeeding section suggests, a central thesis of this book is that standard accounts of the self are mistaken because they treat the self and interpersonal relations as things. If, instead, we understood the self as an acting physical organism we could avoid some of the problems which plague intimate relationships. During the remainder of Part I, I will, among other things, develop and defend an activity view of the self.

Other theses I shall advocate:

1 Many of us confuse affection or attraction with love. Our failure to appreciate the differences between love and attraction may lead us into unsatisfying, detrimental relationships.
2 We are habitual creatures. Thinking, emotions, and morality are all habits. Habits, though, are not mere repetitions which cannot be changed or modified. Rather they are complex patterns of dispositions through which we interact with our environment and with other people. These habits can be changed; reason can prompt and direct these changes. Reason typically changes behavior indirectly.

It audits past behavior and subsequently shapes and redirects our habits, making them more productive, more meaningful. Reason does not standardly dictate how we should behave.

3   Morality and personal relationships are mutually supportive. Learning to care about friends and family typically makes us more sensitive and responsive to the needs of others, including strangers. We are thus more likely to act morally. Conversely, learning to consider the interests of strangers typically makes us more cognizant of the interests and needs of friends and family. This is as Aristotle suggested: the best friends are people of good moral character and those of good moral character are capable of being the best friends.

Many of these claims run counter to popular views about the nature of ourselves and our relationships. Many of these popular beliefs are so deeply entrenched that they will be difficult to budge. No single argument will be sufficient to subvert them. However, I shall offer numerous arguments throughout the book, arguments which should, when taken as a whole, undermine these widespread beliefs.

I will begin by trying to explain more precisely what I mean by "close personal relationships," "love," "friendship," etc. At first glance that sounds about as exciting as oatmeal. Nonetheless, I am convinced that many of our problems in establishing and sustaining personal relationships arise because we are confused about the nature of close relationships.

Acknowledgements

Earlier versions of five chapters have previously appeared in print. Portions of chapters 7 and 8 appeared in "Honesty and Intimacy" in *The Journal of Social and Personal Relationships*, 1986. Thanks to George Graham, who co-authored that paper. Portions of chapters 9 and 10 appeared in "Real Men," which was published in *Rethinking Masculinity*, edited by Larry May and Robert Strikwerda (Rowman and Allenheld, 1993). Finally, portions of chapter 13 were published under the title "Personal Relationships" in Peter Singer's *A Companion to Ethics* (Blackwell, 1991).

Thanks to Steve Smith, Blackwell editor, for his continuing assistance and encouragement. Thanks, too, to Niall Shanks, Peter Singer, and Robert Strikwerda for helpful comments on individual chapters of the book. I also want to thank Anthony Ellis, Gordon Graham – and especially, Larry May, Lester Hunt, and John Hardwig – for thoughtful and detailed comments on early drafts of this book. Finally, I owe a special debt of gratitude to Eva LaFollette, not only for her patience, love, and support, but also for her astute philosophical and stylistic comments on successive drafts of this book.

Part I

The Nature and Value of Personal Relationships

What is a Personal Relationship?

I am married, have three children, parents, one sister, and numerous friends. I relate to them in ways I do not relate to others inhabiting my town, my state, my country, and my world. That partly explains why I consider these relationships personal: they are similar in the minimal sense that those to whom I relate are not strangers. However, they are profoundly different in other respects. I relate differently with my spouse than with my parents. I relate still differently with my friends than with my children. These relationships differ in origin, substance, style, and intensity. I was born into my family; I choose my spouse and friends. I share my body and checkbook with my spouse, but not with other friends. I am candid with some friends, guarded with others. I am carefree with some, solemn with others. In these respects my personal relationships have little in common. Doubtless the same is true of your relationships.

Why, then, do we consider these relationships personal? Is it *merely* that they are not with strangers? No. Strangers are people with whom I never interact. I have not seen, heard, or talked with most of the people in the world, nor will I ever. There are many other people of whom I am aware, but with whom I will never relate.

The Personal and the Impersonal

To those with whom I relate, I may relate personally or impersonally. Relationships are best conceptualized as lying along a continuum with personal relationships at one end and impersonal ones at the other. Likely no relationship is purely personal; probably few are purely impersonal. Rather, they are blends with those nearer the upper end of the continuum deemed personal, those nearer the lower end impersonal. By examining a relationship, we can determine which aspects are personal, which are impersonal, and whether, on balance, the relationship is personal or impersonal. For although few – if any – relationships are pure breeds, those lying near the extremes are profoundly different from one another. Here's how.

A relationship is impersonal if either party relates merely because the other fills a role or satisfies a particular need. Neither party cares who occupies the role or fulfills that need: she is concerned only that someone does, and does it well. I may not care who checks out my groceries; I may care only that someone does it competently. I may be unconcerned about who fixes my auto; I may wish only that someone repairs it for a reasonable price. And I may be content to tell my bad jokes to anyone, as long as she laughs at them. If so, I have an impersonal relationship with my mechanic, my grocer, and the person who hears my "jokes." It is a relationship because we interact; it is impersonal because we interact with each other as a means to our own ends.

However, this does not mean that purely impersonal relationships are necessarily bad: traders frequently do no harm to one another; they may well treat one another with a minimal level of respect. (Of course some impersonal relationships are abusive – e.g. master–slave relationships – but these are best understood and judged by criteria of justice. As such, they are beyond the scope of this inquiry.)

In contrast, a relationship is personal inasmuch as each person relates to the other as a unique individual; the other does not merely fill a role or satisfy a need. If Jane has a personal relationship with Sarah, it is not that Jane wants to have a relationship, and Sarah fills a particular, replaceable role; rather she wants a relationship *with Sarah*. Or, to state it concretely, Jane does not want to walk in the mountains, swap gossip, go to the theater, laugh with, or confide in just anyone; she does not want to be loved and respected by just anyone. She wants to go to the theater *with Sarah*; she wants to confide *in Sarah*; she wants to relate *to Sarah*.

That does not necessarily mean than Jane wants a gushy, touchy-feely, deeply intense relationship. Some personal relationships have that quality. But most – including most very good relationships – do not. Intense relationships may be highly valuable, but they are also emotionally exhausting. Thus, although the desire for a relationship may be deeply emotional, it need not be. Nor need this desire be fully conscious. Jane may simply gyrate toward Sarah at parties and seek her company after work. In short, when I say Jane wants a relationship with Sarah, I simply mean that she tends to put herself in positions where she relates to Jane in ways she does not relate to others.

Rigid vs. historical love

The claim that Jane wants to relate to Sarah as a unique individual is ambiguous. Jane may want to be with Sarah simply because she (Sarah) is the object of her (Jane's) care, not because Sarah is funny or kind or intelligent or moral. If so, Jane's attachment to Sarah is rigid: she wants to relate to the person named "Sarah," regardless of Sarah's traits, no matter how Sarah changes (Rorty 1993: 76). Conversely, Jane's relationship with Sarah could be historical: Jane may relate to Sarah as identified by her particular array of embodied traits. If so, Jane's relationship is based on who Sarah is – right now – as a historical creature.

Most of us have both types of relationships. Relationships with kin are typically rigid: we want to relate to our brother *because* he is our brother. We don't particularly care (or perhaps marginally care) what he is like. We want to relate to him even if he is boring, dull, or crude; after all, he is our brother.

On the other hand, relationships with friends and lovers tend to be historical. We befriend and romance people because of who they are, what they are like. We don't just relate to them as people rigidly identified by some proper names; we relate to them as particular, embodied, historical creatures. We relate to them because they are interesting or intelligent or funny or generous or empathetic – because of who they are.

Of course many relationships have both rigid and historical dimensions. For instance, we may come to like our brother for who he is – not merely because he is our brother; a relationship which was originally rigid thereby assumes a historical dimension. Conversely, after establishing a historical relationship with our friends and lovers, we might begin to relate to them rigidly. That is, we stay together not simply because we like each other, but also because they are our friends or spouses (much in the same way we relate to our brother because he is our brother). Perhaps some people maintain these friendships or marriages even though they no longer like their intimates: their historical attachment has transmuted into a rigid attachment.

5

Both rigid and historical relationships are personal inasmuch as each party does not merely fulfill some role or satisfy some need. But, in other respects, they differ profoundly. Understanding these differences helps illuminate the value of personal relationships, the nature of commitment, and the link between morality and personal relationships. I shall occasionally discuss rigid (extensionally defined) relationships to help illuminate these matters. However, the focus of this book will be on historical relationships. In the future, the reader should assume I am speaking of historical relationships unless I specifically indicate otherwise.

Persons and their traits

In a (historical) personal relationship each person relates to the other because of who she is. Since we typically describe another by identifying her traits, that might suggest Jane's desire for a relationship with Sarah can be exhaustively explained by listing Sarah's traits. Not so. Jane does not want to befriend someone who is funny, intelligent, and morally sensitive – traits Sarah just happens to have. Were that so, Sarah could be replaced by anyone with just those traits: Sarah would be a mere means to Jane's ends. But Sarah is no mere means. Jane wants to befriend *Sarah* in all her particularity. Jane wants a personal relationship.

Saying this might suggest that people are something other than their traits. But what, exactly, would this mean? Suppose, contrary to fact, we could completely describe a person's every trait, fully nuanced. That is, suppose we could *exhaustively* describe and explain her every act. In this non-realizable world what would we imply by saying "she is something other than her traits?' What else is there to know? What else is there to understand? What else is there to care for, to relate to?

Of course in an ordinary sense people are indisputably more than their traits: there will always be complexities of character and behavior which we can never completely describe or understand. Even if we could completely list her traits, understood abstractly, we would not entirely understand her. Identifying a person's traits will not allow us to exhaustively describe her; to assume it would is to misconceive human traits. As Owen Flanagan puts it: "Nor do we understand very well how traits, assuming they are individual dispositions, interact with one another in an overall psychological economy. In part our ignorance is due to that fact that within psychology itself we do not fully understand the nature of traits and dispositions, how they interact, and what typical varieties they contain." (Flanagan 1991: 11.)

Traits, we must remember, neither identify nor entail particular behaviors. Rather they identify tendencies or dispositions to behave. To call someone intelligent is not to say that she always acts intelligently; intelligent people occasionally make obtuse statements and behave injudiciously. To call someone morally sensitive is not to say she is always sensitive; sensitive people are occasionally callous. Rather, to call someone intelligent or morally sensitive is to say that she typically acts intelligently (or sensitively), in a wide variety of circumstances.

Thus, two people who are courageous, morally sensitive, or intelligent may not embody these traits in the same ways. Although Rose and Laura could both be intelligent, it would be ludicrous to assume that they were identical since each has the same trait. Rose might be a math whiz; Laura, a skilled screen-writer. Or, although Josh and Edwin might be morally sensitive, we should not assume they are similar, let alone identical. Josh might be especially concerned about world hunger; Edwin, about his elderly aunt. Even two people who are "moral saints" may not act similarly or be similarly motivated. "Even less does emphasis on some single philosophical principle provide a rich and satisfying portrait of the lives and character of King, Ghandi, Mother Teresa, Magda Trcomé, and least of all Oskar Schindler . . ." (Flanagan 1991: 7.)

Even when two people have the "same" traits, the manner or tone of their traits may vary. Two humorous people may exhibit their humor differently: one may be prone to raucous laughter; the other, to dry wit. Two generous people may embody their generosity differently: one may be generous with her money; the other, generous with her time. In short, to identify someone's traits is not to predict how she will act in each and every situation. Rather traits are after-the-fact descriptions of behavioral tendencies.

Furthermore, any attempt to completely identify someone with her traits masks the historical dimensions of "who she is." To fully understand someone, we should know not only her traits, but also how she has evolved. Our historical dimensions play an especially vital role in the conduct of our personal relationships. For instance, even if two people had exactly the same traits and tended to embody and exhibit them in the same ways (of course, even identical twins are not *identical*), we could still differentiate them by their histories: by the experiences they have had and the people with whom they relate and have related. This history marks a significant difference between these two people, especially for someone who has a personal relationship with only one of them.

Suppose Jane meets Sarah two years before she meets Ruth, Sarah's hypothetical double. Jane and Sarah develop a viable, healthy relationship. They talk, laugh – and perhaps cry – together. They also enjoy similar activities: talking philosophy, playing chess, hiking in the mountains, watching movies, or campaigning for some political cause or candidate. They now share knowledge, experiences, and memories; they have established patterns of relating; they have a history of trust. They are bound together in significant ways. Thus, although Sarah and Ruth have the "same" traits (say, they are both honest, funny, and generous), Jane's and Sarah's reservoir of experiences and their established patterns of relating differentiate Sarah and Ruth. Sarah is unique: she has experiences Ruth does not have; she has a relationship with Jane that Ruth does not have. Put differently, although Sarah shares many traits with Ruth, Sarah also has "relational properties," properties which arise from her experiences, relationships, and memories. Ruth does not share *these* properties, these traits. Had Jane met Ruth before she met Sarah, then Ruth might have had relational properties akin to those Sarah now has. But Jane did not meet Ruth before she met Jane; therefore Ruth does not have these properties.

Consequently, Jane would not drop Sarah as a friend simply because she met Ruth, who has similar traits. At least she would not do so if they had a genuinely personal relationship. Were Jane to abandon Sarah after meeting Ruth, then we should conclude that her relationship with Sarah was not personal, all appearances to the contrary. That is, Jane had wanted a relationship with someone who was funny, intelligent, and morally sensitive – and Sarah was available. Jane was not uniquely attracted to Sarah's particular embodiment of these traits; nor was she interested in Sarah's relational traits. Rather she was attracted to Sarah's behavioral traits, taken abstractly. Put differently, Jane wanted a trade relationship with a person – any person – who had these desired traits. Under the circumstances, Sarah would be correct to think: "Jane doesn't love me, she just loves my humor, intelligence, generosity, etc."

To summarize: personal relationships are not completely explained by an abstract listing of the partner's traits and hence that listing cannot provide the basis for a genuinely personal relationship. Nevertheless, as I shall explain more fully in chapters 3 and 4, traits do provide an especially significant reason why we like those we like.

Impersonal "personal" relationships

Doubtless you have noticed that on this account some relationships standardly described as personal will be more accurately described as impersonal. Marriages (or friendships) of convenience are nothing more than trade relationships in personal guise: the relationships exist only because each person finds the mutual exchange satisfactory. Both want a bowling partner, a sexual liaison, a housemate, or someone to listen to them; the other satisfies that need. However, if someone else would satisfy that need better, then both parties would gladly terminate their exchange and quickly realign with the more suitable partner.

Those whose relationships are primarily of this ilk will find little of practical relevance in this book. I do not discuss exchange relationships – not even exchange relationships which have the air of the personal. I am interested in genuinely personal relationships, and about what these can reveal concerning the nature of the self, the emotions, reason, and morality.

On the other hand, I am interested in understanding the full complement of personal relationships, even those which are only partially so. On the account offered here, some impersonal relationships may evolve personal dimensions. For instance, we will initially interact with an auto mechanic or the salesperson at a local bookstore in a purely impersonal way. But what is impersonal may take on an air of the personal. We may come to seek these individuals when we enter the store or shop, not necessarily because they are the most efficient, but because we enjoy chatting with them about the latest novel or the newest innovation in fuel injection. We may eventually turn to talk of politics, religion, and our families. We may develop an interest in them as particular persons, not merely as the providers of services. We thereby develop some personal attachment. These relationships, though not deeply personal, clearly have personal elements.

Close Relationships

Personal relationships, as defined above, are not necessarily healthy, loving, or valuable. They may be debilitating, contentious, and injurious. That is not an unwelcomed consequence of my view. To say that I have a personal relationship with another is just to say that I relate to them as a particular, unique, embodied individual. I might want to spend time with them, promote their interests, and make them happy; or I may want to shun them, restrict their interests, and do my best to make them miserable. In both cases we relate to the other as particular, embodied people. But in the latter cases we are not close. That is, in a non-close relationship Jane would not want to promote Sarah's interests, even though they relate personally. This is typically the case of two people who hate each other.

Close personal relationships, though, are marked by mutual desire to promote the other's interests. Of course the desire to promote Sarah's interest need not be Jane's foremost thought: she need not spend her waking hours wondering what she can now do for Sarah. That would be obsessive. Moreover, it puts undue emphasis on the role of conscious choice in the development and conduct of our close relationships. For example, we don't need to *decide* to be nice to our friends or to comfort our spouses. To be a (genuine) friend or spouse just is to do those things, and to do them habitually. If Sarah needs to discuss a problem, Jane does not normally say – not even to herself – that she will listen to Sarah so she can forward her interests. Rather, Jane wants to help Sarah, even if it is inconvenient.

Sarah will be likewise inclined to promote Jane's interests. This shows why theirs is not a trade relationship. Since one of Jane's interests is that Sarah's interests be promoted, then one of Jane's interests will be satisfied whenever Sarah's interests are satisfied. It shows why it is difficult to distinguish between egoism and altruism within close personal relationships. Neither Sarah nor Jane can straightforwardly exchange goods or benefits since each desires not only her own well-being, but also the well-being of the other.

Non-standard cases of close relationships

Paradigm close relationships are *reciprocal, voluntary* relationships. They are reciprocal inasmuch as each person has the other as one of her interests. They are voluntary inasmuch as each person chooses to relate to the other. Most marriages and friendships will be both reciprocal and voluntary. However, there are other relationships which, although typically deviations from this paradigm, are close relationships nonetheless. Let me briefly mention three types.

Parents and children Some close relationships are non-reciprocal: one party relates to the other because of the second person's uniquely embodied self *and* she has the other as one of her interests; the latter, however, does not reciprocate. The most common form of non-reciprocal relationship is a parent's relationship with her young child. The parent may deeply care for her young child, but the (very young) child cannot reciprocate. The child may smile, coo, and in other ways respond to her parent, but this does not indicate that she cares for the parent, let alone that she takes her parent's interests as one of her own. The child is incapable of having a personal relationship with her parent; certainly she cannot have a close relationship.

Parent–child relationships further depart from the paradigm in that they are not voluntary. The parents may voluntarily choose to have *a* child, but they do not choose to have *this* child. We select our friends for who they are. We do not know who a child is before she is born, and hence, who she is cannot be *the reason* for our relationship.

Finally, these relationships, are typically rigid rather than historical. That is, the parents love their child *because she is their child*, not because of the child's particular array of traits. Thus, it is not unusual for the parents of a mass murderer to love their son, despite his despicable behavior. After all, their love is not based on the child's traits, but on their blood ties to him. Nonetheless, these are close personal relationships. Nothing is gained by categorically denying that they are.

Indeed, a parent's love for a child is often thought to be one of the highest forms of caring and love, partly because it is unreciprocated and partly because it is rigid. That is, the parents love the child while expecting nothing in return; and they love the child come what may. A rigid, non-reciprocal love is crucial for rearing children, it is essential to prepare them for life as adults. But, while this model of love is entirely appropriate for parent–child relationships, it is not what we want or expect from friends, spouses, or lovers. These latter relationships are paradigmatically voluntary, reciprocal, and historical. And, as we shall see, that is why they are so valuable.

Understanding that parent–child relationships are non-reciprocal, non-voluntary, and rigid helps explain why grown children often have difficulty relating to their parents. After having a non-reciprocal, non-voluntary, rigid personal relationship for many years, both the parent and the child often have difficulty responding to the other as a friend. Both parent and chid are accustomed to being in a non-reciprocal relationship where they care for the other because of their blood ties, not because of who they are. Hence, it is difficult for *either* side to modify their old habits and establish new ways of relating. Those parents and children who can relate successfully as adults do so, I suspect, because some years ago their relationships took on a historical dimension and became (somewhat) reciprocal. For instance, parents who relate to their adolescent children because of their children's particular embodied traits (and not merely because they are *their* children) create conditions which make a more historical, reciprocal relationship between them and their grown children more likely.

Kinship Biological parents choose their children only in some attenuated sense. Children do not choose their parents in any sense. Likewise, none of us chooses our (biological) siblings, cousins, or other kin. But just as a parent's relationship with her child can be close and personal, even though it is neither voluntary nor reciprocal, a person's relations with wider family may also be close and personal. On the whole, though, relationships with wider kin are difficult to characterize, especially in mobile cultures in which there is little opportunity for sustained interactions.

Some relate to their kin in ways as impersonal as any trade relation. Others do not relate to their kin at all – not even impersonally. Still other people may care for their kin in some minimal way. That is, each may relate to kin *as kin* and neither know, nor care to know, who the other really is. Such relationships may be valuable, but they are, perhaps, only marginally personal.

In still other cases the relations between kin are unquestionably close and reciprocal. Sometimes this is serendipitous: two cousins happen to enjoy each other's company and likely would have been friends even were they not related by blood. In most cases, however, kin develop close relationships because they relate regularly. For example, at the prompting of parents, two cousins may spend weekends and summer vacations together. They subsequently come to care for each other in all their particularities; they develop a reservoir of shared experiences and memories which hold them together: they have a close relationship.

In general kin are more likely to relate closely if they relate regularly, and they typically relate regularly if they (or their parents) are part of an extended family that thinks kin should be close. Whether this belief is justifiable and, if so, *why*, are issues worthy of investigation, but are beyond the scope of this book.

Civic friendship   Citizens of the same community may also have some rudimentary form of friendship. They may have some minimal personal attachment to one other and they may take the interests of fellow citizens as their own. When this happens community members have a form of close relationship which is reciprocal, but not voluntary. It is reciprocal because each party takes the other's interests as one of her own; it is non-voluntary because she did not choose to relate to these persons who just happen to live in her community. Rather she relates to them because they live in her community.

Civic friendship, as it is called by Aristotle, can be a glue which "would seem to hold cities together" (1155a23). But whether it plays this positive role depends largely on the beliefs and dispositions of its citizens. Those who think they *ought* to take fellow citizens' interests as their own will be more likely to act in ways which make their interests coincident. To that extent, civil friendship, like close relations between kin, is more likely to develop if our upbringing and education encourage it.

These three types of relationship can be close even though they are deviations from the paradigm. Although interesting and valuable, these are not the focus of this book. I am concerned here with reciprocal, voluntary relationships. Moreover, I am especially interested in *historical* personal relationships. I will have nothing further to say about these or any other non-standard cases of personal relationship.

Placing My Account in Context

Aristotle's theory of friendship

Aristotle's account of civic friendship is but one element of his general theory of friendship. I will briefly outline that theory as developed in the *Nicomachean Ethics* (Aristotle 1985). His theory provides a historical context within which I can locate my account and from which I offer modifications and refinements. Discussing Aristotle's theory also provides an ideal opportunity to forward a principal thesis of this book.

Aristotle divides friendships into three categories: friendships of utility, friendships of pleasure, and complete friendships. Complete friendships are, as the name implies, the ideal form. Friendships of utility and pleasure are incomplete, although they are similar to the ideal in the minimal sense that friends "have goodwill to each other, wish good [for the other] and be aware of it. . . ." (Aristotle 1156a5). However, the exact nature of the well-wishing and the caring varies (Cooper 1980).

Ideal friendships   A complete friendship (or what Neera Badhwar calls an "end friendship") (1993: 16–18) occurs when two morally good people desire to be with each other because the "beloved is who he is . . ." (Aristotle, 1156a15). More particularly, "complete friendship is the friendship of good people similar in virtue, for they wish goods in the same way to each other insofar as they are good, and they are good in themselves." (Aristotle, 1156b7–33.) Aristotelian friendships are thus historical relationships. Each cares for the other because of who she is – and who she is is a person of good character. She does not care for the other because she expects to benefit personally. Of course people in complete friendships standardly do benefit. But the benefits are a consequence of their friendship; hope for benefit neither motivates nor sustains the friendship. A complete friendship is built on the care for each other as particular, embodied people of good character. It is not a circuitous way of making each person feel better or of satisfying her interests.

Non-ideal friendships   Although deviations from the ideal, incomplete friendships are genuine friendships and, as such, are an integral part of a satisfying life. Everyone needs friends. But "no one can have complete friendships for many people" (Aristotle 1158a11). Incomplete friendships provide us with numerous companions; they fulfill our need for congenial social interactions.

There are two types of incomplete friendships. Friendships of utility occur whenever two individuals relate to each other "to gain some good for themselves" – while also wishing the other well (Aristotle, 1156a12). The principal motive for such friendships is the same as that for impersonal relationships: prompting one's self-interest. To that extent they resemble impersonal relationships. But they differ from impersonal relationships inasmuch as each person will, to some degree, take the other's interests as one of her own. Suppose two neighbors who work in adjoining office buildings decide to carpool to work. Each seeks a beneficial exchange. Their only aim is to trade goods – in this case, transportation to and from work. If that continues to be the sole basis for their relationship, then they will not have a friendship – not even a friendship of utility. They will simply have a trade relationship.

However, not infrequently something like the following happens: while riding to and from work, they chat idly about the weather, the stock market, or last night's basketball game. Eventually they discuss each other's work or family life. They subsequently come to know one another and, to some degree, wish each other well. To that extent they have become friends, albeit incomplete friends. The glue which holds the friendship together is not the casual conversation or even the shared secrets, but the shared utility: the carpool. Thus, when carpooling becomes unnecessary or cumbersome, the friendship will likely cease. The friendship served its purpose; in the absence of that purpose, the relationship ends.

Two people who have a friendship of pleasure will find each other's company pleasurable. Perhaps they find each other witty, insightful, clever, interesting, or sexy. Perhaps they share activities: discussing politics, going to the theater, playing poker, having sex, or hiking in the mountains. Within limits these people care for and are interested in one another; they "wish each other well." But the friendship lasts only as long as they enjoy each other's company. If the source of mutual pleasure disappears, or one of the parties ceases to desire that pleasure, then the relationship will end.

The similarities between my and Aristotle's account should be apparent. All three forms of friendship are, using my language, personal relationships. Of course friendships of utility and pleasure are akin to impersonal relationships in some respects: their principal motive is a beneficial exchange. Hence, if the relationship ceases to be useful or pleasurable, it will likely end. That is why Aristotle thinks these forms of friendship are incomplete. Nonetheless, all three forms are personal since each person relates to the other (at least to some degree) because of who she is. Moreover, in all forms each party wishes the other well. However, the extent and nature of well-wishing will be considerably different in incomplete forms. That is why, though personal, incomplete forms of friendship are less personal, less than the ideal.

We should not forget, of course, that few if any friendships are pure breeds: most relationships are mongrels. There is no sharp determinate boundary between personal and impersonal relationships. Likewise there is no sharp, determinate boundary between the various types of friendship. Conceptual classifications rarely distinguish completely distinct types. Nonetheless, these categories do isolate significant, relevant features of our experience. They identify dominant motives for and features of personal relationships. They thereby help us better understand our relationships and empower us to develop and maintain more meaningful ones.

All three types of friendship are valuable and merit further examination. In this book, however, I focus on complete friendships – or rather, relationships approaching this ideal. By understanding complete friendships, we will better understand all three types, since the two inferior forms are variations on the ideal form. But, to remind the reader of an earlier point, complete friendships need not be intense, although, of course, they may be. The hallmark of complete friends is in what they do for and with each other, not in what they feel about each other.

Moreover, I am especially concerned with complete friendships since they are intricately connected to a central thesis of this book. As the preceding exposition suggests, Aristotle thinks that only people of character can relate in ideal ways; he also thinks that only those who have healthy friendships can be people of character. Succinctly, he thinks only complete friends can be good people and only good people can be complete friends. Readers may find this claim mistaken if not preposterous. I happen to think it is true. The defense of this controversial claim, however, is not immediately forthcoming. It will unfold throughout the book and will coalesce in the final chapter.

Love

I have offered a brief conceptual analysis of "personal relationships," and put it in a historical framework. However, I have said little about the more familiar notion of love. I must now explain love's relation to personal relationships, so defined. Otherwise the relevance of my discussion for the conduct of our relationships may be uncertain.

Providing an analysis of "love" will be difficult since people use the term very differently. In Western cultures some people use "love" to identify a *type* of personal relationship; others, to specify an *element* or *feature* of personal relationships; and still others, to indicate a certain *feeling* one person has toward another. There is no realistic hope of providing an exhaustive analysis which completely captures everyone's understanding of the term. Any analysis will inevitably conflict with some ordinary uses.

Perhaps, then, we should eschew attempts to make the term more precise. Perhaps we should assume there is no essence or central core of the word "love," that there are, to use Wittgenstein's language, only family resemblances between these seemingly discrepant uses (Wittgenstein 1958: para. 67ff). On this account a divergence of usage is not a problem to solve, but a reality to accept. To some degree this is undeniable. Since there is no single, univocal sense of even ordinary words like "game" and "chair," it is unlikely that there is a univocal meaning for a more complex notion like "love."

However, I am not trying to identify a single meaning for the word "love." I well recognize that even relatively precise terms have gray areas: cases where we are uncertain if the term applies. This is a commonplace of language. From this commonplace, however, we should not infer that just *any* use of a term is acceptable. Some uses are clearly deviant. The problem is identifying them.

Some deviant uses are innocuous, at least when everyone involved understands that the term is being used by analogy or extension. For instance, when someone says that she loves her car, her new hat, Rocky Road ice cream, or *ER*, it never occurs to (most of) us to assume that she loves her car in the same way that she loves a friend. Usually we interpret this claim as simply a vivid way of saying "I like it a great deal." We quickly recognize this is a non-standard use of the term "love" – that it is not a paradigm case.

However there are cases where we think a word is being used inappropriately, rather than analogously or by extension. When we hear an eleven-year-old tell her friend that she is "in love," we assume she is not *really* in love but, rather, infatuated. Moreover, most of us know an adult who has proclaimed her love for others, when it was evident to all but the blindest observer that she had mistaken sexual desire for love. In such circumstances, most of us would be comfortable thinking – even if not comfortable saying – "But that isn't *really* love!"

Thus, the goal of conceptual revision is not to "lay down the law," telling people how they *must* use terms, but to propose an interpretation which reflects *and refines* ordinarily usage. Hence, conceptual analysis does not *simply* report how people use the term, but explains how we *should* use it if we wish to capture what is significant about the term. Of course it would be insane to offer an account totally divorced from ordinary usage. On the other hand, since most of us recognize that ordinary uses of the word "love" are imprecise, we seek to make the meaning of this important notion clearer – if by doing nothing more than excising the clearly inappropriate uses. If others find the proposed clarification and revision cogent, it will doubtless imply that some ordinary uses are mistaken or misleading. However, since most of us already recognize that, this is neither an unsurprising nor objectionable consequence of this analysis.

I propose that loving relationships are best understood as co-extensive with close personal relationships. That is, they are reciprocal personal relationships in which each party has the other as one of her ends. Thus if Sarah and Jane love each other, then they (1) have a personal relationship (based on each person's particular embodiment of traits) where (2) Sarah is one of Jane's ends, and Jane is one of Sarah's. Put differently, if they have a reciprocal personal relationship where each is one of the other's ends, then they love each other.

One benefit of this analysis is that it not only permits degrees of love, it provides a way to understand this phenomenon. Most of us think we love some people more than we love others. This difference can be explained by the degree to which our relationship is personal (rather than impersonal) *and* to the extent to which each party to the relationship takes the other as one of her ends. Since, on this account, those in close personal relationships have each other as one of their ends, then loving relationships will be exemplified by intimacy, care, sensitivity, and mutual support.

There are, as I noted earlier, other uses of "love," but I think these are deviations from this paradigm use. That is, they are used by analogy or extension ("I love my sailboat.") or they are mistaken, misplaced, or perhaps overly restrictive. For instance, we frequently assume that if two people love each other, then they are romantically involved. This common usage differentiates romantic couples from close friendships in which sex plays no role. There are undeniable differences between these relationships; for example, the former has a sexual dimension the latter lacks. But how does that suggest that "love" applies uniquely to romantic relationships? Why not conclude instead that (some) romantic relationships are one subclass of loving (close personal) relationships, while close friendships are another? Both types of relationship are similar in significant and relevant respects – both are personal relationships in which each has the other as one of her ends. *That* – not sex – is what makes the relationships loving.

This taxonomy seems more plausible. Not every romantic (sexually oriented) relationship is loving; certainly not every romantic encounter is loving. Sex does not a loving relationship make. Adding passion on top of sex does not, by itself, make partners loving, although it does make them passionately sexual. Even sexual partners who, to use Aristotle's language, may "wish each other well" do not thereby have a close relationship. That is, their relationship may be personal, but not close. In summary, although romantic relationships may well be loving, they are loving because the parties care for each other, not because they involve sex.

When I say the partners care, I do not mean to say that each feels overwhelming (com)passion for the other; they do not need to *feel* anything. Caring is not an inner state which, under ideal conditions, we translate into outward behavior. Caring is something we do. If we care for people then we listen, support, and help them; we laugh and cry with them; we intertwine our lives. It is care, and not passion, which is the hallmark of love. Of course we should not belittle feelings or infer that they are totally irrelevant to close relationships. Positive feelings may indicate a tendency or willingness to act lovingly. But they are not equivalent to or even necessary for love. At least that is what I argue in the following chapter.

Conclusion

At the outset of the book I noted that personal relationships are often difficult to establish and maintain. The preceding analysis of personal relationships partially explains why. Close personal relationships are those in which each person takes the other's interest as one of her own. Many people apparently find that difficult. Close relationships also require considerable knowledge – of ourselves and of those with whom we relate. Before we can know if we are in a relationship with someone because we care for them or simply because they promote our personal interests, we must have at least the rudiments of self-knowledge. And before we can care for another, we must be able to discern her interests.

2

Emotions and Feelings

Strong feelings are the stuff of which voluntary close personal relationships are made. They are the first indication that we want a personal relationship with someone: they subsequently motivate us to seek a relationship with them. Feelings also sustain established relationships. They prompt us to demonstrate our love: to spend time with the beloved, to talk with her, to do things for her. But not always. I might love someone, but not show it. Or I might act *as if* I love someone, even if I do not. Since I am the only person privy to my feelings, I am the only person who can *know* if I am in love.

Other emotions central to the understanding and conduct of personal relationships are explained similarly. I am angry if and only if I feel angry. I may act *as if* I were angry, even if I am not. Or I may be angry, but hide it. Normally, though, when I am angry, I act angrily; and when I act angrily, I am angry. Likewise, I am jealous if and only if I feel jealous. I may act *as if* I were jealous, even if I am not. Or I may be jealous, but hide it. Normally, though, when I am jealous, I act jealously; and when I act jealously, I am jealous. Other people may be able to judge from my outward behavior whether I am in love (or angry or jealous). But I am the only one who *knows* whether I am in love (or angry or jealous). Only I know my own mental states; only you know yours. So goes the traditional wisdom.

I reject the traditional wisdom. It is built on a faulty view of the emotions, the self, and personal relationships. This view misrepresents the role of emotions in personal relationships, and thus fosters inappropriate conduct in them.

The Ordinary View

Most laypeople hold that feelings are essential elements of – or even equivalent to – emotions. Love is no exception. It is not difficult to see

21

why. We usually have strong feelings for those we love and befriend; we would be more than a mite suspicious were we devoid of feelings for them. About this there is no question. What is at question is the explanation of this phenomenon – what people think this "fact" indicates about emotions in general, love specifically, and about the proper way to conduct our personal relationships.

Of course what I call "the traditional wisdom" is not a unitary, tightly defined view. Rather, it is a related series of views. Most share common features, although some views are stronger and more contentious than others. Although many philosophers and psychologists have rejected this view in all its guises, it maintains a strong grip on the layperson's understanding of emotion and love. Apparently many laypeople do not find standard academic objections to these views compelling. Moreover, I suspect even many academics who reject the "traditional wisdom" intellectually, remain under its sway personally. What is needed is an account of the emotions which accommodates the phenomenon the traditional view purportedly explains, while exposing the inadequacies of that explanation. Such an account would help us better understand the role of emotion in the conduct of our personal relationships. I will suggest such an account. This account will be best understood in contrast to the traditional view. I will briefly describe what I take to be the more uncompromising version of the traditional wisdom, and then discuss progressively weaker versions.

Some ways the ordinary view is expressed

We are victims of our emotions Most people contrast emotions with reason; many people think emotions and reason are completely at odds. If is not difficult to see why. On the one hand, we speak of deliberating carefully, weighing our options, and choosing intelligently; while, on the other hand, we speak of being smitten by love, overcome by grief, or engulfed by rage. Our ordinary parlance implies that we control reason while we are (often) controlled by our emotions. That is why when we are emotional we are often said to be "out of control;" while, when we are being reasonable, we are said to be "in control." This common view is expressed, albeit in somewhat attenuated form, by a recent psychological treatise on emotions: "Emotions are, to some extent, involuntary. We experience and express them without being able to choose them exactly. They are passions rather than actions. . . . The conclusion that there is something irrational about emotions need not be labored" (Oatley 1992: 9, 131). If emotions are completely beyond our control, then, since we are not responsible for actions beyond our control, we will not be responsible for our emotions or their resultant behavior.

Probably few people think we have *no* control over our emotions or their influence on our behavior. However, fewer still think we are completely responsible for our emotions. Even many of us who intellectually deny that we are victims of our emotions sometimes act as it we were. We often excuse our unkind behavior by citing our anger; we justify our thoughtlessness toward some by implicating our love for another; we rationalize our callousness, claiming it springs from anxiety. However, acting as if we were not responsible for our emotions has lamentable results. As a recent psychology text explains: "The belief that we are not responsible for our emotions or for our behavior when we are gripped by them, permits us to indulge in unbecoming behavior and later to absolve ourselves of blame, at least partially" (Carlson 1988: 362). This belief is so pervasive that it has been preserved in law: persons convicted of "crimes of passion" are given reduced sentences.

We can legitimately excuse our emotions, however, only if we are (at least partially) victims of them – only if emotions force us to act as we do. Imagine how preposterous it would be to excuse my cruel treatment of Beth by saying that I had decided, after careful deliberation, that treating her cruelly was in my best interest. This claim would not justify or excuse my cruelty, it would merely locate it. Likewise, if emotions are an integral part of who I am – as I think they are – then citing an emotion as the cause of my behavior would not excuse that behavior, it would simply locate its source within me. In short, the belief that emotions excuse (or mitigate) behavior is based on the assumption that emotions are forces outside the core of the self, forces which move us, often against our will.

We know our emotions by how they feel Even many of those who deny we are victims of our emotions still believe emotions are (or are constituted by) visceral feelings. On this view each emotion has its characteristic feel. Since we are the best judges of how we feel, we are the best judges of our emotions. I am angry if I feel angry, regardless of how I act. I am in love if I feel lovingly, regardless of how I act. Of course how I behave is some evidence of how I feel. But the behavior is a result of feelings; it is not constitutive of the emotions. As psychologist Carl Rogers states: "The healthy individual is aware of his or her emotional feelings, whether or not they are expressed" (Fadiman and Frager 1994: 435). Each of us can know our emotions simply by looking inside, by introspecting. Since "emotions play a central role in the significant events of our lives" and thus are a potent (if not the primary) cause of our behavior, introspection thus reveals why we act as we do; we are uniquely able to identify our own motives (Lazarus 1991: 3).

Historical roots of the common view

These views of the emotions are embodied in, and were likely advanced by, prominent philosophical and psychological theories. To help understand the underpinnings of the common view, I shall briefly outline two of these theories.

Cartesianism According to Descartes (1596–1650), we are dualistic creatures: some combination of a physical body with a non-material or spiritual mind. We have arms, legs, spleens, and brains. We also have beliefs, feelings, and desires. Though we may not know exactly what these latter "things" are, we do know they are different from spleens and brains. They are parts of our minds. (Substance) dualists disagree about exactly what minds are, but they agree what they are not: bodies. Nonetheless, minds do interact with bodies in two distinct ways. (1) Minds direct bodily behavior: if I decide to go to the store, I get in my car and drive there. (2) Minds monitor the body: if I cut my big toe by stepping on broken glass, then I feel pain.

Emotions, on the traditional view, play both roles. First, emotions are often causes of human action. "The principal effect of all the passions in men is to dispose their soul to desire those things for which they prepare the body, so that a feeling of fear incites in it the desire to fly, that of courage, to desire to fight, and so on" (Descartes 1972: 349–50). Second, emotions monitor goings-on in the body. To this extent, emotions are partially dependent on the body. This link between the emotions and the physical body helps explain why we have limited control over our emotions. "They [our emotions] are nearly all accompanied by some commotion which takes place in the heart, and in consequence also in the whole of the blood, and the animal spirits, so that until this commotion has subsided, they remain present to our thought. . . ." (1972: 352). For example, anger is a visceral sensation which typically causes certain physiological processes associated with anger: increased heart rate, constricted muscles, gastrointestinal upset, etc. These bodily sensations often sustain our anger, despite our best intentions. This tendency of emotions to have a life of their own is a phenomenon to which I shall return. But, for the moment, I want to focus on the Cartesian claim that emotions are differentiated by their characteristic feel.

This claim springs from Descartes's dualism. He claims we identify physical objects and events by our senses: we see them, feel them, smell them, or touch them. Others can verify their presence. Mental events, however, cannot be identified by ordinary senses: they have no qualities our senses could recognize. They can be recognized only by a non-physical sense, namely, introspection – an "inner eye." According to the dualist, each of us looks inside herself and determines her own mental state. Others cannot see or experience our mental states, nor can we see or experience theirs. At most we can see the results of their mental states in their behavior; and they, in ours.

Emotions are mental events. Thus we subjectively distinguish love from joy, anger from resentment, and shame from embarrassment, by introspectively comparing our experiences. As Descartes puts it, "everyone has experience of the passions within himself." Each of us is the only person who can directly identify our emotions. We can only make inferences about the emotions of others. Admittedly some dualists recognize that people may not always know their own mental states. However, these theorists still contend that no one else has direct access to another's emotions.

This asymmetry is pivotal to the conduct of our personal relationships. According to the Cartesians, only we know whether we are angry, proud, or in love. And, since emotions are thought to motivate much of our behavior, each of us is uniquely situated to understand our motives. Each of us is the only person who can know whether we are angry, sad, vengeful, or in love.[1] Each of us is the only person who can directly know why we do what we do.

Freudian theory Other elements of the traditional wisdom, although present in Cartesianism, are best seen as arising from Sigmund Freud's theory. Freud depicts emotions as forces beyond our control, forces to which we are often victim. This view of the emotions springs from his tri-partite division of the self. According to Freud the self is composed of the id (desire), the ego (the rational principle), and the superego (conscience). The id is the source of all desire, all motivation. It is primitive, unconscious, and indiscriminate: it wants what it wants, and it wants it *now.*

Of course society cannot permit everyone to satisfy all their desires; it must prohibit some desires, at least those which are likely to lead to harm of others; otherwise none of us would be safe (Freud 1989). Society must also limit when and where we satisfy other desires which it permits. For example, we could not have a picnic, sex, or a rock concert just anywhere or anytime; that would disrupt other people's lives. To facilitate mutual respect and to guarantee privacy, the state can punish picnics on Main Street, public sex, and loud music at 3 a.m. In Freudian language, the society can constrain the id by making compliance with the law in each person's best interest.

The id is further constrained by the ego. The ego takes the id's chaotic desires and organizes them so as to maximize its satisfactions, given social constraints. For example, although the ego does not condemn sexual desires, it does inform us that there are times when it is inappropriate to act on those desires. It also shows us how to satisfy those desires without interfering with others' interests. The ego understands that if we interfere with others' interests, they will likely interfere with ours. Therefore, to best promote our desires, we must allow others to promote theirs – that is why we are inclined to accede to society's demands. In some circumstances, though, the ego cannot control the id. When that happens the socially created conscience – the superego – comes into play. Through socialization we internalize many social controls: for instance, we rarely desire (consciously) to harm others.

However, neither external threats nor internal controls can repress *all* desires without disastrous consequences. Although healthy people will suppress socially disadvantageous desires (e.g. violent tendencies), they merely delay the satisfaction of other desires to the appropriate time and place. In fact, Freud insists, the ego and superego cannot eliminate primal urges, they can only redirect and restrain them. The urges remain, pressing for satisfaction. If the ego and superego will not permit their reasonable satisfaction, psychological pressure builds up. Emotions are nature's safety valves: they release pent-up and potentially damaging emotional pressure. This release occurs ideally in socially acceptable ways – perhaps yelling at sporting events or getting angry in appropriate circumstances. If those forums for emotional release are unavailable, however, people may indulge in destructive emotions, say violent aggression or insane jealousy.

Hence emotions, most especially destructive emotions, are the result of unsatisfied primal urges which have become redirected in deleterious ways. We cannot control the release of emotional pressure; the emotions move us against our will.

Prolegomena to Any Theory of the Emotions

I cannot offer an exhaustive theory of emotions; I suspect that is impossible. We should not expect to find a single or even multiple characteristic common to *all* emotions. The term "emotion" has evolved over centuries so that it now refers to diverse phenomena such as moods (e.g. depression), conditions (e.g. happiness), episodic occurrences (e.g. jubilance), and pervasive dispositions (e.g. love). As Rorty explains it: "Emotions do not form a natural class. . . . [They] cannot be shepherded together under one set of classifications as active or passive, thought-generated and thought-defined or physiologically determined; voluntary or nonvoluntary; functional or malfunctional; corrigible or not corrigible by a change of beliefs. Nor even can they be sharply distinguished from moods, motives, attitudes, character traits" (1980a: 1; see also Greenspan 1988: 15–20 and Gordon 1987: 21–2).

For our present purposes, however, we do not need a full-blown theory of the emotions, let alone a list of necessary and sufficient conditions. All we need do is isolate paradigm features of emotions with enough precision to inform our discussion of personal relationships. That we can do.

I will begin with the traditional view, since it clearly contains more than a modicum of truth: feelings are usually present in emotions, and they appear to influence how we behave. All of us have occasionally felt as if we were the victims of our emotions, as if we were compelled to act in ways we disavow. We can accommodate these observations, however, without assuming that feelings exhaust – or are even the most important elements of – emotions, and without succumbing to the traditional view's more troublesome implications.

27

Some problems with the traditional view

In its unqualified form, the traditional view is bedeviled by a paradoxical understanding of the role of emotion in our lives. On the one hand, emotions are thought to be essential elements of a satisfying life (Maslow 1973: 85). A life without love and hate, joy and sorrow, pride and regret is not a fully human life. Emotions "provide indispensable color to our lives; we think of emotional experiences as hot, exciting, involving, or mobilizing, and distinguish them from experiences which are routine, cold, and detached . . ." (Lazarus 1991: 19). Thus conceived, emotions are not to be shunned but embraced. According to humanistic psychologist Abraham Maslow, maturity consists in "being able to give oneself over completely to an emotion, not only of love but also of anger . . ." (1966: 38).

On the other hand, emotions are often thought to disrupt an orderly life.

> What happens, especially with a strong emotion, is that we who are experiencing it are often taken over by the emotion; our attention becomes riveted on the harm or benefit and what we can do about it; we are caught up in the charged relationship we have with the environment, the urge to action, the sensations associated with that relationship, and the reaction it provokes (Lazarus 1991: 16).

In this view emotions occasionally force us to act against our best judgement, and to deprive reason of its proper role in directing human behavior. Thus conceived, emotions are not necessarily bad; nonetheless, we must control them. It is difficult to see, though, how these two elements of the traditional view can be reconciled.

The traditional view is also seriously imprecise. Emotions are said to be (or to be constituted by) feelings; it is through these feelings that we know our own emotional states. However, the word "feeling" is ambiguous. Sometimes we use it to identify a visceral sensation (tightness in the stomach, rapid heart beat, etc.), as in "I feel so angry I could scream." At other times we use "feeling" and its cognates to identify a belief, especially a tentative belief, as in "I feel it will rain tomorrow." These latter uses have nothing whatsoever to do with sensations, visceral or otherwise. And I doubt this is what most people mean when they say "I have strong feelings for another" or "I feel jealous." Thus, if the traditional wisdom's claim that "emotions are feelings" is to be more than a claim about what we believe, it must mean that emotions are visceral sensations.

But this stronger claim is beset with problems of its own. Social-psychological studies indicate that most emotions are differentiated not by how we feel, but by our beliefs and our evaluations. In one well-known study, researchers told test subjects they were receiving vitamin supplements when, in fact, they were injected with epinephrine (the adrenal secretion associated with emotion). Some subjects were placed in conditions most people would find offensive; others, in conditions most people would find pleasing. Test subjects placed in the former conditions reported *feeling* angry. Those placed in the latter reported *feeling* happy (Schachter and Singer 1962). That is, although all subjects had the same physiological underpinnings of emotions (caused by the epinephrine), they reported different feelings, different emotions.

More recent studies corroborate Schachter's and Singer's findings. Not only is there no definitive set of feelings associated with each emotion, but even something as physiologically basic as heart rate could not discriminate consistently or fully among emotions (Cacioppo, Berntsen and Klein 1992: 66). Common experience further verifies these experimental findings. Although we have no trouble distinguishing shame from embarrassment, we cannot do so by how we feel. Imagine two situations. In the first I am caught stealing an acquaintance's wallet; in the second I discover I have been walking around all day with toilet paper draped from the back of my pants. Everyone would infer that I would feel shame in the first case and embarrassment in the second.

But if emotions were merely visceral sensations, how could you plausibly predict how I would *feel*? You *might* be able to make that prediction if you had had those experiences. However, most people have not had them. Even if you had, the experiences are not the primary basis on which you would predict my emotion. Rather, you identify the first situation as one in which I would feel shame because I had acted immorally; and the second as one in which I would feel embarrassed because I had violated society's norms for appropriate behavior. *Perhaps* some emotions (say, fear) are standardly identified by a characteristic feel. But most emotions – at least those most important to the conduct of personal relationships – are typically identified by beliefs about what is appropriate or moral, not by the nature of my gastronomical spasms.

Moreover, the traditional view makes the rational assessment of emotions mysterious if not inexplicable. Most people assume you are justifiably angry if I intentionally malign you. Most people assume I should feel ashamed if I am caught embezzling funds from a home for retarded children, but not if I hiccup in public. It is unclear, however, how we could evaluate emotions if they were experiences which just happened to us. For example, on Freud's theory, my anger and my shame are simply the release of pent-up pressure from unsatisfied desires. On what basis could we determine if these emotions were warranted? Yet any adequate account of the emotions should permit their rational assessment.

Finally, although Freud's pressure value theory of the emotions may seem appropriate for some negative emotions like anger, resentment, and jealousy, it is inappropriate for positive emotions like love, compassion, and joy. Is love just a release of pent-up frustrations? Does Mother Teresa spend her life in the Calcutta slums because society unduly constrained her id? If I am joyful, am I merely releasing emotional pressure built-up because I failed to satisfy some more primitive desire? Not likely.

Elements of a Theory of Emotion

I do not intend to offer a full-blown account of the emotions; I have already indicated why I think that is impossible. Nonetheless, I can identify elements of that theory, specifically elements relevant to our understanding of and conduct in personal relationships (Thalberg 1977).

The objects of emotions

Emotions typically make reference to the world. Normally we are not just angry, we are angry at someone or about some situation. We are not just proud, we are proud about something we have done or about something we possess. We are sad, jealous, or joyous *about* some person, event, or thing in the world. Knowing the object of our jealousy is central to knowing that we are jealous. Knowing the object of an emotion empowers us (and others) to reasonably predict how we will act in the future. If I am jealous only of Bob, then you can reasonably predict that I will act differently around Bob than I will act around Gene (Gordon 1987: 22–3).

Emotions and evaluations

Not only do most emotions have an object, they typically include or reflect our evaluations of that thing, person, or event. We are typically angry if we judge that an action, situation, or person is, in relevant respects, bad or detrimental. We are proud if we judge that our work is excellent. Likewise for other emotions. Shame, joy, and love – each is an evaluation that usually "causes the wants or desires which lead to behavior, while the evaluations and wants together cause abnormal physiological changes and their subjective registering, feelings" (Lyons 1980: 57). According to Lyons (and other cognitive theorists) these evaluations are the core of emotions. In paradigm cases, evaluations (1) cause physiological processes we introspectively feel and (2) cause us to act in characteristic ways.

Whether Lyons is right that emotions just are these evaluations is doubtful. Nonetheless, evaluations are normally constituents of emotions. Generally we like people or things we judge to be pleasant, interesting, and available. Generally we are proud when we have performed a task well. Recognizing the centrality of evaluations reveals one way to control emotions. Although emotions are not standardly under our direct control – we cannot merely will them to change – we can sometimes change them by changing our evaluations. I may stop being angry at Joan once I realize she did not wrong me. I may lose my pride once I realize I made a glaring error. Understanding this way to alter emotions can be put to good use in our personal relationships. If I wish to initiate a relationship or to intensify my love for someone, I may spend more time with her. I could also focus my attention on her positive characteristics. By doing so I may change my evaluations, and thereby change my emotions. Of course these maneuvers will not always succeed – we may not enjoy many of the same activities and thus cannot spend sufficient time together. Or I may find insufficient positive qualities on which to focus. Nonetheless, this does suggest one way of altering emotions.

The causal history of emotions: why they appear to be irrational

Although changing our beliefs may lead to a change of emotions, it does not do so invariably. Emotions occasionally have a life of their own, beyond the direct reach of reason. They may emerge in totally inappropriate circumstances; they may be more intense than circumstances warrant; and they may persist even when we change the evaluations which spawned them. We can explain the seemingly irrational nature of some emotions, however, without bringing along Cartesian and Freudian metaphysical baggage. We need only appreciate that emotions have causal histories which formed, conditioned, and sustain them. These histories are embodied in emotional habits which incline us to react in the ways and with the intensity that we do. Let me explain.

An emotion standardly has an object; the object is thought to explain that emotion. Suppose Jack is jealous: he fears Jill is interested in Richard. We might think the object of his jealousy is also its cause. However, its object may not be its cause, at least not its complete cause. To fully understand his jealousy (and, indeed, any complex emotion) we must identify

> an event, or a series of events, long forgotten, and [which] formed a set of dispositions which are triggered by the immediate cause. . . . It requires analyzing the magnetizing effects of the formation of our emotional dispositions, habits of thought, as well as habits of action and response. Magnetizing dispositions are dispositions to gravitate toward and to create conditions that spring other dispositions. A magnetizing disposition to irascibility not only involves a set of specific low thresholds (e.g. to frustration or betrayal) but also involves looking for frustrating conditions, perceiving situations as frustrating (Rorty 1993: 106–7).

Put differently, our emotions standardly focus on some object: a thing, person, or event. Moreover, the emotion typically reflects some evaluation of that object. Our emotions are partly constituted by these objects and evaluations. Partly. For had our causal histories been different, our emotional responses would likely be different. Perhaps we would not become jealous so easily had we felt loved by our parents and our friends. Perhaps we would not become angry so quickly had we not been regularly frustrated as a child.

The distinction between the object and the causal history of our emotions helps answer a significant question about the emotions, namely, whether we ever use them for some purpose, to achieve some end. Some theorists have thought so (Arnold and Gasson 1968; Sartre 1971; Solomon 1976). For instance, suppose Jack wants to have sex with Jill. He might get angry at Jill for spilling the water; she feels guilty and subsequently assuages that guilt by acceding to his demands. Jack thereby attains his goal by circuitous means. Most of us know people like Jack – people who use their emotions to manipulate others.

Many cognitive theorists, however, deny that people use emotions. Lyons, for instance, claims people who appear to use anger for selfish gain are not *really* angry. They are only feigning anger. "If one loved for a purpose or was angry in order to do or to achieve something, then one would not be genuinely angry or in love but would be pretending to be angry or in love" (180).

Certainly people may sometimes pretend to be angry. Usually, though, that is easily detected: their behavior is artificial. Not so in this imaginary case. Although Jack uses his anger to get Jill to sleep with him, we can easily imagine that he is genuinely angry – he gets red in the face, yells, waves his arms, etc. Moreover, his evaluations support the conclusion: he genuinely thinks Jill has wronged him. Lyons, though, claims appearances are deceiving. We could use emotions for our purposes, he avows, only if we could deliberately choose our emotions. However, since we cannot induce emotions at will, we cannot use emotions as instruments of our purposes.

Although this response looks plausible, it commits what I call the rationalistic fallacy: the belief that we intentionally choose all our beliefs, attitudes, and behavior. We don't. Our emotions, beliefs, and attitudes are the products of complex causal histories. Intentional choices play a role in these histories, but they do not produce and direct them.

Take the present case: there are plausible causal explanations how Jack might have acquired the tendency to use anger to serve his purposes. Perhaps once, when he was spontaneously angry at Jill, she felt guilty and gave in to his demands. She thereby reinforced his anger. She (and others) similarly reinforced his anger on other occasions. He subsequently developed a tendency to become angry whenever his desires were thwarted. The causal history reinforced a pattern of emotional behavior; now he uses his anger to achieve his goals.

This form of psychological selection is the way we often acquire emotions. In some situation we become angry or depressed or jealous; others respond sympathetically, thereby reinforcing our response. The more often that response is reinforced, the more deeply ingrained our habit. That is not to say we will always exhibit that emotion, or that we will exhibit it in precisely the same way. Nonetheless, the causal history makes it more likely that we will respond in this manner. Once we have acquired an emotional habit – say, once we have become irascible – then although we do not consciously choose to become angry, we may become angry whenever our desires are frustrated. We thereby use our anger – albeit unconsciously – to achieve our ends.

In short, emotions are habits, and habits are not under direct control. But that should be unsurprising: *most* of what we do is not under direct control. We are habitual creatures – emotions are just one type of habit. Thinking is another. If we are inclined to carefully and critically reflect on important issues, we will, in most circumstances, think critically about an issue; we do not have to decide to do so.

Understanding that emotions are habits explains some phenomena Descartes and Freud sought to explain. For instance, it explains why we sometimes maintain an emotional response which is inconsistent with our evaluations and beliefs. If we want to change our shoes or our hat, we simply change them. Habits, though, are not taken on and off at will. We may decide to control our appetite, restrain our anger, or get in a good mood – all to no avail. Why? Because these are habits, deeply entrenched dispositions, not amenable to direct volitional control.

This best explains why we sometimes feel we are passive recipients of, even victims of, our emotions. The recalcitrant nature of emotions is best explained, not in terms of a Cartesian of Freudian metaphysic, but in terms of the causal histories which shape and sustain them. Once we understand why emotions are sometimes recalcitrant, we may find ways to control them indirectly, for example by altering the objective conditions which framed and now support them (Dewey 1988: 25–41).

Emotions are not just feelings

The preceding considerations explain why emotions are not merely feelings (visceral sensations). Although feelings usually accompany emotions, they do not do so invariably. We may love someone for whom we do not have strong feelings; we may have strong feelings for someone we don't love. People in their early teens, for instance, may experience intense feelings for one another even though they have a limited understanding of love. Older adolescents may have passionate feelings for each other even when their relationships are relatively superficial. On the other hand, couples who have had successful, rewarding relationships for years may not have feelings as intense as they had in the early stages of their romance. This does not imply, however, that they no longer love each other, or that their love has diminished. Depth of love is not measured by height of feeling.

We would, of course, be suspicious were we devoid of intense feelings for those we claim to love. We would fear our love was dead, or at least on the critical list. And so we should – although not for the reasons most people suppose. Many people equate love with feelings; therefore, they construe an absence of loving feelings as an absence of love. A better explanation is this: love is a disposition to act lovingly, a disposition which typically causes, or is associated with, loving feelings. Thus, if the feelings are absent, we have some evidence that the love is absent. Some evidence, but far from proof. In short, although feelings are typically present in emotions, the emotions are not equivalent to, caused by, or exhausted by, feelings.

The failure to properly understand the role of feelings in close relationships has disastrous consequences. We assume that if we have positive feelings for each other our relationship is healthy. But good feelings do not a healthy relationship make. Thus, we may fail to relate, or fail to relate constructively, and our relationship may deteriorate. On the other hand, we may feel badly and thereby infer that our relationship is in jeopardy, even if it is not. Perhaps, though, our bad feelings are not signs of an imperiled relationship, but are caused by conflicts with our parents, pressures at work, or an improper diet.

Moreover, even if our relationship is at risk, a mistaken understanding of the emotions may prompt us to respond inappropriately. If we don't feel as we think we should, we may try various dime-store-novel formulae to intensify our feelings. We assume intensified feelings will miraculously cure ailing relationships and resurrect dead ones. The results are often disastrous: we treat the symptom while ignoring the underlying condition. The proper remedy is to treat the condition: the decline in love. The symptom – the decline in feeling – will respond in due course. In short, undue reliance on our visceral feelings

35

may prompt us to act foolishly – either to assume that a faulty relationship is sound or that a sound relationship is faulty.

Behavior is the acid test of emotions

Behaviorism was once king of psychology and philosophy. However, for several decades it has been in disrepute. Most philosophers and psychologists consider behaviorism so obviously flawed that they mention it only in ridicule. That is regrettable. Certain forms of behaviorism are doubtless defective. Perhaps all forms would ultimately succumb to objections. Nonetheless, behaviorism contains significant insights crucial to our understanding of and conduct in personal relationships. Even B. F. Skinner's version of behaviorism is far more sophisticated than most philosophers suggest (1974). I suspect most philosophers criticize Skinner based on someone else's caricature of him.

The traditional view of emotions claims feelings typically cause certain characteristic behaviors. Thus, when I feel angry, I usually act angrily. When I feel love, I usually act lovingly. According to the behaviorist, however, behavior is not merely a result or an accidental accompaniment of the emotion, it is a constitutive part of it. That is, although an emotion is not exhausted by behavior, it is what it is, in some important measure, because of its characteristic behavior.

The centrality of behavior for emotions comes into focus if we reflect on the ways we first learned to think and talk about emotions, namely, by observing others, usually our parents. Perhaps we saw Dad angry at Sis because she borrowed the car without permission; perhaps we saw Mom angry at the car mechanic because he told her she needed a new clutch – and she knew better. We listened to what they said; we watched how they acted. We thereby gained our earliest understanding of anger.

Normally we think emotions, and perhaps especially anger, existed prior to socialization. We may assume, for instance, that a very young child deprived of her toys screams because she is angry. Although I suspect her reaction is a biological precursor to anger, it is wrong-headed to call it "anger". The child screams not because she is angry *at* the mother or angry *because* the mother removed the toy, but simply because a desired stimulus has been removed. The child's behavior has no object nor does it imply an evaluation – and hence lacks two constituents of emotion. Even those theorists who insist that the child is angry presumably agree that the nature of the anger differs considerably from that of an adult.

This is all the more obvious with an emotion like love. As infants we may have enjoyed being held by our parents. We likely cooed and giggled when they held us. But as infants we do not love our parents. We learned about love later. Perhaps we watched Mom console Dad when his brother died; we saw Dad care for Mom when she was bedridden with a back injury. We saw how they cared for us (their children). We thereby gained our earliest understanding of love. A similar story can be told about other emotions.

More generally, our ability to identify emotions (ours, as well as others) is intricately connected to our linguistic abilities (Skinner 1953; 1974; Ryle 1966). We do not have private schemes for categorizing emotions (Wittgenstein 1958: 243ff). Although we doubtless had visceral sensations before our acquisition of language, we could not identify or distinguish emotions. An infant cannot distinguish frustration from anger; the *feelings* are too similar. Other feelings – say embarrassment or shame – aren't even available to the pre-linguistic child.

How then do we recognize our emotions, if not by feelings? *Pace* the traditional view, learning to recognize our emotions is not something everyone can do; it is more than peering inside to discern some mysterious, ghostly state to which each of us has unique access. Rather, recognizing our emotions is an achievement. We must identify the circumstances which preceded our emotion, be sensitive to our dispositions to respond, discern our evaluations, and observe our visceral reactions. Then we must find the best interpretation of these diverse constituents of emotion. That interpretation must characterize the emotion as an instance of an emotion type, for instance, *as* joy or *as* shame. But we cannot identify emotional types without knowing a language which distinguishes these types. And, as the earlier examples suggest, we learn the language when we learn the conditions which constitute those emotions: causes which often precede them and behaviors which typically follow. As Quine puts it, "Any realistic theory of evidence must be inseparable from the pyschology of stimulus and response, as applied to sentences" (1960: 17).

Of course, even the most astute among us cannot always identify her emotions. Sometimes we say things like: "I feel weird – I'm not sure what I feel." Under these circumstances I may simply not be in any definite emotional state. In other cases I may be able to eventually identify an emotional state, perhaps by studying the circumstances which preceded it, and by examining my responses. ("I wasn't sure at first, but I now see that I am just nervous.") But that requires language.

Think of it this way. Languages have public rules governing their use. We could not communicate if I use the word "anger" one way and you use it another. What determines the rules for the proper use of these words? Do each of us have our own internal rules for identifying anger (or jealousy, or joy)? No. A language requires publicly verifiable rules for the use of words. "Anger" is identified by its constituents, but especially its characteristic behavior, say, becoming red in the face, yelling, waving ones arms, etc. Were anger identified only by some internal state each of us could discern only in her own case, we would have no way to talk about, discuss, or evaluate anger.

"Anger," however, need not be tied to a specific, predetermined set of behaviors. Languages evolve and change. Hence, even if I successfully restrain the standard angry behaviors, my anger would still be partly constituted by my behavior. When I am angry I may not get red in the face, but I may become tense instead. Possibly I do not flail my arms, but I do say nasty things to and about the person who made me angry. Perhaps I am unusually adept at suppressing obvious behavioral cues: my cues are so subtle that only those who know me exceedingly well can detect them. Should you infer that I am not angry, or that anger is merely an internal feeling? No. It would be more accurate to say that I controlled my anger or that the specific behaviors characteristic of my anger are relatively unique to me. However, if I evidenced *no* behavior which others could plausibly interpret as anger, then you must conclude I am not angry – regardless of what I feel or claim to feel.

"But," an objector might say, "you simply haven't envisioned someone with complete control over her emotions, someone who has no behavioral manifestations." Two quick responses. First, if someone has *no* behavioral signs of anger – she does not alter her behavior one iota – then I don't know why she or anyone else should think she is angry. If she thinks otherwise it is because she equates anger with some visceral feeling. Throughout this chapter I have argued that is a mistaken equation.

Second, implicit in this objection is the very point I wish to make. The objector claims that people can hide their emotions. We could not make sense of this claim, however, unless emotions were standardly public. We cannot hide something which is already inaccessible to others. We would not say, for instance, that John hides his pancreas – or that by hiding it he demonstrates self-control. Correspondingly, if pain or joy were merely inner hidden experiences we might choose to express, then it would be senseless to talk about hiding our pain or joy. However, this is not the case: we naturally wince when we are in pain and naturally smile when we are joyous. If in some particular case we do not, it is only because we constrained our natural tendencies. In short, the very idea that people might hide their emotions would be senseless unless behavior were constitutive of emotion.

To more fully explain my view, let me discuss an example which appears to contradict my thesis. Suppose the Nazis kill a Polish woman's husband, children, and parents. She seethes with hatred for the Nazis; she wants revenge. What does she do? She wangles her way into the local Nazi hierarchy and becomes the commandant's mistress. She feigns undying love for him. Her purpose: to obtain valuable military secrets to defeat the Nazis, and to kill the commandant. According to my view her hatred must be evidenced in behavior. Yet a quick observation suggests she loves the commandant: she fawns over him, praises him, and in all outward ways adores him. Doesn't that undermine my claim?

No. Behaviorists do not assert that a person's emotions must be evident to everyone. Although a casual observer might infer that she loves the commandant, her behavior is also compatible with intense hatred for him. We can all understand how and why someone who hated the Nazis might act as she does – after all, we can understand this example. Thus, if the Resistance interrogated her, she would have a ready explanation for her actions. Although they may not accept her explanation (they may think she is lying), they would have no difficulty understanding it. On the other hand, were her behavior not consonant with a hatred of the Nazis, (for example, if she never contacted the Resistance) then they would likely conclude that she was lying. In short, even in this hypothetical case, emotions are embodied in behavior, albeit perhaps in non-standard ways.

It is not merely that we discern others' emotions by their behavior, but also our own. Admittedly this sounds bizarre. We often identify our emotional states introspectively. "I know when I am angry," you might think, "by detecting angry feelings, not by watching how I act. I know when I am in love by discerning loving feelings, not by observing loving behavior. Although I may know if others are happy, sad, angry, or joyous by watching them, that is not how I know my own emotions."

At one level this is indisputable. We typically determine our emotional states introspectively. This does not show, however, that (1) introspection is the *basis* for identifying emotions, that (2) feelings are emotions, or even that (3) feelings always accompany emotion. Although we may identify emotions introspectively, we should not conclude that we identify emotions by how they feel. When I am furious or ashamed or loving, what I introspect are not merely visceral feelings, but tendencies to act in certain ways. If I am furious with John I want to hit him, tell him off, or in some other way, harm him. If I am ashamed of my actions I want to hide them. If I love Juanita, I want to be with her and support her.

These conditions are not identified by feel, but by our thoughts about how we will behave. If I am angry at you I may silently spin scenarios in which I give you your due. If I am in love with you I may envision romantic rendezvous. If I am ashamed of my behavior I may often recall it or think of strategies to regain my lost sense of esteem. Often I do not rely on feelings, but contemplate narratives of past or future behavior.

However, even if we did identify emotions by their feelings, the behaviorist claims we should not infer that emotions are just feelings. Rather, feelings are symptoms of emotions, a subjective awareness of underlying behavioral dispositions. What we recognize introspectively are tendencies to behave, not some well-defined visceral sensation. The emotions are the underlying dispositions, with their accompanying evaluations; the feelings are symptoms of those dispositions. (Perhaps *this* is what Descartes was trying to express.)

Consider the following analogy. You eat a large pizza and subsequently feel discomfort in your abdomen. But this feeling is not the same as indigestion nor is it the cause of indigestion. (Nor can you infallibly recognize indigestion – perhaps you have an ulcer.) Rather the feeling is the result of indigestion, a physiological discomfort caused by improper digestion. Since such feelings are regular effects of indigestion, and since we rarely have other physiological problems which cause these feelings, we standardly identify indigestion by its characteristic feel. But we shouldn't conflate the feeling with the underlying cause. It is at most a symptom of the cause.

Doubtless we do often discern our anger or joy introspectively. But our ability to "see" inwardly is parasitic on our ability to see outwardly

– on our ability to discriminate between different types of behavior. At one level this seems startling; in another respect, a commonplace. At some time or another each of us discovered we were in an emotional state we had initially failed to acknowledge. Most of us have vehemently denied we were angry when everyone present knew otherwise. ("I am *not* angry," said in an especially harsh voice, shows in its tone what it denies in its words.) Likewise for other emotions. We discover what initially eluded us: that we are in love, depressed, or anxious. Usually we make these discoveries not introspectively but by becoming cognizant of our behavior (or our tendencies to behave). You may not recognize your love for Bobbie until you notice your overwhelming desire to be with her all the time. I may be oblivious to my anxiety until a friend asks: "Why are you so jittery?" Discovering we are in an emotional state by observing our behavior would be mysterious, however, if emotions were merely inner, subjective feelings.

Though feelings that follow emotions are typically similar, the feelings are not the same as, the causes of, or even necessary accompaniments of, emotions. Nonetheless, they are constituents of paradigm cases of emotions. They are useful indicators. However, they are reliable indicators only if they are consonant with overt behavior. If I claim to be in a certain emotional state, yet my behavior belies that claim, you should conclude that I am lying, acting, or mistaken. If I claim to love Juanita yet systematically ignore her interests, verbally and physically abuse her, and in general demonstrate no loving behavior toward her, then you should conclude that I don't really love her, regardless of what I say or feel. Perhaps we can tell some elaborate story – like that about the Polish woman who claims to hate the Nazis – which could explain why I love Juanita despite my apparent disregard for her interests. Perhaps. But that story would be plausible only if supported by other as yet unmentioned features of my behavior.

Consequently, even if we ultimately reject behaviorism as an exhaustive account of the emotions, we must conclude that emotions are, in some important sense, irrevocably tied to behavior. Our claims to be angry, embarrassed, happy, or in love are fallible; the claims are plausible only if consonant with our behavior. Recognizing this modest claim would have dramatic consequences for personal relationships. If we look for emotions in the wrong place (inside) then we will often fail to recognize them. And we cannot change what we do not recognize. If we assume that we are infallible judges of our own emotions, we may well overlook the presence of potentially destructive emotions, such as jealousy, resentment, guilt, envy, etc. If, on the other hand, we acknowledge this behavioristic insight, we will become more concerned about how we act, less concerned about what we feel. We will watch what we do and will listen to others' appraisals of us. We will thus be less likely to delude ourselves into believing we are reasonable when we are not, that we are not jealous when we are, or that we love someone when we do not.

Conclusion

Once again we see how a mistaken understanding of ourselves hampers personal relationships. If we are preoccupied with how we feel rather than how we act, we may misdescribe our own emotions. If we fail to recognize that emotions are habits, we may make misguided attempts to alter them. Both of these mistakes will diminish our ability to create and sustain meaningful personal relationships.

NOTE

1 Descartes's view is, of course, more complex than this brief description suggests. For instance, despite Descartes's general assertion that emotions are sensations, in some places he acknowledges the intricate connection between emotions and judgements (1972, Part Second). However, I did not want to discuss all the nuances of his theory, but only to focus on those features which influence the common understanding of emotions and thereby affect the conduct of our personal relationships.

3

Why Do I Love?

Most of us know many people yet we love or befriend only a few. For this there is a ready explanation: we do not have enough time to relate to all of them personally. Is there, however, an explanation for why we love specific people? Are there reasons why we come to love Cherie and Bob, are friendly with Wanda and Ralph, yet relate only impersonally with William and Louise?

This question is difficult to answer, partly because it is ambiguous. Someone who wants to know "the reason for the floods of 1993" seeks their *cause* (global warming, acid rain, and the like), while someone who wants to know "the reason for nuclear disarmament" seeks a *justification* of disarmament, the arguments mustered on its behalf. In these cases the wording of the question indicates which sense of "reason" is operative.

Occasionally we may want to know both the causes of and the justification for some phenomena, for example, Jerry Falwell's belief in God. We might want to know *the reason why* Falwell is a theist, for instance, his upbringing, the historical influences which shaped his beliefs. Or we might want to know *Falwell's reasons* for being a theist, for instance, the arguments he offers for the existence of God. Likewise for the case at hand. You might want to know *the reasons why* I love those I love, that is, the causes of my choices. On the other hand, you might want to know *my reasons* why I love them, that is, whether there is any "reasonable ground" for my choices (Russell 1981: 65). Although the term "reason" can be used to mean either "cause" or "justification," unless I state otherwise I shall use the term to mean "justification."

Three Views

There are three prominent accounts of why we love those we love. The first claims there are no rational justifications for love, only causal explanations of it. On this view we are usually attracted to people whose personalities mesh with ours. Thus, a gregarious person may be attracted to others who are similarly outgoing; a melancholic person, to those who are cheery; an intelligent person, to those of like intelligence; a domineering person, to those who are insecure. In atypical circumstances, however – for example, if we are especially depressed or ecstatic – we may be attracted to virtually anyone. In any event, our relationships are caused, even if we cannot immediately specify the operative causal forces and mechanisms.

The second view acknowledges that psychological propensities and environmental circumstances partly determine the people to whom we relate. But we also have reasons (justifications) for loving those we love. Those who think reasons are (or can be) causes might contend these two views are equivalent (Davidson 1963). However, even if reasons are causes, we can still distinguish between causes which are reasons and those which are not. We thereby show that there is a genuine difference between these views: the first view holds that there are only bare causes of our love; the second view, that some of these causes are also reasons.

The third view claims love is neither caused nor based on reason. Instead love is bestowed: it is a gift from one person to another, a result of personal choice that is neither completely caused nor rationally justified.

As is often the case, each of these captures something significant about personal relationships, something the others are prone to neglect. The exact nature of those insights, however, can emerge only after a closer examination of each.

Causes of love

Similarity and complementarity theories Psychologists studying close personal relationships rarely study (or even mention) people's reasons for their relationships. Instead, they seek causal explanations of them. What they seek, they find. Most contemporary psychologists claim empirical studies reveal that we relate to people similar to us. However, they disagree about the foci of similarity. Some say we seek those with similar personalities; others say we seek those with similar interests; still others say we seek those with similar world views.

Although similarity theories are currently the rage among social psychologists, a minority maintain the theory of complementary needs (Winch 1958). According to them, we do not seek relationships with our clones; rather, we are attracted to those with complementary traits: those whose features allow us to satisfy needs we cannot satisfy in relationships with our clones (or on our own). On this view people with dominant personalities will not be attracted to one another since they will inevitably clash. Nor will submissive people be attracted to one another since each would want the other to take charge. Instead a submissive person is more likely to be attracted to a dominant person, and a dominant person to a submissive one. That way, so the argument goes, both people get precisely what they want. Although this view reflects the old adage that "opposites attract," it has little empirical support. Nonetheless, some psychologists still advocate it; they also offer reasonable explanations for why the thesis resists empirical verification.

A brief look at one theory   The psychologist's assertion that personal relationships can be explained causally merits serious consideration. Although I cannot catalogue – let alone evaluate – each theory and each empirical study supporting those theories, I will scrutinize one prominent theory. That will help us better understand all causal explanations of personal relationships.

According to psychologist Steve Duck, the primary motive for interpersonal relationships is "personality support" (1977; 1983: 27ff; 1991). Most similarity theories isolate one goal of personal relationships – "a sense of community, emotional stability, communication, provision of help, maintenance of self-esteem," etc. (1977). But these features, Duck says, can be understood more broadly as serving "to support and integrate the person's personality." More specifically,

> Each of us is characterized by many thoughts, doubts, beliefs, attitudes, questions, hopes, expectations, and opinions about the current patterns that there are in life. . . . Our personality would fall apart if all of these opinions were not, by and large supported. We would simply stop behaving if we had no trust in our thoughts or beliefs about why we should behave or how we should behave, just as we stop doing other things we are convinced are wrong . . .
>
> Each of us needs to be reassured regularly that our thought-worlds are sound and reliable. A friend may help us see that we are wrong, or

could help to see that we are right about some part of our thinking . . . but our friends are very likely to be similar to us in many of our attitudes and interests so that these discussions are more likely to be supportive than destructive. . . . [In short] we seek out as friends those people who help to support our thought-world-personality (1983: 27–8).

Put more succinctly elsewhere, people "seek consensual validation for their cognition and views of the world" (Duck 1977: 70).

Why are friends often similar?   When respected psychologists like Duck echo a commonly held belief ("Birds of a feather flock together"), we must seriously examine their claims. After all, friends *are* often similar in significant respects. That requires explanation. That similarity can be explained, however, without embracing the view that personal relationships are causally explicable.

Duck claims people enter relationships to obtain "consensual validation for their cognition and view of the world." He supports his claim by citing socio-psychological studies showing that friends and family typically have similar world views. However, these empirical results do not straightforwardly support Duck's contention. When two events are correlated, we cannot straightforwardly infer that one of the events caused the other; perhaps both were caused by some third event. For instance, there is a statistical correlation between ice cream consumption and drowning deaths. That doesn't show, however, that eating ice cream causes drowning, or that drowning deaths cause increased consumption of ice cream. More likely there is a third event, high temperature, which is a contributory cause of both.

Moreover, even if we could infer that one event caused the other, we cannot always discern which causes which. Duck contends the desire for personality support causes the initial attraction and also helps sustain personal relationships. Conversely, I contend the relationship often causes the similarity. Let me explain. Close friends care about one another, listen to each other, and respect one another. Since we are more likely to appreciate a view held by someone we love and respect, one of us may adopt the other's belief, or, more likely, each of us will modify our views so they resemble our intimate's. In short, similarity is frequently a result of close relationships, even if it is not their goal.

There are other reasons why the views of those in close relationships are often similar, especially those in certain types of relationships.

Marriages, for example, are likely to be successful only if the partners generally agree about how to run a house, how to spend money, where to live, whether to have children, and, if so, how to rear them. If Joan wants to live in a large city, does not want children, is a big spender, and likes to vacation on the Riviera, while Jim prefers small towns, wants five children, is frugal, and likes to camp in the mountains, then Joan and Jim are in for trouble. One (or both) of them must substantially alter or suppress their beliefs, goals, and desires. Likely that will make one (or both) of them miserable or resentful. If Joan and Jim are prudent, they should reconsider marriage. But they should do so not because each wants an intimate to reinforce his or her world view, but because each recognizes his or her goals can be realized only in concert with a partner who shares them.

Consider the following analogy: I want to build a house like one designed by Frank Lloyd Wright. Since I lack the time or technical expertise, I hire an architect. But not just any architect. I want one who likes Wright's designs. That does not indicate, however, that I want someone to pat me on the back and tell me what excellent taste I have. Rather I recognize that the architect must generally like the plan if her work is to be timely and of high quality. I do not dislike architects who prefer different styles; rather, I realize I cannot work with them in these circumstances.

Thus, marriages and goal-oriented relationships are generally successful only if both parties have *roughly* similar behavior and *roughly* similar beliefs about matters pivotal to their relationships. But that does not imply that we invariably choose spouses and friends to validate our beliefs. Rather we recognize the futility of establishing certain kinds of relationship with people who do not share certain beliefs and goals – beliefs and goals like those mentioned in the previous example.

These considerations partly explain why people in close relationships are often similar. Partly, but not entirely. After all, everyone occasionally seeks friends who mirror their views; some people seek such friends exclusively. But from this we should not conclude that all relationships are explained by the desire to be with similar people. Still less does it show that relationships built on such desires are especially valuable.

Some problems with the causal view Empirical studies are useful. They can accurately describe people's behavior and beliefs. They cannot, however, prescribe how we *should* behave or what we *should* believe. I suspect many psychologists think such questions are beyond the purview of their discipline. However, some psychologists claim these empirical results reveal not only how people do act, but how they *should* act. Others leave that impression, even if they do not explicitly state it. For example, when Duck says that "each of us needs to be reassured," he implies that we would be healthier and happier with friends who have the same world view (Duck 1983: 28). He thereby implies that the evidence about how people do act tells us how we should act. However, although many of us may choose friends because they validate our world view, why should we infer that this is what we should do – unless, of course, we think the majority is always right?

Of course we do need some friends with whom we agree. We would be miserable if we constantly clashed with all our friends. Moreover, as I argued earlier, those in marriages and goal-oriented relationships need to be similar, in at least certain respects. Nonetheless, we have no reason to believe all or even most friends must be like us, or that we need complete similarity, even in marriages. To suppose that assumes, among other things, that a person cannot support or be supported by those with different personalities and beliefs. But why suppose that? Two friends may be substantially different yet, because they find each other thoughtful and honest, they can support each another.

Of course many of us may dislike relating to people who are considerably different from us, at least when those differences are immediately relevant to our relationship. It is time-consuming and emotionally draining to have friends who challenge what we believe and how we live. It is more comfortable to have friends who agree with us. But that does not mean such relationships are especially valuable. In fact, if most of our friends were similar to us, we would be deprived of the constructive criticism and the exposure to opposing points of view which dissimilar friends can provide. Exposure to different views, different lifestyles, especially by people who care for us, can help us grow and mature (Maslow 1973; 1968). But I must wait until later chapters to fully develop this thesis.

Finally, if our love were causally explicable in the ways these psychologists suggest, our love would be devalued. On this view we could explain love in the same way we would explain tuberculosis or the national debt – as the product of biological, chemical, or psychological causes. However, we do not think our love for others is completely explicable in these ways. We do not think, for instance, that we love whom we love because we were depressed after receiving a D in microbiology or because we had an elevated white blood cell count. Likewise, we do not think others' love for us is causally explicable. Others do not love us because their teeth were aching the day we met or because we reminded them of their fathers. These events may have played some role in determining whether we were open to establishing a personal relationship. No one need deny that. But it would devalue love if these completely explained it.

Those holding a causal account of love would deny their view belittles love. Indeed, they might well argue that it is belittling to love another for reasons. "Loving someone for reasons," they might say, "means we love them simply because they have some characteristic (kindness, intelligences, etc.) we desire. If so, we do not really love *them*, we just love their characteristics."

Someone raising this objection thinks love should be rigid rather than historical. But, as I argued in the previous chapter, although rigid love is the norm for our relations with young children, kin, and fellow citizens, it is not the norm for voluntary, reciprocal relationships – most especially, romantic relationships and relationships with friends. These latter relationships – which are the focus of this book – are typically historical: they are based on the beloved's particular embodiment of traits. Although these relationships may assume a certain rigidity over time, they typically retain their historical flavor – at least those which are especially valuable. Thus, the relationships of special interest to this book will be those based, in important respects, on the beloved's traits.

It is, of course, inappropriate to love someone because of a single characteristic. We should not love someone simply because she is intelligent or funny or kind. But that is inappropriate because love should not be based on a small segment of the person, not because she is separable from her characteristics. I cannot (voluntarily) love someone devoid of characteristics. Thus, for voluntary relationships, we should have reasons for love, and those reasons must be based on the beloved's characteristics.

I should reiterate, however, that none of this implies that ordinary causal forces play no role in the initiation or the sustenance of a relationship. Such forces are clearly operative. Therefore, studies which identify them are valuable. For if we recognize the causal forces at work, we are more likely capable of resisting those which move us to initiate unproductive or unhealthy relationships. For instance, although we may be attracted to depressed people because of some traumatic occurrence when we were infants, we will likely come to resent them because they are too needy. If we recognize our tendency to initiate such relationships, we can more likely resist it.

The bestowal of love

Other people claim love is neither the result of causal forces nor justified by reasons. Loving is a choice, a gift from one person to another. This claim, though, is ambiguous. If it is interpreted as claiming that we have complete control over whom we love, it is false. After all, the causal view of love does capture part of the truth: through no conscious choice we find ourselves attracted to people with certain personalities, smiles, manners, or bodies.

Nonetheless, we are capable of exercising some control over whom and how we love. Although we may be attracted to certain types of people who are bad for us, we need not act on that attraction. We can resist that urge just as we can resist any detrimental urge. Some alcoholics abandon the bottle, some smokers give up cigarettes, some compulsive gamblers forgo the racetrack. Some of us can also eschew detrimental relationships, even if many of us do not.

We likewise have some ability to determine to whom we will relate. If we think there are types of people whom we should befriend, we can choose to act in ways which increase the likelihood we will find them attractive. We can choose to spend time with someone and make a special effort to identify and focus on her positive traits. We may subsequently find we are attracted to her.

In short, even if we cannot choose our desires, we can control how we respond to them. We may also create new desires or suppress old ones. To this extent love *is* something we bestow. How, though, should we exercise this control? Are all forms of control equally good? No. It would be silly to choose someone on a whim. Instead we should reflect on our relationships, and then pursue and deepen the most valuable ones. To this extent we should have reasons for our choices.

Reasons for love

When people talk about *falling* in love, they imply they had no choice in the matter. Although we sometimes speak in those ways, most of us also recognize there are (or should be) reasons why we love those we love. We think it is inappropriate to love someone for no reason at all and we assume some reasons are better than others. We see this belief reflected in Barbara's claim that: "Tom doesn't love me, he just loves my body (or money, or social status, etc.)." Barbara thereby expresses her doubt that Tom *really* loves her; she fears he wants to be with her because of what she has, rather than who she is.

Most of us share some beliefs that certain features of a person are not legitimate reasons for love, that other features provide some, although not weighty, reasons for love, and that still others provide excellent reasons for love. For instance, if Tom claims to love Barbara because she has a baby-blue Ford, we presume he does not have any reason for loving her. If he claims to love her because she dances well, we might think he has a reason, although not much of one. On the other hand, if he claims to love her because she is kind, we might think he has a good reason, although not a sufficient reason. Of course not everyone agrees about what is a reason, let alone a good reason. Someone might think it is appropriate to love another for her body or money, while it is inappropriate to love her because she is kind. Nonetheless, each of us thinks there are some things we could fill into the blank ("You don't love me, you just love my . . .") which expresses our belief that the other does not really love us.

On the other hand, most of us think there are substitutions which make the claim nonsensical: if someone said, "you don't love me, you just love my character, intelligence, moral insight, humor and goodnaturedness," we would not know how to respond. Together these reflect widely held views about appropriate and inappropriate reasons for love. To love others *simply* because of their money is seen as a shallow or no reason for love, while to love them because of their character or moral sensitivity is not only acceptable, but laudatory.

Not only do we want to have reasons for loving others, we want others to love us for reasons. No one wants to be told: "I don't love you because you are intelligent, sensitive, aesthetically tasteful, humorous, pleasantly disposed, or challenging. In fact, I don't like any of your traits. I just love you." We would fear, rightly so, that they didn't love us. That explains why, on balance, we don't want to be loved rigidly, at least not by friends and lovers. If others love us rigidly, we do not receive the personal affirmation we want from our voluntary relationships.

Hence, both lover and beloved want to love and to be loved for reasons – and those reasons must be based on each other's characteristics. But not just any characteristics will do – only those central to who they are. This explains why money is not a good reason for love. Most of us don't see money as part of "who we really are." Thus, if I relate to someone because of her money, we have a trade relationship, not a personal relationship. Conversely, most of us assume intelligence, personality, moral insight, etc. are essential elements of who we are. Therefore if we relate to another (or another relates to us) for these reasons, we have a personal relationship, not a trade one.

Of course, we must be cautious when we assess reasons for love. Suppose Ted loves Tonya because she is rich. Does he thereby have a reason for loving her? We cannot determine that until we know whether he loves her for her money, or because she is the kind of person who has money. In the former case he really loves the money; Tonya is just a means to it. In the latter case, he loves Tonya because she is aggressive, competitive, etc., that is, she is the type of person who typically has money. These latter characteristics are genuine features of the self, and thus are sensible reasons for loving her.

Consequently, we have uncovered a plausible method of distinguishing proper and improper reasons for love. If Frank genuinely *loves* Laurel, then he must love *Laurel*, that is, his love must be based on features central to who she is – even if we disagree about which features those are. This is an important discovery but, it turns out, not one we can easily exploit. The notion of the self is problematic. Neither philosophers nor the general public have a single, incontrovertible view of the self. Therefore, before we can utilize this discovery to evaluate purported reasons for love, we must detour into philosophical territory to survey competing accounts of the self.

Philosophical Views of the Self

When discussing the "problem of the self," philosophers are usually concerned about "personal identity over time." They want to know what makes me the same person now that I was 25 years ago – after all, I do not look the same, talk the same, think the same, or act the same. Moreover, most of my cells have also changed. Yet apparently there is something – the self – which persists throughout these myriad changes. Although that is not the specific issue I want to discuss here, it is intricately related to issues I do wish to discuss, namely "What makes me me?"; "What makes you you?"; "What is it that is central to who I am and who you are?" Answering these questions will help us explain personal identity over time. More importantly for present purposes, it will help us identify and evaluate reasons for love.

Debates about personal identity have been closely linked with philosophical accounts of mind. Some people believe the self – "who they are" – is exhausted by those features standardly identified with the mind: intelligence, character, moral stature, etc. Although others do not think the self is exhausted by these features, everyone acknowledges the self is intricately connected with our "mental" characteristics, however they are described, understood, or explained. Thus, before we can identify those characteristics which provide appropriate reasons for love, we must discuss competing theories of mind.

The problem

We often describe and explain human behavior using mental idioms. We attribute Jane's callousness to her ignoble character; John's shyness, to his fear of groups; and Bill's fawning behavior, to his love of Susan. In other contexts, we describe and explain human behavior using physical idioms: we excuse our foul mood as an (inevitable?) result of physical pain ("Sorry I snapped at you, but I have a throbbing headache"), and we explain some aberrant behavior as caused by a physical defect ("His schizophrenia is caused by a dopamine imbalance").

Although most of us describe and explain human behavior using both mental and physical idioms, these dual modes of explanation and description are intellectually perplexing. I shall briefly discuss several attempts to understand the relation of mind and body, and, of special interest to the current discussion, how these are related to the notion of the self. I shall not even pretend to offer an exhaustive catalogue of all the options or a complete analysis of those I do discuss. My intent is only to discuss the nature of self to the extent that it can illuminate

– and can be illuminated by – our discussion of close personal relationships. To that end, I shall briefly outline four prominent views of the mind and discuss their understanding of the self. Then, in the following chapter, I will sketch an alternative view of the self – albeit a view indebted to several of the more standard options. I shall show, among other things, how this view is uniquely compatible with an informed understanding of personal relationships.

Dualism

For centuries dualism has been the dominant theory of the relation between the mind and body; it continues to be the preferred view of the person on the street. The general idea of dualism is this: a human is a combination of a mind and a body, which, although profoundly different, interact. In the forms of dualism especially relevant to the current inquiry, each of us is said to be immediately and transparently aware of our own mental states. That is, each of us has privileged access to our thoughts, beliefs, desires, wishes, sensations, emotions, etc. Even with Herculean effort, no one else knows what each of us knows about ourselves effortlessly. Rhoda's leg cramp may feel *like* Joe's, but Rhoda can never feel Joe's pain – only Joe can. And although both Joe and Rhoda can think about the Taj Mahal, their thoughts are not identical. In contrast, others can know our physical features as well as we can. Moral considerations and practical difficulties aside, Joe has no more privileged access to the physical states of his body than does Rhoda. Anyone can observe Joe's body as well as, if not better then, he. To take a dramatic example, neurosurgeons can observe the condition of Joe's brain in ways he cannot.

That is because physical objects have size, shape, weight, and spatial location. A chair may be 4 ft. tall with a wooden back, weigh 6 lb., and be located exactly 9 ft. from the closet door. We can specify its dimensions and relationships mathematically. Anyone in the room can verify our measurements. In contrast, thoughts about the chair do not have these characteristics. Your thought is not 9 cm high; it does not have any height at all. It is not a trapezoid; it is devoid of shape. It does not weigh 2 g; it has no weight. Nor is it located 1.3 mm behind your right ear; it is not located anywhere. Physical descriptions (properties) cannot describe mental events. That is why the dualist claims these events must be, or be actions of, some non-physical thing.

Most dualists also think the self is largely if not exclusively identified with the mind. The mind is the seat of reason, desires, thoughts, wishes, and beliefs – all those things we consider central to "who we are." But a non-physical object has no way to move in a physical world, unless, of course, it resides within a physical object: a body. Thus, when others see our bodies, they do not see us, but the vehicle through which we move. By observing the actions of this "vehicle," they can *infer* what our inner selves are like; but the real self they can never see.

Some dualists describe their theory somewhat differently. According to Brentano (1960), the distinguishing feature of the mental is the "intentional inexistence" of mental phenomena. Although the phrase "intentional inexistence" is opaque, the idea behind it is not. It is this: mental phenomena always refer to a content or object. We do not just think or believe or imagine. We think *about* Vienna, believe *that* the moon is spherical, or imagine *that* we won the lottery. We always imagine some object(s), believe some claim(s), desire some thing(s). Not so for physical events or objects. They are not of or about anything. They do not have content. Hence, we can describe physical events in purely physical terms (size, shape, weight, and spacial location). We identify them in ways others can verify.

The notion of intentionality can be made a bit more precise by looking at the way in which we use intentional idioms. If the truth of a sentence is unaffected by the existence of the item picked out by the direct object or propositional phrase governed by the main verb, then the sentence is intentional. For example, the sentence "Many Salemites feared witches" will (presumably) be true even though there were no witches. The intentional object of their fear was witches (what they thought to be witches); that is true even though there are no witches. Similarly, the sentence "Many children believe in the tooth fairy" will be true independently of the existence of the tooth fairy.

In this respect sentences about mental events fundamentally differ from sentences about physical events. Sentences about physical events *are* affected by the existence or inexistence of objects to which they refer. Thus, the truth of: "Salemites killed witches" and "The tooth fairy lives in Detroit" depends not only on people's beliefs, but on the existence of witches and tooth fairies. To identify the differences between these types of sentence is to understand that there is a major rift in the universe. Although we can completely and adequately describe physical events without referring to intentional objects, we cannot describe, understand, or explain mental phenomena apart from their content. We must conclude, the dualist claims, that the mental and physical are fundamentally distinct.

Non-dualistic theories

The remaining theories of the self I discuss are non-dualistic. These theories do not necessarily deny that we often use or need mentalistic terms to describe and explain persons (though some non-dualistic theories do deny this). What they deny is that mental events are properties of some radically different substance. On these views people are not composed of two unique types of things which interact; rather persons are unified creatures. They are bodies behaving in ways we describe using mentalistic language. But from this we should not conclude that mentalistic terms refer to things fundamentally different from physical things.

Behaviorism   The first non-dualistic alternative is behaviorism, a theory I mentioned in the previous chapter. B. F. Skinner has forwarded the most influential form of psychological behaviorism (Skinner 1974; 1953). But here I wish to focus on one of its philosophical cousins, propounded by Gilbert Ryle (1966). I will explain Ryle's theory using a variant of one of his examples.

Suppose you invite a prospective student to visit the local university's philosophy department. You introduce the student to the teaching and support staff, you show her all the offices and classrooms, you arrange a lunch with some of your better students. As she is preparing to leave, she praises the office facilities, claims to be impressed with faculty and students, but then asks: "When will I be able to see the department? The building is attractive, the students are smart, and the staff is pleasant," she says, "but I wish to see the department as well."

Ever so patiently you explain to her that she has seen all there is to see. It is not that there are all these elements of the department, and *then* there is a department. The department *simply is* the building, staff, students, courses, etc., all organized in a certain way. To assume otherwise is a category mistake: it is to treat an abstract description ("department") as if it referred to a specific thing.

Dualists make a similar category mistake. The dualist recognizes that we cannot straightforwardly translate everything from our mentalistic vocabulary into our physicalistic vocabulary. There is no obvious way to describe, understand, or explain beliefs, thoughts, wishes, and desires using just the language of physics and chemistry. For instance, bees have size, shape, weight, and (constantly shifting) spatial location, and thus, can be described using just the language of physics and chemistry. However, fear of bees cannot be described in these ways.

From these facts, though, we should not conclude that the mind and the body are fundamentally different things. After all, says Ryle, the mind is not a *thing* at all. To assume the mind is a thing is to commit a category mistake – akin to our imaginary student's mistake. The student thought "the philosophy department" was a thing. Furthermore, since she could not see this thing, she inferred it must be some non-physical ghostly thing over and beyond its constitutive elements. In like manner, the dualist cannot see minds with microscopes nor describe thoughts using the language of physics and chemistry. She thus infers that the mind must be a non-physical thing hovering near the body. But we do not need ghostly things to explain either academic departments or persons.

The behaviorist claims mentalistic terms do not refer to objects in some mysterious, private realm. We learn to identify and talk about mental phenomena, not by introspection, but by observing our own and others' behavior. We first learned about anger by observing others. Perhaps we overheard mother scolding our brother for staying out all night; we thereby learned how to use "angry" language. We similarly learned about love, pride, hate, and joy. We learned how to use public, physicalistic language to describe not only others' mental life, but also our own. We describe some pains as sharp (like those produced by sharp objects) or throbbing (as in the beating of one's heart), and our ecstasy by referring to some public phenomenon ("I feel like a million bucks"). Without references to public objects, we could not describe, pick out, or individuate our so-called private experiences. (If this sounds wrong, try it some time.)

This explains why the behaviorist rejects the dualist's contention that mental phenomena are transparent. Since there are no mental properties or things for us to see, hear, or experience, we cannot immediately and infallibly know our own mental states. If we know ourselves, we know ourselves in the same way others do, by listening to what we say and watching what we do. If we know ourselves better than others do, it is not because we have incorrigible access to our real ghostly self, but because we are around ourselves more – we have more opportunities to observe how we behave.

In short, the behaviorist says there is no mind – if "minds" are non-physical ghostly substances. But in that sense there aren't any departments or universities either. However, there are departments and there are minds in an ordinary sense: we can talk in such ways to describe organisms (and organizations) which act in complex ways.

Identity theory   Mind-brain identity theory (sometimes simply called "materialism") is a recent non-dualistic attempt to explain the relation between mind and body. Identity theorists recognize that a mentalistic vocabulary is useful for understanding and describing human behavior. For instance, we typically identify beliefs by reference to their intentional objects. However, while the dualist contends this is the only way we will ever be able to identify beliefs, the materialist contends that everything we wish to say about minds could be said by talking about brains. As neurophysiology progresses we will discover that all beliefs are nothing but brain states. This is not wishful thinking, materialists claim; it is a reasonable prediction based on previous neurophysiological findings (Churchland 1979). Neurophysiology has already discovered that certain areas of the brain are the source of specific visceral responses, while others are closely connected to human conceptual abilities. For instance, electrical stimulation of specific areas of the brain can create fear, hunger, sexual desire, anxiety, anticipation, etc.

Our own experience likewise suggests there is a close connection between mental and physical events. When ill, we not only feel badly, we do not think clearly. Head injuries don't merely disturb the circulation of the blood through the brain, they disturb the "circulation" of thought. This would be so, the materialist claims, only if the mind and brain were identical.

It is not surprising that our forefathers thought mental and physical events were distinct. They sought the best available explanation of human behavior; given the information to hand, dualism was plausible. Certainly there are other circumstances where our ancestors failed to recognize that two different words referred to the same object. The materialists favorite example is this: for millennia sky watchers understandably assumed the morning star and the evening star were distinct, after all, they appeared at different times of the day. Later astronomers discovered that the morning and evening star were identical – both referred to the planet Venus. The result: we had two non-translatable vocabularies referring to the same object. Materialists predict that advancements in neurophysiology will have similar results: neurophysiologists will ultimately explain all mental phenomena in terms of brain states. Once they do, we will conclude that the mind and body are identical. Since we have reason to believe neurophysiologists will eventually make these discoveries, we should now acknowledge the identity of body and mind.

Functionalism   The most recent form of materialism is functionalism. According to the functionalist, the dualist is right in thinking there is no straightforward one-to-one correlation between mental states and brain states. That is, we have no reason to believe that for each distinct mental state there is precisely one physical state to which it corresponds. However, the dualist is wrong in thinking the mind is fundamentally distinct from the body.

True, mentalistic language and physicalistic language do not completely overlap. However, that is unsurprising since these languages do not even purport to talk about the same things. Mentalistic language describes the functions of a human being, the way we behave. Physicalistic language describes the physical structures undergirding those functions. We have no reason to think these are inter-translatable. Nonetheless, although these are distinct vocabularies, they need not be about different *things*.

For example, a clock's function is to keep time. Its physical make-up is, if mechanical, a system of gears and springs and, if electronic, a microchip. The function in both cases is the same although the physical structures differ. Put differently, we can have different causal mechanisms for achieving the same function. Thus, even though clocks are simple mechanisms, there is no one-to-one correlation between their function and structure. Why should we suppose there is a correlation between mental function and brain structure when these are clearly more complex than clocks?

From this we should not infer that function and structure are divorced. The function can be ultimately broken down and understood by reference to the structure (often by means of introducing still smaller functional parts of the clock, for example "the function of the spring is to . . ."). Why not presume likewise with the mind and the body?

The functionalist concludes the mind and body are not distinct things. Rather there is a logical link between behavior and the self; the self is what it is because of the way it acts. In this regard, it shares an important feature with behaviorism: behavior is not something which emanates from the self, rather it is a constitutive part of the self. However it differs from behaviorism in the following significant respect: whereas behaviorists are loath to talk about or admit the presence of underlying structures, functionalists are not. They recognize there is an undergirding structure of human behavior and they think we should strive to understand it.

It is now high time that I spell out the implications of these theories for our understanding of the nature of the self, and especially our understanding of persons in personal relationships. That I do in the following chapter.

4

Reasons for Love

Thinking about the self has considerable practical relevance: it helps us understand why we should have reasons for personal relationships, and it empowers us to evaluate competing reasons. Conversely, thinking about personal relationships has considerable theoretical relevance: it helps us evaluate competing philosophical theories of the self. Most philosophers are skeptical: they doubt whether anything as mundane as our ordinary understanding of personal relationships can illuminate anything as mystifying as the nature of the self. They are mistaken. Or so I argue. An informed view of persons in personal relationships provides powerful reasons to reject dualism and to embrace an activity view of the self.

Reasons in Personal Relationships

If Tom loves Barbara, he should have reasons for his love – even if he cannot completely articulate them. These reasons should make explicit reference to Barbara's characteristics. Tom should be able to say, for example, that he loves Barbara because she is funny, or interesting, or insightful, or kind. If he cannot, he would begin to doubt his love. So would Barbara. She will be distressed if he cannot explain his love. If she isn't, it is either because she doesn't realize what his inability indicates, or because she loves him (non-reciprocally) so much that she will tolerate this failure.

However, this is no way implies that our love for others could or should be articulated completely, especially in the early stages of a relationship. To assume it must is to treat decisions about personal relationships as akin to mathematical calculations where reason would *dictate* whom we should love. Reason indisputably plays (or should play) an important role in our relationships. But it is practical, embodied reason, not abstract reason; it is the reason of John Dewey, not Immanuel Kant.

Relationships typically begin because we enjoy another's company (Thomas 1988). Or, to use the psychologists' language, we are attracted to them (although attraction does not imply anything sexual). This attraction is usually best explained causally. We may be unable to articulate any reasons for the attraction; reasons we can articulate may be little more than guesses. As we relate to the other, however, we should be able to offer some, albeit still not exhaustive, reasons for our interest in her. Certainly we expect to have such reasons in well-established relationships.

In these respects loving others is akin to other likes: we can explain them, but only partially. For example, I happen to like my job. I can explain why. It is challenging, allows interaction with interesting people, and provides a forum to spout my beliefs. Nonetheless, these reasons do not completely explain my fondness for the job. Almost certainly they do not explain how I originally chose it. Most of us do not choose friends – or jobs – the way we choose a car. When purchasing a car many people know generally what they want and how much they are willing to pay; then they search for a car that meets their requirements.

However, we do not look for friends who match some predetermined set of characteristics – or if we do, we will likely be disappointed. We sometimes discover we have reasons for liking a person only after discovering that we like her. I may find myself inexplicably intrigued by someone who is a bit impudent. Later I discover she helps me see my blind allegiance to and fawning behavior toward people in authority. Or I may be inexplicably attracted to a shy, self-conscious person, and later recognize she exposes my desire to be popular.

In short, reason often plays little role in initiating relationships. But after relating to a person, we can rationally evaluate our relationship to decide if we should abandon, preserve, or alter it. Put differently, reason does not command behavior; rather it audits or commends it. It is in this sense that people should (and often do) have reasons for love.

The role of reason

Many philosophers will think the previous account denigrates reason. Not so. Reason is exceedingly important in the conduct of our personal lives. However, reason is not some external power which dictates how we should behave, but an internal power, integral to who we are. To attain knowledge is not the sole end of human action. Humans are primarily active creatures, not passive knowers. Practical reason audits action so we (can) make action more meaningful, more successful (Dewey 1988; Rorty 1979). Consider, for example, what it would mean to say that we selected our friends because reason dictates. If reasons for love were like reasons for believing mathematical statements, rational people could not choose their loves, rather they would *be rationally compelled* to love those with the requisite characteristics.

However, neither love in particular nor practical reason in general functions this way. Reason does not command that we love anyone. Nonetheless, reason is vital in determining whom we love and why we love them. We may begin relating with someone for any number of reasons. But after we have a relationship, we should rationally reflect on it to determine if we should sustain it and, if so, whether and how to alter it. Put differently, practical reason does not compel action; rather, it evaluates, justifies, and subsequently redirects it. Reason tell us whether our choices are moral or prudent, thereby helping us decide how to behave in the future. This is the sense in which we have reasons for love.

Understanding practical reason in this way highlights the importance of one specific reason we sometimes have for loving another (a reason discussed in the first chapter), namely, that we have a history of relating with them. There are many people we admire, many people whose traits we find attractive or interesting. We might even think that, under the proper circumstances, we could be friends, long-time companions, or lovers. However, aesthetic appreciation does not a relationship make. A relationship is formed and shaped by relating: the sharing of activities, ideas, peeves, jokes, and, in deeper relationships, money and bodies. The interaction is the glue. The more we relate, the more intermingled our lives become. The more intertwined our lives become, the more each of us has a reason to continue the relationship; the separation would, in some significant sense, tear us apart. If we have a successful relationship it is generally imprudent to abandon it to pursue a relationship with another, even another with traits similar to our current partner. This is true not only of profoundly deep relationships but also of friendships of utility and pleasure. Reason cannot predict that we can relate satisfactorily to any potential friend. The only way to know we can relate successfully is to successfully relate.

Of course these historical dimensions of personal relationship do not require that we maintain friendships forever or that we seek unconditional commitments. Though there are demonstrable benefits of long-term relationships (which I discuss in later chapters), not all personal relationships need be permanent. If we are in a woefully inadequate relationship, we should fix it or abandon it. And we needn't make heroic efforts to maintain all our relationships, even if they are entirely adequate friendships of utility and pleasure.

Personal Traits

We should – at least eventually – have reasons for our personal relationships, especially deep and abiding ones. And those reasons must make reference to the other's traits. And not all traits will serve as equally good reasons. Suppose I said I liked *The Brothers Karamazov* because the book cover was aesthetically pleasing. You could plausibly infer that I did not grasp what it means to like a novel. The cover, after all, is not part of the book; it is merely an appendage, an accidental feature. (Even if we think all books must have a cover, they needn't have any specific cover.) Correspondingly, I cannot be said to really love a person unless the love is based on who she or he is, on her or his central characteristics. But how do we determine which traits are central? That was one question the philosophical theories of the self were supposed to illuminate.

Characteristics are identified by behavior

There is only one reliable basis for ascribing character traits to another: her behavior. We don't decide if another is intelligent, kind, or patient by consulting an ouija board, the local soothsayer, or even the person in question. Rather, we watch and listen to her, we see how she behaves. Intelligent people typically act intelligently; kind people regularly do kind actions; patient people persevere.

This is not to say that kind people are never cruel; intelligent people, never silly; or judicious people, never impulsive. To say that Joan has certain character traits is not to imply that she always exhibits them; it implies merely that she usually does. Thus, we do not deny that someone has a trait simply because she failed to act in a certain way in a single situation. However, we do deny that she has a trait if she never exhibits it. Belinda is not intelligent if she consistently fails intellectual tasks which others her age find easy. She is not kind if she is regularly cruel to her friends, family, and pets. And she is not patient if she usually becomes frustrated whenever she is forced to delay a few minutes.

At first glance this is so obvious that it does not require defense. However, many people object to identifying a person's character traits by how she behaves. They claim the agent's attitude is an essential element of her characteristics; some even equate traits with attitudes. Suppose, for example, Ruth gives money to the poor, not because she cares about them, but because she is a senatorial candidate who wants the electorate to think she is kind. Such a woman, so the objection goes, is not kind, no matter how she acts.

If Ruth's reasons for charity are as described, then I agree: she is not kind. But this just shifts the debate one level higher. We must now identify Ruth's attitudes or reasons. But attitudes, in my view, are not mysterious ghostly entities to which only the actor is privy. Rather, they describe the agent's dispositions to behave. Thus, we discern Ruth's attitudes and reasons not by asking her for a report of some inward experience, but by seeing how she regularly acts in a wide variety of circumstances. If she typically ignores others in need, then we have reason to say she is unkind, no matter what introspection reveals. On the other hand, if she regularly gives to charity and is sensitive to the needs of her neighbors and colleagues, then she is kind, no matter what introspection reveals. Entertaining mean thoughts does not make a mean person. If that were so, there would be no difference between a mean person and someone who was tempted to be mean.

If attitudes are relevant to the evaluation of others, they must be reflected in behavior. Merely internal attitudes – if there were such things – would have no moral significance. Suppose, for a moment, that Rick regularly runs roughshod over the interests and needs of others. Further suppose we could investigate Rick's inner space (whatever this would mean) and discover that Rick was filled with kindly feelings toward those he harms. We would still maintain our conviction that he is callous. His feelings would be irrelevant to our evaluation.

65

This does not imply, of course, that we can straightforwardly determine an individual's traits by a cursory glance at her behavior. There are numerous reasons why we may misunderstand another's character: (1) We may see only a small part of that person's behavior, or (2) we may misconstrue or misinterpret the behavior we do see, because (3) we may also be unduly influenced by faulty factual or moral beliefs. In short, it is often difficult to know another. I do not wish to explain here how we can know another – that I do in chapter 6. Here I claim only that we cannot know another's character traits by consulting some internal mental state accessible only to her. Of course we may consider an individual's self-reports in determining her attitudes and traits, but only if her reports are compatible with the behavioral evidence to hand. If her reports are incompatible with her public behavior, then we believe the behavior, not the self-ascriptions.

"But surely," someone might say, "we can imagine someone to be intelligent even though she appears feeble-minded. Consider Helen Keller, who was, since infancy, blind, deaf, and mute. As a child she behaved erratically; she threw ferocious tantrums. Her family judged, not surprisingly, that she was mentally defective. But surely she was intelligent," the objection continues, "even though her intelligence was not evidenced in behavior." The argument has plausibility, but only because she eventually acted intelligently – after she learned sign language. If she hadn't, we could not justifiably claim she was intelligent. "But," someone might continue, "suppose she had never learned to communicate. Wouldn't she still have been intelligent?" I think not, although perhaps she might have had the *capacity* for intelligence. Even if we could have looked inside her skull and found the biological structures which support intelligence, we should not conclude that she *was* intelligent before she acted intelligently. A capacity for intelligence is not intelligence.

We all have unrealized capacities for complex behaviors. Given my size, for example, I might have had the capacity to be a professional football player. But I never developed that capacity. Hence, it would be inappropriate to say that I *really was* a professional (or professional quality) football player. Nor could we even confidently predict that I would have been had I only tried. There is only one way to know if I had those abilities: if I had in some way evidenced them in my behavior.

Some objector might try a different tack. She might claim that whereas intelligence is identified by behavior, morally significant traits like selfishness are best identified by an individual's underlying attitudes, and attitudes are best identified by the agent in question. On this view selfishness is an attitude, for example, a selfish person is someone who sees her interests as more important than others. This attitude then prompts her to act selfishly. The behavior is a result of an inner attitude, and is thus derivatively deemed "selfish." The real measure of whether someone is selfish is this inner attitude, not her outward behavior.

Consider Ron, a hard-working fellow who is generally decent to his family, friends, and neighbors. But when Ron is forced to take a considerable cut in salary, he changes. He pursues his personal interests at the expense of his family and friends; he verbally stabs co-workers in the back in order to endear himself to his supervisor. Two years later, after landing a huge promotion, Ron reverts to his "old" self.

Ron claims that during this two-year period he maintained kind feelings for and positive attitudes toward his family and friends. Assuming Ron honestly reports his feelings, then, according to this objector, he is (and was) not selfish. His behavior, although less than ideal, was understandable under trying circumstances. Since he maintained a selfless attitude, he was not selfish, no matter how he behaved.

This contention is mistaken. For selfishness (and kindliness) is not a matter of what one thinks or feels but what one does. If Ron acted selfishly for two years, we should conclude that he was selfish, at least during this period. Of course that does not mean Ron is unqualifiedly selfish – after all, his behavior before and after this incident suggests otherwise. It is, though, accurate to say that Ron has a penchant for being selfish *when the going gets tough.* That is, he is selfless when it doesn't cost much, but selfish when personal costs are more substantial. Recognizing this is not only more accurate, it empowers Ron to be more selfless even when times are tough. If, on the other hand, Ron really thinks he was selfless simply because he had selfless thoughts, then he is unlikely to change.

In summary, there are circumstances in which we reasonably describe ourselves or others as having traits not evidenced in current behavior. However, when we do, we must have (1) independent behavioral evidence to suggest that we (or they) have the trait in question and (2) a plausible explanation of why our (their) inclinations were not exhibited in those circumstances. Otherwise, we have no reason to ascribe the trait in question, no matter what the agent reports.

A philosophical objection

There is a common philosophical objection to the view I have for-warded. I have argued that a person's traits are unalterably tied to her behavior. Some have asserted that this is tantamount to saying that we can say everything we meaningfully wish to say about ourselves and each other without any reference to personal characteristics or thoughts or beliefs or attitudes. Or, to put this objection slightly differently, I am presuming that for each statement about a person's characteristics or mental states there is a completely equivalent statement about that person's behavior.

· That is not what I am saying. Mental and behavioral ascriptions may not be equivalent. Indeed, I think demand for an equivalence or reduction is a bugaboo. Nonetheless, some behavioristically inclined philosophers thought they had to provide an equivalence, that they had to explain how each and every statement about the mind could be translated without loss into statements about behavior. It is not appar-ent why (Dummet 1982).

For the present purposes, at least, I claim only that we can say virtually everything significant about a person's traits using behavioral language. However, I would be astonished if all statements about traits were completely translatable. Once we develop two different vocabu-laries to describe the same phenomenon, each vocabulary takes on a life of its own. Each evolves as languages do: each mutates in different ways; each experiences different selection pressures. Subsequent modi-fications may well have "survival" value: while using one language we may devise new and interesting ways of speaking, ways the other language cannot easily capture. Even some sentences in two similar languages, say English and German, are not easily translatable. Yet we all assume English and German speakers are living in and talking about the same world.

We can likewise see this same phenomenon within regions of the same language. H_2O is the chemical symbol for water. Yet chemists cannot say everything they want about water – for example talk of molecular structure – in everyday language; that's why they developed molecular symbols. On the other hand *we* cannot say everything we want about rain, sleet, and snow using the language of chemistry. For instance, we do not interpret claims about crystalline H_2O as equiva-lent to claims about snow. However, the fact that these statements are not quickly translatable does not imply that these phenomenon are fundamentally (ontologically) distinct. Snow is not a different substance from H_2O.

Or to take another case, we cannot say all we want about the American or the British government merely by itemizing the choices or behaviors of people within those governments. Governments function in ways individuals cannot; their actions are understood only as the actions of an institution. But we should not therefore conclude that the government is some *thing* over and beyond individuals.

The core of the view: the self is embodied

To summarize the argument so far: people should have reasons for love. Those reasons must be based on the other's central characteristics. We identify these people's characteristics by how people behave. Therefore, since behavior is inevitably embodied, so is the self.

Some people would balk at this conclusion. Yet our own experience in personal relationships provides ample reason to accept it. While some dualists typically see the body as an appendage or a vehicle through which our selves move, lovers do not relate to their bodies as things some inner self directs or manipulates. Rather, they experience their bodies as an integral part of who they are. Lovers are not inclined to say: "Gee, dear, our bodies had sex last night; I hope they enjoyed it."

Of course, there may be times when lovers say things like this. But when they do, it is not because they are separable from their bodies, but because one or both of the partners were inattentive to the other – perhaps because he was preoccupied with *his* involvement in the activity. Self-conscious attention to an activity changes that activity. If I say to myself, "Oh, look, I am having sex," I change the action. Usually I diminish the enjoyment and value of the activity. Likewise for self-conscious writing, walking, talking, or sports. Self-conscious attention to a current activity makes the activity stiff, not genuine (try walking while being acutely conscious of every step). The activity is more genuine, more effective – more *us* – if we just act without self-consciously thinking about what we are doing.

This in no way denigrates self-consciousness. Self-conscious reflection allows us to audit our behavior, to evaluate and modify our action so it is more meaningful, more productive, and more focused. But self-consciousness and reason are not valuable unless they have activities to evaluate. To put a twist on the well-known Socratic slogan: "The unlived life is not worth examining." So we return to the same conclusion: humans are active, embodied creatures, not disembodied self-conscious knowers.

What exactly does it mean, though, to say that we are embodied? Although I cannot say in detail, I can say enough for current purposes: to illuminate our understanding of persons and relationships. Our bodies limit the range of our characteristics. We are circumscribed by our physical size, intellectual capacity, the nature of our vocal cords, and the balance of our endocrine system. If I have enormous or tiny hands, I cannot become a concert pianist; if I have an IQ of 60, I will not become a professional philosopher (well . . .); and if I am hyperactive, I should not join the bomb squad.

The body not only limits the range of our traits, it also dictates their style or tone. Consider Rough and Ready: Rough is 7'2", Ready is 5'4"; Rough weighs 195 lb., Ready weighs 350 lb. Their size is not a peripheral feature of who they are; it constrains their options; it modulates their style or tone. Suppose both are comedians. Their physical appearance will influence the tone of their humor. For example: Ready could tell fat jokes which wouldn't make sense if told by Rough.

The idea that the self is embodied is made vivid if we consider seriously the possibility of brain transplants (or mind transfers) discussed by science fiction writers and philosophers of mind. What *would* happen, for example, if we switched the brains of Shaquille O'Neill and Margaret Thatcher, or Mother Teresa and Robin Williams?

The results would be laughable: Mother Teresa's calm character trying to animate Williams's frenetic body; Thatcher speaking to the House of Parliament in O'Neill's body. This makes for interesting science fiction – with the emphasis on *fiction*. The reason these swaps seem so preposterous is that *these* specific personality types won't fit with *those* bodies. The resultant Mother Teresa might still be kind; but not *in the way* she currently is. And O'Neill might be Prime Minister, but not in *the way* Thatcher was. Our bodies are not mere appendages to the self or vehicles through which the self moves.

Many dualists conceptualize the self's relation to her body as analogous to the scuba diver's relation to her aqualung. Just as the aqualung is merely a means for surviving under water, the body is merely a means of surviving on this physical earth. Neither the aqualung nor the body are part of who we are. However, I contend the more apt analogy is this: the body is to the self as gills are to a fish. I may don an aqualung for a particular purpose; when I am finished I can remove it. Moreover, there is no particular aqualung I must wear. I can use one today, a different one tomorrow. But a fish cannot live without gills; nor can it trade in used gills for new ones. Gills are not mere appendages for fish; bodies are not mere appendages for persons.

Imagine we were forced by circumstances (say, a nuclear holocaust) to live under water. We devise a means to permanently affix (or grow) aqualungs. Having done so, the aqualung would become part of us. We would learn to move, think, desire, and love as underwater creatures. Our present bodies resemble these fictional aqualungs; they are essential parts of who we are.

Implications for Our Understanding of the Self

The argument so far suggests dualists have no plausible account of personal characteristics. And since reasons for love must be based on the beloved's characteristics, dualists cannot explain love (close personal relationships). That's one strike against dualism. Our understanding of personal relationships creates still further problems for dualism. To see how, we need only remember one motive for dualism: its apparent ability to explain personal identity over time. Philosophers want to explain why George Bernard Shaw was the same person at 84 that he was at four. According to biologists virtually every cell in his body had changed during eight decades; his beliefs were different; he likely had no direct memories of his early years. Why, then, should we think he was the same person? The dualist response: there is something inside Shaw which persisted unchanged throughout all the outward changes. George Bernard Shaw was the same person at 84 that he was at four because he had the same unchanging ego. That is why it was appropriate to identify both as different moments of the same person.

Although this response might ease some people's concerns about personal identity – and thus survival after death – it creates insurmountable problems for our understanding of personal relationships. Dualists explain identity over time by claiming that our real selves persist unchanged throughout our seemingly ubiquitous changes. That

71

is, they treat changes in bodily shape and size, ideas, beliefs, desires, wishes, personality, as peripheral to who we really are. But we cannot think of ourselves – or those with whom we have close relationships – as some "thing I know not what." Our bodies, personalities, beliefs, desires and wishes are not accidents. Rather, they are significant personal characteristics, essential to our sense of self. Perhaps more importantly for present purposes, they are the basis upon which we explain our love for others, and others' love for us.

Dualism might be modified to blunt the force of this objection. For instance, some dualists might claim that the mentalistic self, though distinct from the body, is causally inseparable from it. This is an option, but not one that would be widely accepted even by many contemporary dualists, for example Swinburne (Shoemaker and Swinburne 1984). But this maneuver would blunt the current objection only by sacrificing much of dualism's initial appeal. The modified dualism would no longer be especially capable of explaining personal identity over time; nor would it (easily) permit the possibility of personal survival after death (since the body is an ineliminable part of the self).

Finally, most forms of dualism make knowledge of others mysterious. If we are distinct from our characteristics, then Barbara could never directly experience or know Tom. She can watch his body, listen to him talk, and observe his behavior. But these, the dualist claims, are not Tom, but are the results of Tom's actions. The real Tom, Barbara cannot see, experience, or relate to. She can only *infer* what he is like. Perhaps her inferences are correct. But since she can never compare her beliefs about Tom with the real Tom, she cannot know that. Not even Tom could know. Tom, on the dualist's model, can know who he is. But he cannot compare his introspective understanding with *her* account of who he is; the veil which denies Barbara access to Tom also denies Tom access to Barbara. He can infer – but he cannot know – how Barbara understands him. Hence, even he cannot verify that her views are correct.

This makes personal relationships impossible in most forms of dualism. Since we cannot love what we cannot know, if dualism were true we would have to radically alter our understanding of persons and personal relationships. Love becomes not just mysterious, but impossible.

Doubtless some dualists think I am overstating the problem. They may argue that since there is a (non-standard) causal connection between the mind and body, we can reasonably infer the nature of the self from observed behavior. But given the fundamental distinction the dualist draws between the mind and body, this is not an inference she can reasonably draw. She has no reason to think there is a causal connection in her case; still less in the case of others.

After all, we do not generally correlate our thoughts with our behavior, primarily because we do not experience behavior as something we do, but as something we *are*. When we speak it is *we* who speak; we do not experience ourselves as some inner person borrowing vocal cords the way we might borrow a megaphone. When we walk it is *we* who walk; we do not experience ourselves as an inner person going for a ride. If we do, we are inarticulate, bumbling, or psychotic.

Even if, contrary to fact, we were confident of a causal connection between our own thoughts and behavior, we could not infer a similar connection in others. The inference would be even more questionable than trying to infer the precise nature of a puppeteer simply by observing her puppets. We know from experience that people manipulate puppets. But suppose we had never seen a puppeteer: we were unable to look above the curtain. Further suppose puppetologists told us we could not, in principle, see, hear, touch, or smell puppeteers. Under such circumstances we would have no reason to believe there were puppeteers, still less could we know anything about them.

Yet the dualist suggests we can know other selves even though we have never seen one – only the bodies those selves animate. Nor could we, in principle, ever directly experience another self; search all we want, we can never see anything more than an animated body. Others' selves would thus be as mysterious as invisible puppeteers.

It might seem all theories of the self face the same problem: after all, the self is unquestionably elusive. The dualist's problem, however, is unique. Behaviorists, functionalists, and most materialists think we can know others, even if it is difficult to do so. But their explanation of the self's elusiveness is more plausible than the dualist's. The dualist claims we cannot know others since the self is some hidden inner thing accessible only to the person in question. Non-dualists deny the self is hidden. They claim we can see and experience others, even if we do not see all of them, and even if we fail to understand what we do see. In non-dualists' views, coming to know another resembles assembling a jigsaw puzzle. Just as we arrange the pieces of the puzzle to yield a coherent picture, we likewise arrange "pieces" of a person's behavior to yield a coherent picture of her. Of course, we may have seen the other person only occasionally, and then in tightly prescribed circumstances; thus, we do not have enough pieces of the puzzle to detect even a vague pattern. Or we may have seen her in a variety of circumstances over an extended period of time, yet don't know how to interpret her behavior: thus, although we have enough pieces of the puzzle, we don't know how to put them together.

Put differently, materialist views of mind claim we can know others because selves are embodied. However, since the self is not a specific *thing*, trying to know the self is often difficult – like trying to know "the United States government." The "object" we want to know is diverse and continuously changing. Hence, it cannot be known in its entirety. Moreover, it has conflicting elements. Nonetheless, we can know governments – and we can know people – by how they behave.

Behavior does not just reflect who we are, it constitutes who we are. To paraphrase Aristotle, people become builders by building; they become just by doing just acts. If we desire certain traits, we must act accordingly. We don't become great pianists merely by thinking about being pianists – we must practice. We don't become honest by think about being honest – we must be honest. And we don't become kind by closing our eyes and wishing we were kind – we must act kindly. To believe otherwise is to believe in magic (Dewey 1988: 3–7).

Accounting for intentionality

Before developing the claim that we are constituted by our activity, I should examine one specific feature of personal relationships which appears to support dualism. Intentional states, as you may recall from the discussion in chapter 3, are states with an object or content: they are *of* or *about* something. Mental states are prime examples of intentional states: I have a thought *of* Loch Ness, you believe *that* Merrill Lynch is your stock broker. Only dualism, some philosophers claim, can permit and explain intentional states. Thus, they argue, since we inevitably view those to whom we relate intentionally, the existence of personal relationships suggests dualism is true.

This argument is unconvincing. Although it is true that we view those to whom we relate intentionally, we also describe other things intentionally, including things with which we could not have personal relationships because they are inanimate objects. We say, for example, that *The Prophet* is *about* love. Or we ascribe beliefs and desires to a chess-playing computer. We say, for instance, that the computer believes its opponent plans to capture the computer's knight or that it desires to checkmate its opponent. According to the dualist, however, these ascriptions are parasitic on human intentionality. We should not conclude that the book and the computer really *are* intentional. *The Prophet* is not really *of* or *about* anything; the computer does not really have beliefs. We interpret the book intentionally only because it was written intentionally. We consider the computer's moves intentional only because it was designed to operate *as if it were* intentional. Thus, we should not be surprised to learn that the book and the computer are best described intentionally.

Why, though, should we share the dualist's disdain for describing a computer intentionally? Suppose I am watching you play chess. I assume you have certain beliefs and desires (e.g. the desire to pin the opponent's queen or to place the king in check or to win). I would assume the same for a chess-playing computer. How else could we understand its moves? According to Dennett, we *must* understand the computer's moves intentionally – there is no other way to understand it (1978). Even the grammatical rules for using intentional idioms are applicable to computers. For example, the sentence "The computer thought it was best to capture the knight" would be true even though that was a rotten move.

There is, of course, one difference: the human is conscious while the computer (apparently) is not. However, that is beside the point. The particular objection we were considering was that intentionality – not consciousness – is the mark of the mental. Perhaps the dualist's point, however, is that only conscious states can be genuinely intentional.

This maneuver, however, backfires. This response asserts that all intentional states are conscious. Yet we frequently ascribe intentional states to others even when we know they are unaware of them; we sometimes ascribe intentional states to people who would disavow them. For instance, more than once others have recognized that I was angry even when I have vehemently denied it. This would be nonsense if all intentional states were conscious (and if, as all would agree, anger were an intentional state). More generally, if all intentional states were conscious, we could make no sense of self-deception; moreover, self-knowledge would be a given, not an achievement. Thus, since some of our non-conscious states are intentional, then why can't a chess-playing computer also have intentional states?

Perhaps the intentionalist will simply assert that purely physical objects cannot be intentional. But why should we suppose that? Are there *a priori* reasons for saying that objects cannot be intentional? I cannot imagine what they would be. Even if we once thought physical objects could not be intentional, our experience with computers should force us to reconsider this claim. Current computers can only be understood intentionally, and future developments will surely result in ever more complex behavior which will be incomprehensible unless interpreted intentionally. In the face of such developments, why should we continue to suppose that the computer is not *really* an intentional system? And, if we do not need a dualistic metaphysics to explain intentionality, then viewing our intimates intentionally will not give us any reason to embrace dualism. The objection fails.

A Proposal: Self as Activity

Although standard materialist accounts of the self are preferable to dualism, they are not without their problems. Neo-behaviorism and functionalism are on the right track in recognizing the centrality of behavior for the self. But many (most?) theorists make what I take to be a cardinal error: they search for a *thing* which is a person: they try to understand persons in terms of the substance of which they are made. In so doing they ignore Ryle's lasting insight. I would like to end this chapter by proposing, in a more formal, though still abbreviated way, what I earlier suggested: that we should understand persons in terms of embodied activity.

We must first distinguish persons from human beings (Tooley 1972). "Human being" is a biological classification. To be a human being is to be a certain type of organism, a member of a particular biological species. ('Human being" does have a more normative usage, but that is roughly equivalent to the notion of "person" described below.) To be the same human being over time is to be the same biological organism. Period.

"Person" is not a biological category. It is a term we use to describe organisms which behave in certain complex ways – say, like a mature adult. All persons we current know are human beings. But they needn't be: sophisticated aliens would be persons if they are not human beings. Moreover, not all human organism are persons – we sometimes say of someone in an irreversible coma: "She is a vegetable."

Thus, although we typically identify the same person with the same organism (since the requisite complex behavior is usually associated with the same biological organism), the two categories are distinct. But that does not imply that there are two things, a person and an organism. Rather, there is one *thing* described in two ways. As it turns out, we can best understand the behavior of well-functioning organisms if we see them as persons (just as we can best understand computers if we see them as intentional systems).

Put differently, "person" is an honorific; it is not a biological classification. To understand much of Queen Elizabeth's behavior we need know only that she is a person. But that will be inadequate for understanding other behavior, most especially, her actions *as monarch*. From this, though, we should not conclude that she is really two things (a queen and a person), let alone three (queen, person, and human being). She is a single creature that can be evaluated and understood in different ways, described in different ways. Were she to abdicate, we would say that she had been queen, but is now "just" a person. This does not imply, however, that a queen is some type of peculiar metaphysical object. Rather "queen" is a category for understanding and evaluating part of an organism's behavior. It is not a category which even purports to describe a metaphysical entity.

Try a different example. Suppose you ask: "Who is Hugh LaFollette?" I contend there is no straightforward answer, since the request is ambiguous (though the context would likely clarity it). You might want to know how to recognize me in a crowd, in which case the answer would be: "He's the tall red-headed fellow with the beard." Or you might want to know: "What kind of person is he?", in which case the answer should be: "Look and see. Observe how he acts. Listen to what he says."

A similar ambiguity arises if you want to know if I am the same person who was once a part-time fundamentalist preacher. If you want to know: "Is this the same organism?", the answer is a simple yes. We have biological laws to explain the development of the organism which was once a preacher and is now a teacher. On the other hand, if you want to know "Does this organism act in the same ways?", the answer will vary, depending on your purposes. Someone might plausibly respond: "Yes, he is the same person: he retains certain central elements of his personality", or they might say: "No, he is not the same person: although some characteristics remain, certain vital characteristics have changed."

Neither answer is unqualifiedly correct; it all depends on our purposes. Once we recognize that persons constantly change, it does not matter whether we say we are the same people despite changes or that we are different successor persons (just as I am the son of my parents, I am the ancestor of the Hugh LaFollette of yore). Not much hangs on it.

If, in a particular case, something practical *does* hang on it, we can give an answer, depending on the circumstances which demand an answer. Suppose we need to ask: "Is this the person Jones designated to receive his inheritance?", then if she is Jones's daughter (the same biological organism he fathered 42 years ago) the answer is "Yes." Or suppose we need to ask "Is this the person (Juan Corona) who killed two dozen migrant workers 20 years ago?", the answer will vary depending on our purposes (and our available psychological information). For instance, we should not base our decision to continue incarcerating him based on a contentious issue of metaphysics. We might decide that he *really is* the same person (whatever that means in this case), yet conclude that incarceration is inappropriate since he has changed so radically. Or we might decide he is *not* the same person, yet think we should punish or restrain him anyway since he is a "successor person" who continues to be a threat to society.

Understanding selves as activity has profound implications for our personal relationships. Since we constantly change, self-knowledge is now an ongoing effort, not a one-time achievement. Moreover, since both you and I continuously change, a one-time commitment *now* will not help us *then* – after all *then* we will not be the people who committed ourselves to stay together. Consequently, if commitment is to be more than an empty gesture, we should not merely commit to "love, honor, and cherish." Rather, we should commit ourselves to act in ways which enhance the chances we will stay together; for instance, regularly communicating. These are themes I shall pursue in more detail in chapter 12. Finally, understanding that knowing others is difficult should make us wary of jumping to quick conclusions about what someone is like and why they act the way they do. These are themes I consider in more detail in chapter 6.

Which Reasons for Love are Best?

Given the argument so far, which reasons for love are best? Reasons, as you may recall, must be based on a person's characteristics. Since dualism cannot permit genuine characteristics, the dualist cannot have any reasons for love; *ipso facto* the dualist cannot explain why some reasons are better than others. Even if dualism were modified to countenance accidental characteristics, this would not help her since all characteristics would be equally accidental. But reasons for love must be based on the beloved's *central* characteristics.

What about functionalists and behaviorists? These theorists contend that persons have genuine traits. Hence, we can evaluate reasons for love according to the centrality of those traits. To this extent these theories are superior to dualism. But they are not without their problems. Traits which these theories consider accidental, e.g. money, fame, social standing, etc. could not provide reasons for love. Yet in some circumstances these might be reasons for love, even if they are not ideal reasons. An activity view of the self *could* countenance these traits as providing reasons for love. For instance, if I spend my entire life desiring, thinking about, and acquiring money, then acquiring money *would*, on the activity view, be a part of who I am. Thus, having money could be *a* reason for loving me, even if it were not a very good reason.

There are still other traits (intelligence, kindness, aggressiveness, etc.) which most of us agree could provide reasons for love; after all, these traits are central to who we are. But which reasons for love are best? Personal relationships must be founded on a recognition of each other's unique characteristics. As long as the identified characteristics are deep and stable – that is, as long as they are genuine parts of who we are – then they are a basis for love. But as it stands, this answer is incomplete. If Eva loved Adolf because he was cruel, she may have had a plausible basis for her love, since he was infinitely cruel. If Pat loved Richard because he was ruthless, she, too, may have had a plausible basis for her love. However, neither cruelty nor ruthlessness is a desirable trait. Thus, we may be suspicious that although these are reasons for love, they are not particularly good ones.

To say anything more definitive, however, we must first determine the value of personal relationships. Only after we know which relationships are valuable will we be able to specify which reasons for love are best. Those features which promote the best relationships will be the best reasons for love. That, at least, is what I argue in the next chapter.

5

The Value of Personal Relationships

Close personal relationships are extremely valuable, some of the most significant elements of our lives. We cannot entirely understand personal relationships unless we understand their value. Understanding their value will empower us to develop and sustain good relationships. It will also help us resolve the question raised at the end of the previous chapter, "What are the best reasons for love?"

Intrinsic vs. Instrumental Value

Some people claim personal relationships are intrinsically valuable – valuable in and of themselves. Others claim personal relationships are instrumentally valuable – valuable because they promote other values. For those who hold the former view, this chapter should contain a single sentence: "Friendship and love are intrinsically valuable." Although I have some sympathy with this claim, I am uneasy with the distinction as typically drawn; I am also uneasy with what it often implies. By putting substantial weight on the distinction between intrinsic and instrumental values, we construe human values as distinct, relatively independent. We thus fail to appreciate, in general, the interdependence of human values and, in particular, the network of values which promote and are promoted by personal relationships. Let me explain.

Many people draw the distinction between intrinsic and instrumental (or extrinsic) value like this: some things are intrinsically valuable; for example, friendship, knowledge, health, and virtue. These are valuable – and ought to be desired for their own sake, not because they promote any other values or ends. In contrast, money is instrumentally valuable. It is not valuable for its own sake, but because it enables us to obtain other valuable things; for example, food, shelter, and health care.

As a psychological distinction, this is clear and relatively uncontroversial: some things we desire because they help us achieve specific ends or goals; others we desire without having any specific end in mind. Money seems to fit the first category; health, the second. The error comes in treating this psychological distinction as marking a fundamental difference in value. It ignores, and perhaps masks, the interconnectedness of human values.

Consider. Health is something all or most of us presumably desire for its own sake. However, do we want health regardless of its consequences? Would we desire health if, when healthy, we felt miserable and were incapable of productive activity? The objector might claim I am confusing the matter. "It is not," she might say, "that health is a means to good feeling and increased activity. Health does not cause us to feel better; to be healthy *just is* to feel good and to be capable of productive activity. These notions are conceptually related." This objection hinges on a distinction between causal relations and logical or conceptual relations. A brick's falling on my head causes pain and perhaps death. But a coin's landing heads up does not *cause* it to land tails down; its landing heads up *just is* for it to land tails down. "By the same token," the objector claims, "being healthy does not cause us to feel better; being healthy *just is* to feel better. Thus, we do not desire health as a means to some other end. Rather, we desire it as an end in itself."

Again, although I am sympathetic with the thrust of this response, as stated it fails: "being healthy" and "feeling good" are not conceptually related in any strong sense. Suppose by "health" we mean "the well-functioning of a biological organism in the absence of any specific disease" (a standard lexical definition). Some people who are healthy claim to feel badly, and some people who are unhealthy – say, people who have high blood pressure or are cancer ridden – claim to feel just fine. Unless they are fibbing or horribly mistaken, we should conclude that health and feeling well are conceptually distinct.

Even if they were conceptually related, problems remain. Part of what people mean when they say something is intrinsically desirable is that all people desire it. Yet not everyone desires health. Some people are masochists. Others are chronic whiners; perhaps they are inveterately lazy and being ill provides a ready excuse for their inactivity. Still others may like feeling badly since if brings the attention they so desperately want.

Of course those who claim health is intrinsically desirable may not think all people do desire it; they may think instead that people *should* desire it (or that *rational* people do desire it). But this permutation does not solve the problem at hand since not all rational people do desire health. Indeed, there are circumstances in which people have good reason for not desiring health. Chronically ill slaves may have been treated better than healthy ones. In such conditions it would be arguably rational to desire to be unhealthy. Of course these are unusual circumstances. I wish to show only that health occasionally undermines other values and, to that extent, is not unqualifiedly valuable. Generally, though, we do desire health, and we do not desire it for any *particular* reason. That is why health is typically a constituent of a satisfying life.

To fully explain why, let's take the previous suggestion one step further. Are feeling good and being active (which are, in this view, conceptually related to health) intrinsically or instrumentally valuable? Do people desire these in and of themselves, or do they desire them as a means to still other ends? Admittedly most people do desire them. But would they desire them if they had no activities they wished to pursue? I doubt it. Certainly they would desire them less than they would if they had activities they wanted to pursue. Health is valuable not merely because we like feeling good, but because it empowers us to act as we wish, to pursue activities and goals we desire. Its value, however, is not tied to any particular activity, but to the possibility of pursuing virtually any activity.

Likewise for other presumably intrinsic values. Although from one perspective they appear basic, they are part of a larger network of values. To this extent, *some* of their value is instrumental. Consider knowledge. Knowledge appears to be valuable even when we cannot identify any *particular* value it promotes. Nonetheless, knowledge unquestionably promotes other values. Knowing about the world empowers us to avoid dangers and to provide goods necessary for survival. Knowing ourselves makes us more able to direct our own lives, to achieve our goals, and to establish and maintain meaningful relationships. Knowing others enables us to design sensible social and political institutions which will make our lives more productive, more satisfying. In short, knowledge empowers us to pursue virtually every interest we have.

This suggests a different way to distinguish between intrinsic and instrumental values – a parasitic way on Aristotle's account of value (1094aff). Knowledge and health are intricately tied to almost every value we have; they are basic to who we are and what we want to do. Contrast these with a VCR. VCRs are nifty devices, but their uses are limited. They contribute to only a few interests and values. That is why we consider health and knowledge are intrinsically valuable, while we consider VCRs only instrumentally valuable.

Values which serve one or only a small number of purposes we deem "instrumental." Those which are intricately connected to a large number of values we deem "intrinsic." That is, intrinsic values are promoted by and contribute to so many different values that we reasonably think they are valuable even when we cannot see any specific value or purpose they serve. In that sense, intrinsic values are constituents of a good life.

Thus, in the world you and I inhabit, it is reasonable to suppose that knowledge and health are intrinsically valuable. There is no specific reason to value them, no single goal they allow us to achieve. Rather they promote most values we have. Still, from *some* perspective their values are subordinate to others. In other circumstances they may not be valuable at all. Thus, it is best not to take the intrinsic/instrumental value distinction, in its original guise, as isolating a fundamental cleavage between types of values. If we wish to salvage the distinction we should redraw it along the lines suggested here: instrumental values have limited connection to other values, while intrinsic values are strongly interwoven with a large number of other values.

Using this distinction, personal friendships are intrinsically valuable. They are a central value of life; they are not mere means for other ends. I cannot envision a valuable human life devoid of close relationships. But that does not mean we cannot specify the values they promote. Indeed, given this new way of drawing the distinction, we can identify the large number of values which personal relationships promote and are promoted by, while still maintaining that they are, in this important sense, intrinsically valuable.

What are these values personal relationships are especially apt to promote? I shall mention four. Healthy personal relationships tend to (1) increase an individual's happiness, (2) elevate each intimate's sense of self-worth, (3) increase individual self-knowledge, and (4) develop character – especially moral traits. I will briefly explain why each of these is a value and will show how they are promoted by personal relationships.

Value of Personal Relationships

Increases happiness

Happiness is generally valuable. Both common experience and psychological studies confirm that personal relationships are an important source of happiness. Generally people in satisfactory, on-going personal relationships are happier and healthier than those who aren't. The psychological studies supporting this claim are legion (Argyle and Henderson 1985). To give one example:

> People with fewer friends are more prone to tonsillitis and cancer; while people who are in the process of divorcing actually stand an increased risk of heart disease, injury in traffic accidents, and being attacked by muggers. . . . People who are poor at making friends have been shown to have worse teeth and to get more serious illnesses. . . . Some researchers are starting to claim a direct connection between friendship problems and breakdown of the body's defenses against invasion by viruses. So it is not merely for reasons of enjoyment and satisfaction that we need to keep our friendships in good repair and try to let them help us; we need friends for life . . . (Duck 1983: 7–8).

This is not to say that happiness and health are the only or the highest values. But neither should we underrate them. All moral theories enjoin us to promote the happiness of others. Some, like utilitarianism, do so directly; others, like Kantianism, do so indirectly (Mill 1979; Kant 1981). Anything which promotes individual happiness without simultaneously promoting other values is undoubtedly valuable.

Elevates sense of self-worth

It is important for each of us to have a positive sense of self, to see ourselves as people whom others enjoy and respect. Those who have no regard for themselves are typically miserable, depressed (and

85

depressing), often guilty, and morally impotent. If we have no positive regard for ourselves, we naturally assume we have nothing to offer others. We are less inclined to be kind or sympathetic since we assume others neither want nor need our sympathy. Thus, self-esteem is a significant value which enhances, among other things, our ability to care for others.

It is imperative, though, to distinguish self-esteem from conceit. Despite some tendency to confuse them, self-esteem and conceit are not identical, or even related. Someone who esteems herself has a reasonable sense of her worth (or what we might call non-pejorative pride). She knows who she is, what she is capable of doing and doing well. Therefore, she can utilize her talents. She is able to help others as well as herself.

In contrast, a conceited person has an undue sense of her importance; she assumes she has a significance she does not have. A conceited person is not merely aware of her strengths and successes (real or imaginary); she thinks about, relishes, and focuses on them. Conversely, she ignores her weaknesses. But, as I noted in the previous chapter, constant self-reflection often diminishes those strengths we do have. If, for example, we are unduly proud of our oratorical skills, we will likely be less effective as orators; we will become more concerned with *our* having the skills, and less concerned with *using* them. Or if we think ourselves kind, we will become more concerned with *our* being kind and less concerned with *being* kind. Conceit is not just an awareness that we have certain skills or traits; it is the frequent self-conscious attention to them. The result: conceited people are not only haughty, they are often inept as well.

Relatedly, we must distinguish humility from self-deprecation. For although some people might think they are similar, I think humility is more closely related to self-esteem than to self-deprecation. A person likely to accurately identify her strengths is also likely to accurately identify her weaknesses. And someone well aware of her weaknesses is likely to be modest, humble. That is, modesty is a recognition of our limitations, or faults; it is a recognition that we are not all that important in the scheme of things. All of us have limitations; therefore, all of us should be modest. But we should not deprecate ourselves. Self-deprecation is more than just an awareness of our limitations; it is a tendency to focus on them. A self-deprecating person spends more time worrying about and brooding over them and less time trying to change them. Moreover, she is often oblivious to her strengths. And someone unaware of her strengths cannot make good use of them.

Consequently, it is detrimental to be obsessed with either our strengths or our weaknesses. If we pay undue attention to ourselves, we thereby divert attention from what we can do – for ourselves and for others. Hence, I think an appropriate sense of self-worth (which, on my account, is mingled with modesty) is crucial for well-being, for personal development, and for moral maturity.

Personal relationships play a crucial role in developing that sense of self-worth. We care for our friends because they are who they are. If they know we care for them, they are more likely to see themselves as lovable. That will enhance their self-esteem. They likewise care for us; that promotes our self-esteem. Without these relationships, it is difficult to imagine what grounds we would have for esteeming ourselves; we do not gain self-esteem in a vacuum, or, if we do, we are self-deceived.

It might appear that I am surreptitiously supporting a view I earlier denigrated, that the principal reason for personal relationships is per-sonality support (see chapter 2). My claim, however, differs from Duck's (1983) in several notable respects.

Personality support is not a suitable *motive* for personal relationships, although it is doubtless a *result* of many of them. If we enter close relationships simply to gain personality support, then not only will the relationships fail to be close, they will also fail to fulfill their intended purpose. If Bridget loves Bernie because she wants a heightened self-image, she will plausibly assume (or fear) that he wants the same. She will infer he does not really accept her for who she is; rather, he pretends to accept her because of what she can do for him, namely, boost *his* self-image. Realizing this, she has no reason to see herself as someone who is accepted for who she is. Thus, she has no reason to accept herself.

I can make the same point in a slightly different way. By selecting friends and lovers who support my personality, I will likely select those who constantly pat me on the back. However, I can esteem myself only if I know others accept me with all my faults. I can be confident that someone wants to befriend me faults and all only if she knows my faults. Hence, genuine self-esteem can come only inasmuch as our intimates are aware of our faults. So our self-esteem cannot be promoted by someone who constantly agrees with us, someone who "supports our personality." Close friends will disagree, criticize, and occasionally get furious with one other; but they accept each other nonetheless. By so doing each intimate learns she is worthwhile and lovable even with her blemishes.

In fact, our self-esteem is stronger when we can accept ourselves despite criticism. If all our friends regularly boost our ego, we might assume that we esteem ourselves. But if we have never been subjected to criticism, our so-called self-esteem may crumble the first time we are challenged. On the other hand, if we maintain a strong sense of self even after criticism, then we likely have a more lasting, more significant sense of self-worth. And it is difficult to imagine how we could achieve this sense of self-worth without intimates.

Promotes individual self-knowledge

Being a close friend both requires and promotes self-knowledge. If you are to relate openly and honestly with me – if you share intimate details about who you are – then you must first know to some degree who you are. You cannot share information you do not have, whether the information is about you or something else. (These claims are clarified and qualified in chapter 11.)

More relevant to the present discussion, close personal relationships promote self-knowledge. This happens in at least two ways. First, if Belinda is honest with Boris, she will not tailor her thoughts to impress Boris; rather she will be candid. She will, at least on occasion, say what comes immediately to mind: she will voice her immediate reactions about herself, Boris, other friends, and world events. This will increase Boris's knowledge of Belinda; it will also increase Belinda's knowledge of herself. While openly sharing with Boris she will hear herself make comments she will likely find surprising, comments which reveal aspects of herself she had heretofore not noticed.

Secondly, close friends want to help each other grow and mature. Thus, if Boris notes that Belinda is unduly sensitive to professional criticism, he will tell her. Though she may not be thrilled to hear his comments, they can help her better understand – and hopefully change – herself. He may also tell her that she is an exceedingly talented writer, something she failed to notice or appreciate. She may thus be more willing to submit her short stories for publication. These two forces work in tandem to enhance her self-knowledge.

Of course there are other ways we learn about ourselves: through introspection, feedback from mere acquaintances, psychological profiles, and even harsh comments from our worst enemies. But most of us, most of the time, learn more about ourselves from close friends than from anyone else. Our friends are in an especially good position to know us and can therefore provide the most accurate perceptions. Perhaps more importantly, since we know they care for us, we will be more willing to seriously consider their criticisms – after all, we assume they do not wish to hurt us. And we assume they care for us despite our flaws.

Develops character

As I have mentioned before, close friends do not cavalierly approve of each other's behavior or character. If you and I care for each other, each of us will want the other to be the best person possible. Each will want the other to change, to mature, to realize her potential. Consequently, each will help the other identify her weaknesses. This will heighten our self-knowledge. But we will not be interested merely in some abstract knowledge of ourselves. Each of us will encourage and help the other to use that knowledge to become a better person, to overcome her character flaws. This is a potent, perhaps essential, way we can build our characters and develop moral sensitivity. Loving criticism and personal assistance from our intimates can help us change in ways we cannot – or do not – change on our own (Friedman 1993; Blum 1980).

Moral character is also developed more indirectly. If Belinda has a close relationship with Boris, she will care for him. She will want to comfort him when he is hurt, to laugh with him when he is happy, to cry with him when he is depressed. She will want to be honest with him, and to trust that he will be honest with her. In short, the best way to care for him is to develop and refine moral traits like honesty, trust, benevolence, sympathy, etc. Without these she will likely be unable to care for Boris as she should. However, once she has developed these traits she will generalize them: she will likely become sensitive to people other than Boris. Consequently one of friendship's important values is its ability to promote moral character.

Which Reasons for Love are Best?

We are now in a position to answer the question first posed in chapter 3: "What are the best reasons for loving a particular person?" At the end of chapter 4, I concluded that any reason based on a genuine characteristic of the beloved constitutes an appropriate reason for loving *that person*.

But, as I suggested, there is another question lurking in the background. When we ask why we should love some particular person, we must discuss, as we have in this chapter, the value of close personal relationship. Otherwise, we may come up with an inappropriate answer to the question which prompted this inquiry. Suppose Pat loves Richard because he is devious. If her love is based on one of his central characteristics, then she has a reason for loving him. However, deviousness is both morally objectionable and detrimental to good relationships. Hence, I would contend she does not have a *good* reason for loving him. She would have a good reason only if she loved him because of his traits *and* those traits were conducive to the relationship. Let me explain.

Some relationships are better than others. What makes them better? Better relationships are those which best promote the values of close relationships. The best relationships will be those in which each party's characteristics are conducive to valuable close relationships. Therefore, these traits will provide *better* reasons for love than will traits which hinder relationships – traits which fail to promote relationships' values. Thus, if we want to have not only relevant reasons for loving someone but also *good* reasons, then the beloved should have traits which promote close relationships. More specifically, she should have characteristics which promote, or at least do not undermine, some of the values cited earlier in this chapter.

Can we specify traits which promote these values? Most assuredly. For instance, certain personality traits seem especially likely to promote the happiness of the beloved: even-temperedness, kindness, good humor, sensitivity, etc. Others appear to be detrimental: irascibility, egoism, depression, etc. Thus, the former traits provide good reasons for love; the latter do not. We should also note that most of these traits have marked moral dimensions: those conducive to happiness are generally moral traits; those which diminish happiness are generally immoral traits.

Hence, it seems a relationship is likely to promote happiness only if the partners have moral traits. That should not be surprising. As I have noted on several occasions, close relationships are non-egoistic. It is impossible to have a close relationship unless we can care for the interests of others, and that we cannot do unless we are moral.

Consequently, the first value of personal relationships is dependent in some significant measure upon the partners' having moral traits. Of course having these traits does not guarantee that we will be happy or that we will make our intimates happy. If that were so, any two people with well-developed moral characters could be close friends. They can't. Two people's personality styles might be radically different. One person might prefer to spend calm evenings at home while the other wants to go to local pubs and dance halls. Both might be fine people; but their personalities may be too different for them to establish and maintain a lasting close personal relationship. So moral traits alone will not guarantee that the people can be good friends or be happy together. Moral traits are a necessary but not a sufficient condition for close friendships.

Close relationships are also valuable because they increase a person's sense of self-worth. What traits are likely to promote the partner's sense of self worth? Those traits which allow us to accept another as she really is, faults and all. These are likewise moral traits: tolerance, acceptance, honesty, courage. Again, this is as we should expect since we cannot even have a personal relationship with another unless we are able to care for her, unless we have her as one of our ends. And we can do that only if we are somewhat moral.

Likewise for self-knowledge. I will reiterate here only what I have earlier suggested, that self-knowledge is best fostered if our partner has certain moral traits, most especially honesty, empathy, kindness, and tolerance. Finally, intimates who are themselves moral will be more likely to help their intimates cultivate, refine, and heighten their characters.

Conclusion

The value of close relationships is not tied to any particular value. Rather, their value is intricately connected with a wide range of important values, most notably happiness, self-knowledge, a heightened sense of self-worth, and the development of moral character. At least in this sense, close personal relationships are intrinsically valuable.

We can now bring together the arguments of the last three chapters: (1) love should be based on reasons; (2) reasons must make explicit reference to the beloved's traits; (3) the best reasons for love will make reference to those traits most conducive to close relationships; (4) the traits which will do *that* are generally moral traits. Therefore, the best reasons for love will be those which make explicit reference to the moral character of the beloved.

Consequently, I have offered the first line of argument for the Aristotelian thesis that only moral people are capable of establishing and maintaining close personal relationships. But I cannot complete the argument for this view until the end of the book.

Part II

The Personal Bond

6

Interpreting Another's Behavior

This chapter bridges the two major divisions of the book. In part I I discussed the nature and value of close personal relationships. In part II I discuss the conduct of ongoing relationships. How can we sustain and deepen them? How can we best be intimate, honest, and loving? Should we treat intimates equitably? Does jealousy damage close relationships? Is it desirable to explicitly commit ourselves to long-term relationships?

Knowing how to interpret and evaluate the behavior of others is crucial to understanding issues in both parts of the book. For instance, it is intimately connected to our having reasons for love. And, as I argued throughout part I, reasons for love must be based on who the beloved really is – on her characteristics. We can know those characteristics only by accurately interpreting her behavior. Therefore, our love will be justified only if we accurately interpret her behavior. Interpreting another's behavior is equally critical for the initiation and the conduct of relationships. Our interpretation of her behavior determines whether and how we relate to her. Therefore, our relationships will be successful only if we accurately interpret her behavior.

In several earlier chapters I argued that we can know others, but only by carefully observing what they say and do. But it is one thing to acknowledge we can know others, and quite another to specify how we do so. For it is not easy to know other people. Indeed, any adequate explanation of how we can know others must acknowledge the difficulty of knowing them.

The difficulty of knowing others has often been thought to vindicate dualism; after all, central to dualism is the claim that other selves are elusive. The dualist, however, does not explain why it is *difficult* to know others; rather she explains why it is *impossible* to know them. According to the dualist we are never directly acquainted with anyone other than ourselves. All we see is the behavior which the self causes

– not the self itself. Consequently, we can never compare our perceptions of someone with "the real her" to determine if our perceptions are veridical.

Hence, in the dualist's view it is not merely that we cannot *completely* know another person – everyone recognizes that. Rather we cannot know them at all; certainly we cannot know we know them. According to the dualist, all of us could be systematically mistaken about every one of our intimates: every belief we have about them could be erroneous. This is a most troublesome implication of dualism; it is one of the principal reasons I argued in chapter 4 that we should reject it as an adequate account of mind.

In that chapter I proposed an activity view of self. In that view the self is not some thing which inhabits a body; rather, it is a way of understanding the behavior of a complex, acting organism – ourselves as well as others. Hence, to know a person is to understand how that organism behaves. Here I want to explain both how we can know a person, and why it is difficult to do so. This will give further reason to favor the activity view of self. It will also enhance our understanding of close personal relationships.

Knowing Others

A person's behavior, in my view, is not a mere result of the self, it is a constituent of the self. The self is constituted by the whole of a person's explicit behavior and her deeper-disposing traits. Of course, no isolated piece of behavior exhausts a person. Hence, observing anyone only occasionally cannot produce an accurate understanding of her. How could it? Watching a session of Congress or the House of Commons will not yield an accurate understanding of them either. We can construct an adequate account of a person – like an adequate account of Congress – only by observing her over a reasonable length of time, in a variety of circumstances. Exactly how we do this is a process I will outline here.

Think, for a moment, about the ways in which we begin relationships. Serendipity brings two people into geographical proximity: they bump into each other on the train, they live in adjoining apartments, or they find themselves seated next to each other in a classroom. Sometimes serendipity conspires with unique psychological factors (stress, recent loss of a close friend, etc.) to make it more likely that the two will be attracted to each another. Other times an individual may not have any *special* psychological need for a relationship, but may, after observing someone from a distance, think that person might be a potential friend.

Whatever the circumstances, in all these cases each party begins to see the other in a positive light: she interprets the other's behavior as exhibiting positive traits or characteristics. This distinguishes the prospective friend from those about whom she has either a negative or no opinion, and from those she thinks worthy of befriending but for some reason chooses not to pursue. At the time we may not be fully aware of this attraction, or its psychological or rational basis. We may simply notice we enjoy the other's company, that we seek her out whenever feasible.

The role of background beliefs

Why, though, are we attracted to some people? Why do we see some folks "in a positive light?" At the initial stages of a relationship it may be difficult to say. It may simply be that the other person's behavior is reinforcing. We enjoy being around her, listening to her, watching her. Regardless of the precise explanation, our attraction is strongly influenced, if not determined, by our background beliefs – whether general, fine-grained, or particular.

Suppose Trevor is interested in establishing a close relationship with Roper. If Roper is witty and Trevor has shown a penchant for witty folk, we can plausibly surmise that Roper's wit at least partially explains Trevor's interest. On the other hand, if Trevor has no historical proclivity to witty folk, then we can conjecture that his interest in Roper is not based on Roper's wit. Of course if he appreciates Roper for other reasons, Trevor may eventually come to appreciate Roper's wit as well. If so, Trevor may learn to also appreciate wit in others.

Trevor's background beliefs and attitudes – whatever they happen to be – will shape his understanding of, interest in, and interactions with, others. So it is with all of us. Background beliefs influence current beliefs, attitudes, and perceptions; they provide a context within which we can understand the significance of others' behavior. Unless we understand that context, how can we make sense of their behavior? We cannot.

Think about it. We cannot understand the behavior even of inanimate objects without the appropriate background beliefs. If I know nothing at all about the earth, the planets, the sun, and the stars, then exactly what would I see when I look into the heavens on a clear night? To the untrained eye, a giant red star looks neither giant nor red. Neither does it look to be millions of times the size of the earth, or millions of light years from the earth. So without the appropriate background beliefs, I can make little sense of what I see. (The ancient Greek myths interpreted celestial lights as chariots of the gods – doubtless a reasonable explanation given their evidence and background beliefs.)

The need to understand the context is even more evident once we shift from the behavior of inanimate objects to the behavior of intelligent, purposive creatures. To understand why persons behave as they do, we must understand the behavior's significance, role, or purpose. That we cannot do unless we have the appropriate background beliefs which put that behavior in its proper context.

Let me offer an example: while living in Scotland on sabbatical, I occasionally watched cricket on television; I wanted to understand this game which so thrilled many Brits. Initially I could make no sense of the game (after a year I was not much better off). I could detect patterns of action, but could not understand their purpose or function – after all, I didn't know the rules of the game. So I interpreted their actions in light of my knowledge of a seemingly related game: American baseball. Clearly there were some similarities – one person pitched or bowled a "ball" while another batted; the batter was out if a fielder caught the ball before it hit the ground, etc. These gave me *some* way to interpret the players' behavior. However, there were also critical dissimilarities between the games: one batsman might bat for several hours; the bowler (pitcher) bounced the ball off the ground, etc. These differences hindered my understanding of the game.

This example illustrates the difficulty (if not impossibility) of interpreting complex behavior in a vacuum. The only way I could make any sense of the game was to rely upon my background knowledge. Since baseball and cricket are somewhat similar, I had some basis for understanding the game; since they are also different, my understanding was constrained.

These difficulties arise whenever we seek to understand a practice or behavior radically different from our own. The average Christian perceives Islamic or Buddhist practices and beliefs as weird, incomprehensible; I can only surmise the reverse is likewise true. The differences are more radical, and understanding more difficult, between, say, a modern-day American or European and a member of a primitive South American tribe. The lesson to be learned from these examples is not that Buddhist, Islamic, Christian, or tribal practices *are* weird or incomprehensible, but that human behavior and social practices are relatively inscrutable in the absence of appropriate background information. Even detailed acquaintance with the relevant background information is often insufficient to permit a *unique* interpretation of the other's behavior. Theory and even observation statements are generally underdetermined by the evidence (Quine 1960: 1–5, 26–35, 73–9).

More relevant to the present point, the same is true for understanding the behavior of someone within our own culture, including those with whom we relate personally. However, since most of us share *roughly* similar background information and have inherited *roughly* similar cultural patterns of behavior, we usually behave in *roughly* similar ways and interpret each other's behavior accordingly. These commonalities make communication between members of the same culture easier; they make it easier to interpret the other's behavior. But they also mask the role background beliefs play in our interpretation of others, especially others within our culture. We may interpret rough similarity as complete similarity, and thereby be insensitive to the ways slight differences in behavioral patterns and background beliefs may lead us to misinterpret others' behavior. This hampers the creation and sustenance of personal relationships.

The influence of background beliefs runs deep. It affects even "simple" perception. That is especially significant since most of us assume perception is "pure," untainted by beliefs or experiences. This assumption is unjustified: there are numerous psychological studies demonstrating the influence of background beliefs. In a famous experiment by Bruner and Postman (1949), researchers told subjects they were being tested on their speed of perception. The subjects were shown a series of playing cards and asked to identify them. Initial exposure to the cards was very brief; time of exposure was later increased. Without the knowledge of the subjects, the researchers placed several anomalous cards throughout the deck. The anomalous cards had an inappropriate color for the given suit; for instance, the deck might have included a black queen of hearts or a red ten of spades.

Researchers discovered that subjects initially ignored the anomalies and identified the cards according to pre-established categories. When confronted with the black queen of hearts, subjects would identify it as the queen of hearts – ignoring its color – or as the queen of spades – ignoring its suit. Virtually no one recognized the discrepancy immediately; a significant number of subjects never identified the anomalous cards, even after lengthy exposure.

In short, background assumptions and beliefs influence and shape perceptions and experiences. This finding has had a significant influence in the history and philosophy of science. Historically philosophers and scientists assumed science was based on unfettered observation – that scientists simply observed the world "as it is," without any predispositions or theoretical beliefs. Only then did they construct theories to explain the observed data.

This once popular view is now in retreat – in fact, it has been completely discredited. Numerous historians of science have shown that scientific progress requires certain background scientific beliefs and theories. Indeed, background beliefs make scientific observation possible; they don't undermine it (Kuhn 1961; Shapere 1980).

Thus, although we must be attuned to the power of background beliefs, and we should protect ourselves from the ways these can mislead us, we should not try to shed our background beliefs and to experience the world, or other people, without them. Background beliefs may distort experience, but they also make experience of the world possible (Quine 1953; 1960). If we were devoid of background beliefs about colors and playing cards, we could not identify the cards *at all*, let alone incorrectly. If we had no beliefs about street signs and traffic lights, we would probably not even "see" them (what would make us focus on an octagonal piece of aluminum?), and even if we did perceive them, we wouldn't know their significance. And, if someone unfamiliar with baseball tried to observe (without explanation) a cricket match, she would have little chance of understanding what she saw. More importantly for present purposes, background beliefs are essential for interpreting and understanding human behavior. Therefore, we must understand how background beliefs function, if we are to use or alter them, as circumstances demand.

Which beliefs are especially important for interpreting and understanding human behavior? Certainly our general beliefs about human motivation are pivotal. Suppose Tony believes all people are selfishly motivated – that even when people appear to be altruistic, they are, in fact, simply striving to promote their own selfish interests, albeit indirectly. Gordon, on the other hand, thinks some humans are motivated by selfish interests; others, by more benevolent urges; and most of us, by both selfishness and altruism.

Tony and Gordon have a mutual friend, Chris, who donates a substantial sum of money to a local orphanage. How will each interpret Chris's behavior? If either has previous specific beliefs about Chris, these will clearly influence his interpretation of Chris's donation. But their general beliefs about human motivation will be equally important, especially in forming their initial specific beliefs about Chris. Thus, all things being equal, Tony will likely see Chris's donation as a circuitous way of promoting his selfish interest, for example by raising his standing in the community. Gordon, on the other hand, is more likely to see the donation as genuinely altruistic.

Our general beliefs about human motivation will strongly influence our interpretations of others' behavior. Those who see (most) people as competitive or cooperative or acquisitive or prideful or insecure or confident or sexually depraved or stupid will interpret others' behavior in light of these general beliefs. Our general beliefs about rationality will likewise shape our interpretations. For instance, someone who conceives of rationality as a simple means–ends calculation will likely interpret people's behavior differently from someone who conceives of rationality more broadly.

Of course background beliefs need not be so broad; we also have more fine-grained beliefs about subclasses of people. Thus, Tony might not believe that all people are selfish, just that all rich people are. This background belief will affect how he perceives the behavior of each rich person, even if it plays no role in interpreting a poor person's behavior.

How did Tony come to hold these general and fine-grained beliefs? He doubtless thinks they are founded on careful observation of people. If he has occasionally observed greedy folk, those observations will play a significant role in shaping his current beliefs. But these observations do not tell the whole story. In particular, they do not explain how he initially acquired his general beliefs about human motivation and rationality. These he did not choose. No did we ours. Rather, they emerged from early instruction by our parents, peers, church, and society. Even if modified by experience, these "inherited" beliefs usually exert a long-term influence.

Sometimes for the worse. Most of us were taught (verbally or by example) that people with crew cuts (or long hair or orange hair), or dingy clothes (or three-piece suits) are unscrupulous or closed-minded. Others have been taught that liberals (or conservatives) are insensitive manipulators, that religious folk are closed-minded or that atheists are immoral. Those who weren't taught these particular beliefs were taught others. These initial beliefs affect our perception of and encounters with individuals so described. They often make it difficult for us to seriously consider evidence which undermines them.

Social-political beliefs function similarly. For instance, the average Westerner is told that the Iraqi government is untrustworthy. She has also been warned that deceitful people can sound honest and reasonable. Thus, she is unlikely to believe anything an Iraqi government official says – no matter how reasonable it seems. In fact, she is unlikely to listen sufficiently carefully to Iraqi officials so that she could seriously reconsider her earlier beliefs.

More important to current purposes, background beliefs also shape our more personal interactions. For instance, many adolescents in some parts of the United States were taught that atheists are unscrupulous. When one of these adolescents meets atheists, she will be wary of them. She may assume they are trying to take advantage of her. If they are overtly friendly, she may infer they are feigning amiability so that, having gained her confidence, they can undermine her faith. Thus, she is unlikely to trust atheists enough either to develop a personal relationship with them or to question her beliefs about them. In short, our initial beliefs strongly influence our decisions about whom we relate to and how we do it.

Strongly influence, but not completely determine. Occasionally we meet someone we cannot readily classify (e.g. as a theist or an atheist, as a liberal or a conservative). When this happens, our background beliefs about certain types of people cannot operate; only our more general beliefs about what all people do can come into play. Or sometimes we meet someone who so obviously deviates from the stereotype that we are forced (perhaps after some time) to rethink our background beliefs. None of this shows that we can view people open-mindedly, devoid of background beliefs. However, it does show that we can question our beliefs.

A detailed example

Let me use a detailed illustration to make this discussion more concrete. (If all this seems painfully obvious, then proceed to the next section of this chapter. I have provided a long example to make the point perfectly clear, since the point is, in my view, essential for understanding and having personal relationships.) After Debra first meets Pat, Debra forms a tentative impression of her. This impression will be shaped by Debra's background beliefs (both general and fine-grained) and her recent observation of Pat's verbal and bodily behavior. This impression will likely be vague, perhaps no more than: "Pat is funny" or "Pat is a bore." Debra's first impressions will then become an element of her background beliefs which influences how she subsequently interprets Pat's behavior. That is, Debra's next observation of or encounter with Pat will be seen and understood through: (1) Debra's background beliefs about all people, (2) her background beliefs about specific people resembling Pat, and finally, (3) her first impressions of Pat (which were themselves shaped by those more general background beliefs).

Debra will interpret Pat's subsequent behavior as strengthening, diminishing, or modifying this first impression. She might decide, for instance, that Pat isn't all that funny or that Pat is not the bore she supposed. After each successive interaction, the new "data" will be merged with the old to render a somewhat revised understanding of Pat. This need not be achieved consciously; often it is not. But whether consciously or not, we learn from experience: past experiences become part of the information we use to make future decisions or interpretations. If Pat's subsequent behavior supports or is compatible with Debra's first impressions, then those impressions will likely become fixed. Once that happens, then even if Pat's future behavior is at odds with Debra's settled view of her, Debra is unlikely to dismiss that view out of hand. Indeed, if Debra's settled view of Pat can be changed at all, it can be changed only if Pat's current and future behaviors regularly (and dramatically?) conflict with it.

Suppose, for example, that when Debra first observed Pat, Pat was arguing with June, one of Debra's best friends. Debra did not hear the particulars of the disagreement, but when June later explained that Pat had "attacked" her, Debra quickly inferred that Pat was irascible.

A month later Debra observed Pat having a disagreement with another of her friends, Yolanda. Pat's behavior was consistent with Debra's original impression. Thus, her view of Pat became stronger, more resistant to change. Still later Debra observed an argument between Pat and Vickie, a woman Debra does not know at all. Without knowing any of the details, Debra quickly surmised that Pat was at fault. Debra concluded her impression of Pat was well established.

But several months later Debra observes Pat working as a volunteer aide in a local hospital's geriatric ward. She cares for patients who have lost control of their basic bodily functions. Moreover, she is exceedingly kind to the patients; they obviously appreciate her presence and concern. What is Debra to think? How can she understand this "new" behavior in light of her earlier view of Pat?

She might find a way to interpret Pat's present behavior as an odd variation of her (Debra's) original assessment. For instance, she might think Pat has some selfish motive for acting benevolently; perhaps she is trying to impress her ailing uncle so she will receive his sizeable inheritance. Or Debra might think Pat has a split personality. Perhaps she will simply surmise that Pat is a complex person with both good and bad features. Or she could even conclude, especially after further thought and examination, that June, Yolanda, and Vickie – not Pat – were at fault in the original disputes.

Debra's perception of Pat can also be altered by additional background information. For instance, after discovering that Pat's parents had been murdered prior to her arguments with June and Yolanda, Debra might infer that Pat's reactions were caused by depression. Or after learning that Pat had recently been released from a mental hospital, she might conclude that Pat had a split personality.

Putting it All Together

I cannot specify all the details that might affect our interpretation of others' behavior; there are an indefinitely large number of them. My point is simply that our interpretation of strangers, family, friends, and spouses is a constant interplay between presently observed behavior, background beliefs, and the observer's current physical and psychological condition.

Until now, though, I have talked as if our background beliefs were static, and relatively immune to change. Not so. Just as we can change our impressions of individual people, we can also alter our more general (or class) beliefs about human motivation or rationality. If I have been taught that everyone is selfish to the core, yet I repeatedly observe people acting benevolently, then my original views about human selfishness may moderate. This moderated view subsequently affects how, in the future, I interpret others' behavior. I may be more likely to see benevolence where I once saw thinly disguised egoism. I may thereby further moderate my original view that all humans are selfish.

Learning from experience

Intelligent creatures learn from experience. Knowledge gleaned from experience is embodied in our background beliefs. These inform and give shape to current observation and experience. It could not, indeed should not, be otherwise. Nonetheless, it is essential that we recognize ways in which our attributions of others can misfire. Suppose Joanne believes that Kurt is devious. She will understandably be guarded around him: she will look for ways in which he might try to take advantage of her. Thus, she will be less likely to trust or be honest with him. Consequently, she is less likely to find any evidence which alters her initial suspicions. Rather she is more likely to interpret Kurt's present and future behavior as reinforcing her initial belief that he is devious.

In principle, there is nothing sinister here. If experience teaches Joanne that Kurt is devious, then, unless she has good reason to believe he has changed or her initial perceptions were mistaken, prudence demands that she be wary of him. We must not forget, however, that our background beliefs are often based on inadequate evidence. Frequently we form impressions of people based solely on the testimony (gossip?) of others. There is nothing wrong with relying on testimony, as long as we critically evaluate our sources and are willing to take even the most reliable sources with several grains of salt. Unfortunately, most of us are prone to believe gossip about others, particularly gossip about someone we already have some propensity to dislike. Testimony, however, is not always accurate. Sometimes people exaggerate or lie about others. But even when someone is honest, their claims about others are fallible. People whose testimony we believe can be mistaken. So can we.

How interpretations can go awry

Our observations can go awry in at least three distinct ways. First, our current mental states influence our perception and interpretation of others' behavior. Thus, if I am depressed or ticked off when I first observe someone, I may well identify that person as a cause of my ill feelings. I am therefore less likely to befriend her.

Second, no one is perfect. We all occasionally say stupid things; we all occasionally act unkindly; occasionally we are all loutish. If I first notice someone being insensitive or cloddish, I am likely to assume she is unkind, self-centered, or unsophisticated. If I first observe her giggling incessantly, I may conclude she is a buffoon. If I first hear her making inane comments in class, I may infer that she is dimwitted. However, first impressions are not always reliable. After all, we have no evidence that this person's current behavior is representative.

Third, as I argued earlier, human behavior, like everything else, is explicable only in context. If I do not understand the context, I will likely misinterpret the behavior. To use the earlier example, Debra saw Pat scolding June and surmised that Pat was irascible. Suppose, though, that Debra observed only part of the altercation: she was looking the other way when June slapped Pat. Debra failed to see Pat's anger in context, and thus misunderstood its import.

In short we must remember that our impressions, and especially our first or isolated impressions, may be mistaken, unrepresentative, or out of context. If we first observe Robert when we are ill, when he is behaving atypically, or if we are ignorant of the relevant context, then we may form an erroneous impression of him which governs our future observations of and encounters with him. Conversely, we could develop mistaken positive impressions of Robert – impressions which make us trust or like him more than we should. Consequently, we must be wary of our first impressions. Although it is only natural to form them, we should be willing to scrutinize and alter them. That we can do only if we are genuinely receptive to behavior at odds with them.

Specific implications for personal relationships

It is now time to spell out the precise relevance of this account for the initiation and conduct of our personal relationships. Knowing how our views of others are formed and maintained can help us initiate and sustain close relationships. Ignorance of (or inattention to) the intricacies of interpreting others' behavior can impede close relationships. We could have numerous false, or at least seriously misleading, general or fine-grained background beliefs. For instance, we might believe all people, or all people of a certain type, are untrustworthy. Consequently, we avoid these people; we do not even consider them as possible friends. Or perhaps we believe that everyone, or everyone of a certain social or economic class, is trustworthy, and thus strike up a relationship with someone who is, in fact, unscrupulous.

We must also be attuned to ways background beliefs can create problems within ongoing relationships. This can happen in either of two ways. One, we all have a tendency to be blind to the other's faults when we are in a well-functioning relationship. Perhaps we are afraid that acknowledging her faults will daunt our enthusiasm for the relationship; perhaps we are afraid that, by bringing our reactions to light, we might upset the other person and somehow damage the relationship. This is a mistake. Eventually, the defects – and our reactions to them – come to light. It may well be difficult to deal with them openly and productively after they have been allowed to fester for so long.

On the other hand, when a relationship is in crisis, most of us have a tendency to interpret the other's behavior negatively. Rather than deal with the immediate conflict or problem, we have a tendency to make grand generalizations ("I knew all along that she was devious, unkind, insensitive, etc."): this may damage the opportunity to repair and re-establish a productive relationship.

In short, unless we are aware of the process of knowing others, we may find ourselves in detrimental relationships, or we may irreparably damage sound relationships by over-reacting to relatively insignificant problems.

7

Intimacy and Trust

Throughout part I, I made several allusions to intimacy, but I made no attempt to elucidate the concept. Now I must make it more precise, specifically the notion of intimate relationships. However, we do not form intimate relationships instantaneously. Rather, they emerge over time; typically they arise from a series of intimate encounters or exchanges. So to understand intimate relationships, we must first understand intimate encounters.

Intimate Encounters

An encounter or exchange may be verbally or behaviorally intimate. An exchange is verbally intimate when one privately tells another something significant about herself or shares personal information she rarely shares with others: for instance, Elaine might tell Lucretia, "I am dying of lung cancer and I am terribly afraid." An exchange is behaviorally intimate when one person acts with or allows herself to be seen by others in ways which reveal significant information about her: for instance, Elaine might weep in front of Lucretia or allow Lucretia to observe her (Elaine's) conversations with her doctors. Of course, exchanges may be both verbally and behaviorally intimate, as when one reports revealing information about oneself while also sharing experiences or behaviors which are revealing.

Encounters are intimate inasmuch as one person reveals her personality or deeper-disposing traits to the other. These revelations provide a context which helps the other interpret her behavior, which helps the other understand why she acts as she does. For instance, having heard or seen Elaine's fear, Lucretia now has a context to better interpret Elaine's behavior – she now understands why Elaine has been irascible and preoccupied. Elaine has thereby disclosed her self – she has shown Lucretia who she (Elaine) really is. That is why we consider the encounter intimate.

When revealing ourselves to another we need not reveal a permanent, fully formed, or even a distinctive trait. As I have argued throughout the book, the self is not a permanent, fully-formed thing. Rather it is constantly changing, evolving. So by revealing features which are temporary, unfolding, or emerging, we may nonetheless reveal the self. Sharing certain temporary features may help others understand *how* we change. That gives them a sense of where we came from and how we are likely to develop.

However, not just anything we disclose reveals who we are. Margaret might tell Warren about her acne pattern as a teenager. If this information discloses little or nothing of Margaret's personality or deeper-disposing traits, then she has not been revealing. It is not enough to share information about oneself. Unless the information is revealing, the exchange is not intimate. Not all information about us is revealing; not all that is revealing is equally revealing. Of course our judgements about what is revealing are fallible. If we fail to see the significance or importance of someone's disclosure, we may think it is not revealing. For example, if I fail to see how Margaret's disclosure about her acne patterns helps explain her shyness or preoccupation with physical appearance, I might erroneously conclude that Margaret has not been revealing, and thus, not intimate.

In short, the listener's judgements are fallible. So are the speaker's. We are sometimes mistaken about who we are and what is really important to us. My thinking that information is revealing doesn't make it so. Margaret might share information she thinks trivial, but be mistaken. Others might see and appreciate a deeper significance she has not recognized. On the other hand, she could share information she thinks vital, but be mistaken. Others might see, for example, that she is simply rationalizing her selfishness. Thus, it is not always evident whether information disclosed is revealing. Nonetheless, if it is not at all revealing, then it is not intimate.

Further elements: privacy, trust, and sensitivity

Intimate exchanges must not only be revealing, but private. Privacy helps distinguish intimacy from mere openness. If Susan announces her fear of reptiles to a large crowd of people, her report might reveal significant features about herself, but she is not being intimate. She is merely being open or frank. However, if over a quiet dinner, Susan tells Betty about her phobia, then the encounter would be both revealing and private, and thus intimate.

I once knew a woman who, without the slightest provocation, would describe her most recent sexual exploits to classes and to unsuspecting students standing in the hallway. Sharing such information, although typically thought to be private and deeply personal, was not, for her, private, nor its disclosure intimate. It was not offered to reveal who she was, nor did she have the interests of her listeners in mind. The nature of the encounter – *how* information is shared – is an essential element of intimacy. In intimate encounters we reveal ourselves; but we must do so in ways which are sensitive to the other. Openness can be harsh; candor, brutal; frankness, inconsiderate; whereas an intimate encounter cannot be brutal, harsh, or inconsiderate. The revealer must be sensitive to the intended recipient. She can be sensitive in two ways.

A revealer demonstrates communicative sensitivity if, in her desire to be understood, she tailors her revelation to the capabilities and background of the listener, for example by expressing herself using language the listener can understand. A revealer demonstrates interest sensitivity if she responds to the recipient's general interests and desires, for example by expressing her views so as not to remind the listener of a recent tragedy. Ideally revealers will demonstrate both forms of sensitivity. Presence of neither form, however, means that intimacy is absent. Suppose Elaine is a medical lexicographer. She discusses her cancer with her best friend, Lucretia, using nothing but incomprehensible medical idioms. Elaine's insensitivity would surely be forgivable, their encounter private, and even in some sense personal. However, her exchange is not intimate since it lacks sensitivity.

An exchange is not intimate unless it also evidences trust. Like the woman I mentioned earlier, people may openly (frankly, candidly) reveal themselves without trusting the listener(s) in the least. In fact, they occasionally reveal themselves to others precisely because they do not trust them. In some circumstances, revealing oneself to another makes one less of a threat ("I had to put an end to Frank's gossip. 'Frank,' I said, 'your wife and I *are* having an affair. Sue for divorce if you will, but stop spreading vicious lies about her being a slut and my being a grand seducer'."). In intimate exchanges, however, the revealer assumes the listener will respect the privacy of the exchange. The revealer trusts that the listener will not harm her or abuse her welfare. She thereby makes herself vulnerable to the listener: she exposes herself to the possibility of exploitation.

In short, trust and sensitivity heighten intimacy; their absence diminishes it. But we must be careful before judging that trust and sensitivity are absent. These elements are sometimes difficult to identify, especially in ongoing relationships. For instance, it is difficult to see how Bonnie is being sensitive when she yells at her husband. Perhaps, though, she is sensitive, but her sensitivity is apparent only in the context of a troubled, ongoing relationship: she may be crying for help or calling desperately for the renewal of trust. Nonetheless, although it is sometimes difficult to decide whether someone is sensitive or trusting, the fact remains that if sensitivity and trust are absent, so too is intimacy.

The foregoing analysis helps explain the common-sense view that there are degrees of intimacy. Not all intimacy is created equal; some exchanges are more intimate than others. Intimate exchanges reveal significant information about the speaker, and do so in ways that are sensitive and trusting. An exchange is more intimate the more each of these elements is present; an exchange is less intimate the less each of these elements is present.

Finally, sensitivity and trust are not only crucial elements of intimate exchanges; they help explain the exchange's value. Recall the discussion in chapter 4. We all occasionally need others' assistance or emotional support. We are more likely to seek the help of someone we trust, someone who has demonstrated her reliability and sensitivity. Furthermore, intimacy enhances self-knowledge. If we trust our intimates – if we feel secure sharing our thoughts, reactions, fantasies, etc. with them – then we will likely learn more about ourselves. We may hear ourselves say things which enhance our self-knowledge. And we are more likely to heed their honest appraisal of us.

Until now, I have glossed over the distinction between reciprocal and non-reciprocal exchanges. In a non-reciprocal exchange, both parties participate in the exchange in the minimal sense that one listens while the other speaks; nonetheless, only one of the people is intimate – only one of them reveals herself to the other. In a reciprocal intimate exchange, each party reveals herself to the other. Although intimate exchanges *need* not be reciprocal, social-psychological studies say they typically are (Derlega and Chaiken 1976). Two reasons for reciprocity are worthy of note. First, intimacy is an expression of sensitivity and trust. If you confide in me, then I am likely to conclude that you trust me and expect me to treat you sensitively. Since I am also likely to conclude that you are trustworthy, I am more likely to be intimate with you. Second, most of us think we are obliged to return favors and gifts; intimacy is frequently viewed as a favor or gift. We are thus more inclined to be intimate with someone who is intimate with us. Conversely, we are more likely to be closed with those who demonstrate no interest in intimacy. If we distrust people or find them insensitive, we are unlikely to seek intimacy with them.

Intimate Relationships

Personal relationships, as you may recall, are those in which the people relate to each other because of who they are. Our reasons for love – our reasons for having a close personal relationship with them – should be based on their characteristics, especially those at the core of their self. I have just argued that intimacy is the sensitive sharing of information which discloses the self. Hence, close personal relationships will be intimate relationships.

Intimate exchanges can occur outside intimate relationships, although they are most at home within them. Occasionally we may have intimate exchanges with a neighbor or a colleague with whom we share an occasional beer. If we begin to have these exchanges frequently, we will likely form an intimate relationship. Once we are in an intimate relationship, we become still more likely to have regular intimate exchanges. And the more frequently and more intimate our exchanges, the more intimate the relationship. (Remember the earlier comments about degrees of intimacy.) Thus, lovers and close friends regularly disclose themselves, and they are especially sensitive to one another's interests and needs.

This does not imply that intimates spend their lives in intense conversations, gazing soulfully into each other's eyes. Intimates can and do reveal themselves by sharing common activities (playing games, walking in the park, or shopping) and ordinary conversations (about politics, mutual friends, and "the day at the office"). Indeed, I suspect we reveal ourselves more in these seemingly mundane interactions than in those intense (and often pre-fabbed) conversations whose stated purpose is to "be intimate".

Indeed, it is important to recognize that intimates do more than disclose revealing information about themselves. They often share time (and sometimes property), engage in mutual projects, make mutual promises, and (in romantic relationships) have contact with one another's bodies. These additional features of intimacy give close personal relationships a structure over time; they create a personal bond; they provide a history lacking in mere encounters. This history leads both parties to expect continuing intimate exchanges. Without continuing exchanges, the relationship might persist, but it will cease to be intimate.

Although intimate relationships are sustained by intimate exchanges, people may reveal themselves too frequently, in inappropriate circumstances, or at inappropriate times. If I spend our evenings together detailing my life in summer camp, you will quickly find me boring. And if I constantly badger you to be similarly forthcoming, I thereby demonstrate my insensitivity. That is why thinking of intimates merely as frequent self-revealers – as people who often report this or that experience or belief – is an over-simplification. Intimates must also demonstrate sensitivity for their intimates, a sensitivity which underlies their revelations and modulates their frequency.

To summarize, a relationship is intimate if both of us regularly (a) share significant information about ourselves (either verbally or behaviorally), and do so (b) privately, (c) sensitively and (d) with trust. If any of these aspects increase, our relationship will become more intimate; if they abate or disappear, our relationship will become less intimate.

This reinforces an earlier argument that close personal relationships (and thus intimacy) are not one-time achievements, but ongoing processes, forever in need of revitalization. The fact that you and I have an intimate relationship now does not ensure that we will have one later. People change. Our interests, ideas, attitudes, character, etc., evolve (sometimes radically) over time. Unless we have regular intimate exchanges – unless we continuously reveal our emerging selves to one another – we will no longer know each other as well as we once did; perhaps we may lose touch altogether. Since love is based on knowing the beloved, our reasons for love will diminish, if not evaporate. Of course if we have related for years, intimacy will not vanish overnight. Each of us has residual background information about the other. We also have established patterns of relating which symbolize and reinforce some level of intimacy. Moreover, since we presumably still spend time together, we will likely know much about each other, merely by observing each other's behavior. But the central point remains: if we cease sharing ourselves, we will eventually cease being intimate, even if we continue being partners.

Intimacy will likewise diminish if we cease being sensitive to each other. If I lose interest in you or your interests, then our relationship will deteriorate. And by "losing interest in you" I do not mean that I lose some internal mental state ("loving feelings") I once had. Rather, I cease spending time with you and listening to you; I am no longer disposed to be around you or to discuss my life with you. To repeat the conclusion of earlier arguments (especially in chapter 2), it is one thing to feel sensitive and quite another to be sensitive. You may be sensitive to me even if you do not particularly *feel* sensitive. It would be regrettable were it otherwise. We cannot always control what we feel; we do, however, have considerable control over what we do. Indeed, if we act sensitively toward each other, we may well find that we now feel sensitive.

In the remainder of this chapter I focus on the role of trust in intimate relationships. As I have argued, trust is an essential element of intimacy, which partially explains intimacy's value. Hence, if we understand the nature of trust, we can better understand intimacy. We will also be better equipped to create and maintain trust within our close relationships.

Trust

Trust is essential for personal relationships. But not only personal relationships. In some sense trust is essential for life. As Sissela Bok puts it, "*Whatever* matters to human beings, trust is the atmosphere in which it thrives" (1978: 31). No one is completely self-sufficient. Not only must I trust my friends, I must trust my grocer, my auto mechanic, and my postal carrier. I trust my grocer to sell quality food at a reasonable price; I trust my auto mechanic to repair all and only defective car parts; I trust my postal carrier to deliver all my mail, unread. Moreover, I must trust that most people – the doctor, the newscaster, the government official, etc. – tell me the truth (or at least something approximating the truth) most of the time.

Trust, in this sense, is the foundation of social order. Sociologist Bernard Barber claims this trust is evidenced when we assume (1) that others will act within a persistent moral order, (2) that they will perform their technical roles competently, and (3) that roles that require a special concern for others will be faithfully fulfilled (Barber 1983: 9). Doubtless this captures the sense of trust necessary for a well-functioning society. We all must trust other people; without it, a fully human life would be impossible. Nonetheless, there are important respects in which this trust differs from my trust of friends. Both the scope and nature of social or impersonal trust is limited. I trust my mechanic not to install a clutch I do not need; I do not trust her with details of my private life. I trust the grocer not to sell rotten produce or charge exorbitant prices; I do not trust her to listen sympathetically while I rhapsodize about my son's new job. Conversely, I do trust my close friends with what is dear to me. I trust friends in ways that are quantitatively and qualitatively different from ways I trust mechanics, grocers, and postal carriers.

For people in public roles, my trust is not so much trust *in* these people, but rather trust *that* these people will – to use Barber's language – fulfill their roles, and thus, not mistreat me. Or, perhaps more accurately, I rely upon these people. Usually I rely on them without knowing anything personal about them. Why? The explanation is fairly straightforward: I assume most people will seek to promote their own interests (even if they do not do so exclusively). Since I further assume most businesspeople can best promote their interests by promoting their customers' interests, then, unless I have a specific reason to think otherwise, I expect them to offer satisfactory service. People are either altruistic or selfish. The former people will protect my interests because they do not want to harm my interests. The latter people will tend to protect my interests as a circuitous way of promoting theirs.

For instance, most of a mechanic's business comes from returning customers. If my auto mechanic does shoddy work and charges outrageous prices, I will not take my car to her in the future. Nor am I likely to recommend that others take their cars to her. Indeed, I am likely to discourage others from doing so. Much social trust can be explained in this way: it is not so much trust in the person, but trust that, given appropriate social constraints, most people will act in ways which promote, or at least do not inhibit, my interests.

Although this explains most impersonal trust, it cannot explain it all. Most of us recognize that some businesspeople feign an interest in their customers so they can manipulate them. Nonetheless, even an unprincipled businessperson recognizes she should not be perceived to be unscrupulous. The truly unscrupulous person wants to appear to be a person of integrity, a person worthy of trust, even if (or perhaps especially if) she is not. Thus, we must somehow distinguish between an unscrupulous businessperson who will not harm my interests *unless she can get away with it*, from the grocer, auto mechanic, and postal carrier who will not harm my interests even if she can get away with it. I assume these latter people have either some personal interest in me, or that they have moral scruples. Either way, these additional elements of trust have obvious moral dimensions. That is why it is appropriate to speak of them as genuine instances of trust. Nonetheless, they still fall short of what I would expect from a close friend.

Personal trust

What, then, is *personal* trust? How do I, how should I, trust close friends? I don't trust them, for example, to repair my television or to design software for my computer. But that does not mean that I don't trust *them*. Rather it means I do not think they can perform those particular tasks. This gives us a clue to the nature of personal trust. To say that I trust someone is not to say that I trust her to do everything. What I trust is that she will be a certain kind of person, who, among other things, will not intentionally harm my interests. Thus, I trust she will not undertake a task she knows she cannot do. Were I to say to her: "Would you fix my stereo?", I trust that she would refuse, unless of course, she could repair it. That is, at least in part, what I mean by saying I trust her.

This is an important corrective to the standard account of trust in the philosophical literature. Baier argues that trust is best understood as a three-place relation, such that one person (say, June) trusts another (say, May) with something she (June) values (1988; 1986). For example, June intimately tells May some secret, that is June trusts May with something she values (her secret). Clearly this captures important elements of trust. Among other things, it recognizes that personal trust requires action and not merely belief. June may truly believe that May can and will keep secrets; that is, June might believe May is trust*worthy*.

But June cannot be said to trust May unless and until she actually trusts her, that is until she is intimate with her, until she makes private revelations to her. Trust is putting one's confidence in another, to rely on her, to entrust something to her.

However, Baier's account fails to emphasize one crucial element of personal trust. June might trust May with some private information or aspect of herself, without personally trusting her. For instance, June may trust a banker with her life savings (something quite valuable), but that does not show that she personally trusts her banker. Likely this is just a vivid example of impersonal trust. She is simply confident that there are extensive regulatory checks on bankers, so that even if the banker were totally unscrupulous, her money would be safe. This is not (standardly) a case of *personal* trust (although if she also had a personal relationship with the banker, it could be).

Being confident about how another will behave is insufficient for trust. It is not enough even to rely on her. I believe the local Ku Klux Klan will continue to embrace its racist policies, even if it masks them in more attractive garb. I not only believe that, I rely on that belief. I assume they will maintain these policies come what may. My confidence in these matters is exceedingly well placed. I have reasons for this belief, and I am willing to act on that belief. But all of this does not yet show that I personally trust Klansmen.

Minimally what is missing is this: I don't trust them to take an interest in my interests. I don't expect that they will guard information shared in confidence; nor do I rely upon them for help or assistance. However, if I personally trust people, I must have confidence in them, I must assume they will protect and promote my interests. I expect they will not harm me because they care for me, not because there are external forces (legal or social sanctions) which forbid them from harming me.

The moral dimensions of trust

We are almost home. The above account of trust seems to accurately describe the personal trust we expect in close relationships. But I am inclined to think one further element of trust is missing; at least as part of ideal trust. Consider the following scenario: June privately tells May something in confidence. June would prefer that this information be kept secret, though let us suppose that it is not horribly embarrassing or earth-shatteringly private. On a later occasion when May and April are talking, May finds that sharing this confidential information with April would be *extremely* helpful to April. Perhaps April is very depressed and it would conquer her depression. What should May do?

If June's trust is nothing more than a belief that May will never share privileged information, then if May wishes to retain June's trust, May should not share the information, no matter how much it would help April, no matter how trivial that information. At least she should not share the information without first receiving June's explicit approval. Although in most cases I think May should not share that information, the conclusion is reached prematurely, without duly considering an important element of the strongest forms of trust.

Certainly May should be careful not to reveal information given her in confidence. Nonetheless, she should consider whether, in some circumstances (for example, if the information is not terribly private and sharing it would do April *substantial* good), she should divulge that information to April. Moreover -- and more central to the present point -- June should want and expect her to tell April. In fact, in the best of relationships, June might well be hurt if May did not share the information.

An important element of trust is trust in the moral sensitivity, insight, and judgement of our intimates. In this case June would trust May to be sensitive and kind enough to know when she should override the normally stringent constraints on sharing confidences. Moreover, she would assume that May likewise recognized that she (June) was morally sensitive and, therefore, would approve of May's sharing the privileged information with April, under circumstances so described.

In short, the trust we have in our closest friends is not just a trust that they will keep confidences; it is not just a trust that they will never hurt us -- though doubtless these are crucial elements of trust. Rather, we trust the character of our intimates, we trust they have sufficient moral integrity to discern how they should act. If this trust is well founded, then they can be trusted to look after and promote our interests.

To trust or not to trust

There is one further question about trust which merits discussion, especially when considering trust in personal relationships. Should trust be self-conscious? Should we be consciously aware that we trust another person? Should we have clearly articulated reason for trusting? From one perspective, the answer is obviously yes. It seems imprudent to trust someone we have no reason to trust. It is manifestly stupid to trust someone we know is untrustworthy. Likely she will take advantage of us. Perhaps, too, it is better for the untrustworthy person if we do not trust her. For if we did trust her despite her being untrustworthy, we might well reinforce her unscrupulous behavior.

However we must be wary of going too far. Though it is obviously imprudent to trust those who are demonstrably untrustworthy, we should not therefore refuse to trust people simply because we are not certain they are trustworthy. More important to the present discussion, neither should we constantly re-evaluate trust for our intimates. To do so is to "ask one question too many" (Baier 1988; 1986) By questioning trust too often or too intensely, we diminish the chance that we can initiate personal relationship. It will virtually ensure we cannot sustain intimate relationships.

Trust breeds trust; distrust breeds distrust. If June trusts May, she demonstrates to May that she sees her as honorable and trustworthy. Few people are inclined to directly abuse that trust. In fact, numerous studies and ordinary experience show that May will likely reciprocate by trusting June. On the other hand, if June demonstrates her distrust of May, May will likewise reciprocate. She will plausibly assume that June is not trustworthy, or is at least incapable or uninterested in trusting her (May). Hence, if someone is generally distrustful of others, she will be reluctant to trust any specific person and, thus, will find it difficult to establish intimate relationships.

The same problem arises within ongoing relationships. If June demonstrates that she distrusts May, for instance, by constantly challenging, questioning, or testing May, then May is likely to do the same. "Why," May may plausibly ask, "should I trust her if she is unwilling to trust me?" Consequently, the presence of distrust will often set off a spiral of further distrust. Now that is not to say that one should never express distrust. But it is to say that a person should cultivate an attitude of trust if she wishes to initiate and then maintain close personal relationships – especially once we remember that the "evidence" on which our distrust rests can be misinterpreted or out of context, and thus, unreliable.

8

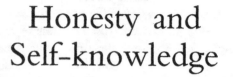

Honesty and
Self-knowledge

Two people can be intimates only if they regularly disclose themselves to each other. That they cannot do unless they are honest with each other, at least most of the time. But must they always be honest? Many people think not; they think we can be intimate even if we are occasionally dishonest. Concern for our intimates appears to require that we sometimes be less than forthcoming with them. Honesty can hurt intimates, and close friends should not intentionally hurt one another. Therefore, to avoid hurting our intimates, we should, at least in certain circumstances, lie. Or so goes the traditional wisdom. Dishonesty is permissible and occasionally even mandatory. As Solomon puts it: "honesty is sometimes the obstacle [to] rather than the essence of love" (1981).

There is an important insight in this traditional view. Bare honesty is insufficiently rich soil in which to grow intimacy; intimacy cannot flower without the fertilizer of sensitivity. Moreover, if we are preoccupied with honesty, we may become blind to other dimensions of intimacy. Nonetheless, honesty is more important for close relationships than most people suppose. Indeed, I think complete honesty is essential for an ideal intimate relationship. Honesty need not be blunt or callous: intimates should be sensitive with each other, even (especially) when they are being honest. From this we should not infer, however, that sensitivity trumps honesty. Sensitivity should not constrain honesty, although it should modulate it: it should shape how we are honest.

I begin by examining two cases many people think excuse or justify lying. These represent two types of reason people typically give for lying in personal relationships. Discussing these cases provides an opportunity to articulate reasons for complete honesty within close personal relationships.

Why Honesty is the Best Policy: Two Cases

The scarlet sweater

My intimate comes home wearing a chartreuse sweater, proud as
Punch. "Look, honey, I got a great buy on this sweater and I'm crazy
about it. Don't you just love it?" I don't. I think it's a bit gaudy. How
should I respond? According to traditional wisdom: "Yes, dear, it is
quite nice."

The tendered justification for lying goes something like this: it
is crucial that intimates reveal those features, beliefs, emotions, etc.,
which are central to who they are. However, not all of a person's
features are central; some are peripheral. Thus, disclosing these latter
features is not revealing, withholding them is not detrimental. If my
reaction to my intimate's sweater is peripheral to who I am, then
honesty achieves nothing and costs much. It achieves nothing since I
would be revealing only peripheral information about myself. It costs
much since it hurts my intimate. Thus, there is no compelling reason
to be honest and good reason to lie.

This argument, although initially plausible, is dangerous. If allowed
much sway, it will encourage dishonesty, which, even when motivated
by sensitivity, will bar the formation of new intimate relationships and
subvert existing ones.

First, I suspect that this proffered justification is often nothing more
than an unconscious attempt to avoid conflict. Many intimates will do
whatever is feasible to avoid a "fight" with their intimates. Certainly I
have rationalized my dishonesty with intimates in just this way; I can
only surmise others have as well. One indication that this is nothing
more than a rationalization is that the justification conflicts with my
reaction to her sweater. If I didn't care about apparel, why would I
notice, let along make a judgement about, the sweater? Is not the
presence of a negative judgement a prima facie reason for thinking it
is *not* peripheral? As I have argued throughout the book, we know our
beliefs and attitudes not simply by introspection, but by observing our
behavior and our propensities to behave. I may *think* apparel doesn't
matter to me, but discover it does matter when I notice that I respond
differently to people depending on how they are dressed. Consequently, the reason I am dishonest about the sweater is not that it

121

doesn't matter, but that it does – and I don't want my intimate to know.

Suppose, however, that my reaction were peripheral in some sense. Nonetheless, my disliking the sweater will likely shape how I relate to her when she wears it. I may be less affectionate or even curt – and she will not know why. Moreover, we must remember that one lie is seldom sufficient. On future occasions she will expect me to compliment her on the sweater; I must also be careful not to criticize others wearing similar sweaters.

We must also be wary of the claim that my intimate will be hurt if she discovers I dislike her sweater. She might be momentarily bothered, even miffed. But hurt? Unlikely. She is more likely to be hurt if she discovers I deceived her because I thought she could not handle my honesty. Suppose, however, that she were hurt. Barring circumstances which would explain her reaction (for example, if she just learned she did not receive the big promotion she deserves and desperately wants), if my telling her that I disliked her sweater caused her great pain, she is not the type of person likely to establish deep and abiding relationships. She is too emotionally fragile. If I fear this criticism will terribly upset her, then I will be disinclined to discuss issues or ask questions which might bother her. This will substantially limit the range of our discussions and, thus, the possibility of intimacy.

Additionally, this rationale will be a quickly spreading cancer. All of us are annoyed by some features of our intimates. Similar reasoning would lead us to lie about those matters as well – e.g. her hair, mannerisms, beliefs, or personality. To protect our intimates, we will need to advance and then maintain a network of interrelated lies. That we can do only if we are constantly on guard about what we say and do. And if we are guarded with our intimates, we will not long be intimates. Certainly the range and depth of our intimacy will be severely circumscribed.

Finally, even if such information were trivial to me, and even if voicing my reaction would hurt you, that does not show that I should hide my reaction. Although such matters may be trivial to me, they may be exceedingly important to you. If so, then if we are going to relate intimately, you should know that something you think is important, I think is trivial. Both of us should know the relative interest each of us has for various activities, goals, or beliefs. If we lie about such matters, we will be hiding significant portions of our lives from each other. Thus, we cannot be completely intimate.

This helps isolate a general problem with lying. Suppose I know apparel is important to you. Although irrelevant to me, I feign an interest in apparel so you will like me. By doing so, I do not respect you: I have deprived you of information you may want and need to make an informed decision about me and our relationship. This is an inevitable result of dishonesty: if I deceive you, I limit your options (Bok 1978: 20–2, 30–1). I indicate my lack of respect for you. I thereby violate the presumption of trust on which our relationship presumably rests. I treat you as an object to be manipulated, not as an equal.

The reader should note that this proffered justification for lying usually rests on the dualistic view of the self rejected earlier. Its dualist underpinnings are especially apparent in psychologist Sydney Jourard's discussion of self-disclosure. Jourard claims the self is relatively fixed and determinate, and that each of us has direct access to our "transparent selves" (Jourard 1964: 1–7). Thus, we know what is peripheral and what is central to our selves. We just look and see. I should disclose the "real me" to intimates. But that does not mean I need disclose everything. For instance, since I *know* that I have no real interest in apparel, then I can intentionally withhold my reaction to your sweater. By doing so I do not fail to reveal my self, since my lack of interest in apparel is not, on this view, part of my self.

Jourard is right that people sometimes intentionally hide their true beliefs and thoughts. But his belief that hiding peripheral beliefs is innocent is based on his assumption that we know what is central and what is peripheral about ourselves. However, the self is difficult to discern: we are opaque to ourselves as well as to others. The self is also constantly evolving. Even if we may know ourselves better that others do, we are not transparent. Even an insightful individual may be oblivious to significant features of herself; other features she may misrepresent or misunderstand. In fact, others will know her, in at least some respects, better than she knows herself. This should not be surprising. We come to know ourselves in the same way others do: we watch how we react, we listen to what we say. Our self-descriptions are reliable only if they are consistent with observable behavior.

Using the language of chapter 4, the self is a complex, acting organism. Like any complex subject, it is difficult to understand fully. The self changes constantly and thus eludes complete description. Our selves emerge from decisions we make and things we do; it is not a pre-existing, non-changing thing we can discover. If my arguments against this view of the self have been telling, then Jourard's advice – that everyone should share her true self – is of little help. We do not always know what is central to us; we do not know (precisely) who we are. Indeed we do not have completely determinate selves to reveal. The self not only changes but is constantly (re)created by our choices and actions.

Understanding the self as malleable, evolving, and opaque gives us reason to be honest, even about matters we think peripheral. Regular and detailed sharing with our intimates is often the best (and possibly the only) means to uncover indistinct though relatively fixed elements of our selves, and to forge the self's amorphous elements. Put differently, by being honest in an intimate relationship, we not only uncover our selves, we help constitute ourselves. As intimates we should commit ourselves to the mutual uncovering, refurbishing, and creating of our mutable, amorphous selves. In this way we help each other have a semi-determinate self to reveal or to share with others.

The scarlet letter

People sometimes justify lying to their intimates about significant matters if they think honesty will damage or destroy the relationship. A common example: while away on a convention, I have a one-night stand. I did not love my sexual partner; my hormones simply got the better of me – at least that is what I tell myself. Should I tell my spouse? Absolutely not. Why? Because she will be devastated; the relationship, forever damaged.

Certainly this is a tough case. The argument for lying is forceful. However, the argument proceeds too quickly. Many of the previous considerations suggest why I should be honest even here. For instance, by denying my spouse this information, I fail to treat her with due respect. I am effectively coercing her – making decisions for her – by withholding information presumably relevant to her continued participation in the relationship. This lie will have to be regularly reinforced by still other lies. I must be careful around her lest I let some telling detail slip. This will create an air of distrust which will inevitably limit our closeness. Or, if I can blithely lie to her about something which is, *ex hypothesi*, so important, then our relationship is already in jeopardy.

Thus, I could view my action in two different ways. I could see the affair as indicating my dissatisfaction with the marriage, even if I recognize the dissatisfaction only in retrospect. Or I could think promiscuity is compatible with a strong and abiding love for my spouse. Either way I should be honest. In the first view I must be honest to rebuild a deteriorating relationship. How else could we regain intimacy with this secret between us, polluting the atmosphere of trust? On the other hand, if I think I can have extra-marital affairs without any detrimental effects on our marriage, then I should tell her that. If she agrees, fine. I would then have no reason to lie. If she disagrees, however, she has a right to know my beliefs on important matters; otherwise, I have control over her and over our relationship.

There are two variations on the above case in which temporary dishonesty might be justified. In the first variation I realize the affair signals trouble in the marriage but I want to "work things out." I conclude, however, that given our current lack of intimacy, sharing details of the affair would destroy our chances of regaining intimacy – I predict she will be so angry that she will simply leave. What should I do? Perhaps this. Tell her my misgivings about the marriage, assuming that if intimacy blossoms I can then share details with her about the affair, along with an explanation for my momentary deception. Such a maneuver would arguably be honest in the long run, even though I would momentarily suspend honesty until we strengthened our relationship. At that time the relationship could withstand the momentary trauma of learning about the affair.

I do not intend to consider this argument in detail – although it does have a surface plausibility. But even if it justified temporary dishonesty, it does not undermine my contention that complete honesty is essential for ideal intimacy. Our relationship will be fully intimate only after I am completely honest with her. Moreover, the time when honesty is suspended is the very time when the relationship is admittedly less intimate.

In the second case I conclude our relationship is beyond repair and plan to leave without telling her about the affair. To tell would only hurt; it would not help. This too seems plausible. However, this case does not undermine my thesis either. Our relationship is dead and my thesis does not consider whether we should be completely honest with former intimates.

What is Honesty?

I have tried to suggest why honesty is essential for intimate relationships. Now I must more closely examine the concept of honesty. We
often assume people know what is honest; they need only decide to *be*
honest. Certainly we can choose to be honest or dishonest. But we can
be honest only if we know what *is* honest. Determining that is not
easy.

Sometimes people talk as if honesty were just "speaking the truth."
Not so. For instance, honesty cannot require sharing *every* thought I
have. Even if you could endure this running commentary, it would not
enhance your understanding of me. Indeed, it would preclude understanding. You can know me better, you can understand me – if I
selectively share relevant details. For instance, the details of what I ate
for breakfast will likely tell you nothing about me, except, perhaps,
that I am inconsiderate. But details about my first love or the death of
my parents – events which helped shape my deepest-disposing traits –
are revealing.

Thus, to be honest we must disclose our thoughts and feelings
which are genuinely revealing, and we must disclose them in ways the
other is likely to understand. That we cannot do unless we know our
intimate's perspective, background beliefs, predispositions, etc. As in-
troductory logic teachers tell their students: the context of our utter-
ances affects their meaning. Why presume matters are different in
personal relationships? The context of our relationship, including our
beliefs and attitudes, determines whether and how you understand my
disclosures.

For instance, every teacher knows that she must present material in
an order students can comprehend. Explanation of basic terms and
simple concepts must precede presentation of more complex concepts. Hence, to be honest with her students the teacher must present
the simpler material first. To prematurely present the more complex
material – even if it is "closer" to the truth – would fail to communicate and, thus, would be dishonest.

Jack would not be honest with Jill if he told her how he felt in
Portuguese – unless, of course, she understood Portuguese. Or a parent
who answered her seven-year-old's ill-formed questions about sex with
a lecture summarizing sections of Gray's *Anatomy* would likewise be
dishonest.

Thus honesty occasionally demands telling different people different stories. By so doing we are not dishonest; rather, to communicate we must say different things (or say the same thing differently). Is this surprising? No. Rather it is something ordinary experience teaches us.

Honesty is an achievement or, more accurately, an attempted achievement. I cannot merely mouth statements which, according to my interpretation of them, accurately reflect my views. Rather, I must speak so that I am understood. Thus, I must know my audience. For instance, I must know their backgrounds sufficiently well to know how to effectively communicate with them. It is not enough to *tell* them the truth, I must *communicate* the truth. Among other things, I must pace my revelations so that I can reveal myself in a way they are likely to understand.

Moreover, we should recall that a person can be honest (or dishonest) in her actions as well as her words. I am verbally dishonest if I intentionally mislead you by what I say. I am behaviorally dishonest if I intentionally mislead you by what I do. I might deceive you by saying, "I am benevolently inclined," even when I am not; or I might deceive you by donating to charity in your presence.

In an intimate relationship we should also be behaviorally honest with our intimates. Although the reasons for doing so parallel those offered for verbal honesty, there is one striking difference. The more time we spend together, the less likely it is that we can behave dishonestly with each other. It is far easier to tailor our verbal discourse than our actions – after all, non-verbal behavior is more habitual, less under our conscious control. We can maintain an artificial posture in front of each other only so long. Eventually our façade will drop and we will see each other for what we are. In short, sustained behavioral dishonesty is difficult – if not impossible – in an ongoing personal relationship. This provides still another reason for verbal honesty. In long-term relationships we reveal ourselves to others by how we act. This will doubtless expose verbal lies to a discerning partner.

Meta-honesty

When most people say that "John is honest," they mean that John reveals himself to others – that he does not mislead them about who or what he is. Suppose John informs his intimates that he is selfish, smokes dope, or once worked as a CIA agent. If John is selfish, smokes dope, and once worked for the CIA, then he has been honest. But perhaps not entirely honest. Honesty is more than just revealing our tastes and history. Meta-honesty, or honesty about our overarching traits, may be especially important for building and sustaining an intimate relationship.

For instance, even intimates who are attuned to the contribution honesty plays in a relationship will feel the appeal of dishonesty and will, at least on some occasions, succumb to it (Baxter and Wilmot 1985). To be completely (meta-)honest we should share this information with our intimates, to explain why we chose, in a specific situation, to be dishonest. This would require exploring our motivation for dishonesty – be it fear of rejection, the desire to appear faultless, or whatever. This honesty about our more general overarching traits can uncover details about us, details we have heretofore withheld from everyone, including perhaps ourselves. This disclosure provides our intimates with a different level of understanding and thus opens possibilities for real growth – for us, for them, and for our relationship.

Meta-honesty is particularly important once we realize that in some cases there is no "fact of the matter" about what we are feeling or thinking. Suppose Ron asks Judy "Do you love me?" Judy cannot answer the question merely by looking inside herself for something which is or designates her love (or lack of it). Even if she had strong loving-like feelings for Ron, that would be insufficient for an unqualified affirmative response. Ron wants more than a report about her inner states; he wants to know, among other things, whether Judy thinks their relationship is viable. Perhaps she has doubts whether the relationship would endure, or she may find herself repulsed by some of Ron's personality traits. Perhaps she has an overriding commitment to Joseph. On the other hand, Judy may not have strong feelings for Ron, yet finds she wishes to be with him since she enjoys his company, revels in his sense of humor, and is titillated by their conversations. Should Judy, therefore, say "No" since she does not have strong feelings for him?

The earlier discussion of the role of feelings in the emotions provides the beginnings of an answer. In this latter case, Judy should not *automatically* say "No" since feelings are neither the same as nor unmistakable signs of emotions. Moreover Judy does not have a well-defined emotion; rather her emotions are blurred – she has seemingly antithetical beliefs. A simple "Yes" or "No" will not do. An unqualified affirmative will only indicate her intent to love and spend time with Ron; an unqualified negative, her intent to break off the relationship.

To be meta-honest Judy should share the details of her reactions, as well as her reactions to the reactions. To be meta-honest she should candidly respond to him, for instance by saying, "It bothers me that I really want to be away from you sometimes even though I have such strong feelings for you." Or Ron might say: "I find your revulsion to some of my traits inconsistent with your purported commitment to tolerance."

Genuine honesty requires sharing meta-observations, hunches and random thoughts – and labeling them accordingly (for example, "I am not confident about this, but...."; "I do not like so and so, and it bothers me"; or "I wish I didn't think this, but...."). Such qualifications provide intimates with a more accurate picture of our beliefs, a context within which others can more plausibly interpret our behavior.

The need to share these meta-observations becomes all the more significant once we recall that the self is opaque. Inasmuch as who we are is indeterminate or undetermined, mutual sharing of such thoughts, appropriately qualified, will improve the chance that both of us will gain knowledge of ourselves and of each other.

Quest for Intimacy

Honesty is vital for intimate relationships, although its importance is usually unrecognized, ignored, or compromised. Nonetheless, there are cases where temporary dishonesty seems justified. For instance, suppose Rhonda is miffed at Sonny, who is momentarily depressed. He asks Rhonda: "Are you angry or upset with me?" Given his depression, Rhonda decides to lie now and then discuss her anger later, along with an explanation for the lie.

Rhonda's decision seems reasonable. But it can be plausibly argued that this momentary suppression is not really dishonest. That is, since Rhonda will eventually tell Sonny the truth, she is not trying to give him a false picture of herself. Instead, by telling him about the lie later, she is actually giving him more details about herself. Furthermore, given the contextual view of honesty, there is another reason for recharacterizing the lie. I argued that honesty requires communicating the most accurate portrait of oneself. Under the circumstances, telling Sonny *now* about her quibble might not succeed in communicating with him. It might only tell him that she is more concerned to "get it off her chest" than to communicate. As long as the pledge to share later is fulfilled, then it does not seem Rhonda has been dishonest.

If I recognize the legitimacy of withholding the truth in these cases, however, I may be inclined to also withhold the truth when it is inappropriate. It is easy to let sensitivity suppress our desire to be honest. The result of doing so is detrimental: we begin to drift away from our intimates. This usually happens in one of two ways. The first involves a psychologically slippery slope. We recognize that sensitivity may demand temporary suppression of feelings, beliefs, attitudes (as in the case above). Slowly but surely, our concern for sensitivity becomes more important, or at least more psychologically powerful, than honesty. ("Why," Rhonda asks herself, "should I tell Sonny about my disgruntlement now? I am no longer upset." Consequently, the disgruntlement gets repressed.)

Slowly people begin to equate sensitivity with coddling: we assume that any criticism will hurt our intimates. Consequently, in the name of sensitivity we repress all our complaints. Likely our intimates are swayed by similar reasoning, so they repress their complaints as well. So we daintily tiptoe around each other, avoiding fights, but also avoiding the growth which comes from creative conflict. We thereby close off lines of communication which can enhance intimacy and promote self-knowledge.

The second way is often just a bastardization of the first. Here we claim to be concerned with the feelings and needs of our intimates (and such concerns may be present to some degree). In fact, however, the principal reason we lie (or suppress information) is self-protection. Frequently we deceive our intimates because we dislike conflict or fear they will reject us (Baxter and Wilmot 1984; 1985).

We must scrupulously avoid this temptation. Although we might suppress our troubles or disgruntlements now, we cannot do so forever. They may emerge surreptitiously, in snide comments or avoidance behavior. Or we may "gunny sack" so long that we finally explode, dumping all our gripes at once, with an embellishment that comes only from stewing over complaints for a long time. Our intimates – victims of these embellishments – will not understand our concerns or complaints, and thus will be unable to respond appropriately. Therefore, the disclosure will not be honest.

In short, what often happens in intimate relationships is the opposite of what should and could happen. As relationships persist, we should become closer and more honest with our intimates; in fact we often become progressively closed and distant. We should be developing habits of honesty; instead we are cultivating habits of suppression and deceit. We could be learning that honesty can promote personal growth probably unachievable in any other way; instead we are learning to endure relationships which are stunted or even detrimental. In short, here we vividly see the truth in the words of Somerset Maugham: "It is a funny thing about life. Those who refuse to accept anything but the very best very often get it."

Self-knowledge

Throughout the book, I have suggested that self-knowledge is intricately connected with personal relationships. I have argued that (1) self-knowledge promotes and (2) is promoted by personal relationships, (3) that self-knowledge is one of intimacy's principal values, and (4) that self-knowledge and our knowledge of others are intricately connected. Earlier in this chapter, I further argued that we know ourselves better if we are completely honest with our intimates. It is now high time to discuss self-knowledge explicitly. What exactly is it for a person to know herself? Why is it valuable? How is it achieved?

At first glance knowing ourselves seems simple. After all, most of us assume we know ourselves not just better than others do know us, but better than others could know us. This appears to support Cartesian dualism. Dualism gives a univocal account of self-knowledge; it is to know our transcendental egos, the mentalistic "thing" which constitutes us. The dualist also has a clear procedure for knowing ourselves: introspection.

Unfortunately, virtually every major thinker throughout history thought self-knowledge was a stunning achievement, not a foregone conclusion; it was the result of hard work, not a simple act of mental perception. From the beginnings of civilization, philosophers, religious leaders, novelists, poets, and statesmen have extolled the value of self-knowledge. According to the Cartesian dualist, however, self-knowledge is easily achieved: we need only look and see; the self is, so to speak, right in front of our mental eyes.

If self-knowledge were achieved effortlessly, most influential thinkers in history were not only wrong, but profoundly wrong. Socrates would have spent most of his life imploring people to do what all but the biggest fool do with ease. Similarly, John Stuart Mill would have made an unbelievable blunder when he said that the vast majority of mankind live their entire lives without even a whisper of self-knowledge. Could these great thinkers have been so wrong?

I think not. Although we sometimes fall into the trap of thinking self-knowledge is a given, at other times we recognize clearly just how elusive it is. All of us have discovered aspects of ourselves we had previously missed, sometimes to our embarrassment. Not infrequently we realize our failure to understand or appreciate our motives. We sometimes discover glaring faults (or obvious strengths) we had previously overlooked.

The dualist cannot account for this common experience. The functionalist and the behaviorist, however, can explain what self-knowledge is, and why it is elusive. They claim we can know ourselves only by knowing our deeper-disposing traits (our tendencies to behave) and the interrelationships between those traits (tendencies). Moreover, we must not only know that we have certain tendencies (compassion, sensitivity, and honesty), we must understand the connections between them, for example a general tendency to do what we think moral. Perhaps more importantly we must also know how we change, what I have earlier called "meta-traits." For instance, perhaps you are flexible; you cope effectively with external changes; you modify your first-order traits when appropriate. By knowing this meta-trait, you know the ways you are likely to change.

But *how*, according to the functionalist and behaviorist, can we know our deeper-disposing traits? We cannot just look and see – there is nothing to see. We come to know ourselves in more or less the same way we come to know others. We must carefully observe what we say and do; then we must interpret this data in light of our general knowledge of human psychology (why and how people act as they do). The resulting view of our self must be consistent with others' perceptions of us. If not, then unless we have compelling reason to think everyone else is confused, blind, malevolent, or dishonest, we must re-evaluate our self-portrait.

Any resultant view of our self must then be subject to further scrutiny and tested against the collective understanding of others. This process continues *ad infinitum*. There will always be elements of our behavior that elude capture; there will be pieces of the puzzle that just don't fit. However, when they do fit, we are justified in saying we know ourselves. The mere fact that we do not know *everything* about ourselves does not show that we are devoid of self-knowledge. We do not make these stringent demands on other forms of knowledge. For instance, we would not deny that Albert Einstein knew about particle physics just because he did not understand everything about atomic particles.

According to the functionalist and behaviorist, the self is constantly changing, evolving. As we have new experiences we will learn from them; we will change because of them. Since these changes are often minor and may occur subconsciously, we may not immediately notice them. But change we do. There is always a "new" me to rediscover. The knowledge of ourselves yesterday will be (slightly) outdated today. Nonetheless self-knowledge is attainable. Even the rudiments of self-knowledge can be exceedingly valuable.

The value of self-knowledge

Self-knowledge is a fundamental value. This belief has been the cornerstone of Western thought since Socrates proclaimed that "The unexamined life is not worth living." But why, exactly, is self-knowledge so valuable? Is it intrinsically valuable, valuable for its own sake? Or is it valuable because it promotes other values? As I argued earlier in the book, the traditional way of distinguishing intrinsic from instrumental values should be rejected. Intrinsic values are not valuable independently of their connection with other values. Rather, they are intrinsically valuable, in part, because they are intricately connected with a wide range of other values. In this sense, we can partially explain any intrinsic value by citing these other values which it promotes and by which it is promoted. Because of its role in this network of values, we can be confident of its value, even when we cannot, in a particular case, specify that value. That is why we say it is *intrinsically* valuable.

Self-knowledge is a vivid example of an intrinsic value, so understood. We think of knowledge as intrinsically valuable; self-knowledge thus seems equally (or especially) valuable. We can identify the network of values it promotes, and which promote it. For example, many ethicists think personal autonomy is supremely valuable. Some ethicists, like Kant, make autonomy the linchpin of their ethical theories. These thinkers claim a person's life is uniquely valuable if it is self-directed. Our lives are self-directed only if we choose how to live, and if our choices are rational, based on an assessment of the available evidence. If we are genuinely self-directed, then, barring bad luck, our lives will be more pleasant, more productive, and more successful. However, autonomy is impossible without self-knowledge. We cannot do what we really want to do unless we know what we want to do. We cannot fashion a sensible life plan unless we know our desires, attitudes, beliefs, and inclinations. Without self-knowledge we cannot make informed decisions about our vocation, friends, political alignments, marriage, or children.

It is especially relevant for present purposes that self-knowledge is not only promoted by close personal relationships; it also makes those relationships possible. I have already indicated ways in which close relationships promote self-knowledge: we learn more about ourselves if we honestly share our views and reactions with our intimates, and if we receive their honest, caring feedback.

Self-knowledge also promotes close personal relationships. Before we can respond sensitively to our intimates, we must know their needs, desires, and emotions – that is obvious. But we must also know our strengths and weaknesses, our abilities and our propensities. Otherwise, we may respond improperly to their needs. But to say we should know our strengths, weaknesses, and abilities is just to say that we must know ourselves. Furthermore, we can be honest and benefit from our intimates' honesty only if we already have rudimentary self-knowledge. Without some self-knowledge, we cannot reveal ourselves to our intimates; nor can we modulate our conversations to effectively and sensitively communicate.

It might seem I have been inconsistent, or at least stated a paradox, i.e. that we need self-knowledge for personal relationships, and that we need personal relationships to obtain self-knowledge. Not so. We need not completely understand ourselves to be intimate with others; nor must we have completely intimate relationships before we can attain any self-knowledge. Rather self-knowledge and personal relationships are mutually supportive. People with the most meager self-knowledge may establish minimal forms of personal relationships; people who have yet to form personal relationships may have the rudiments of self-knowledge. But both self-knowledge and personal relationships are limited without the other. Knowledge of ourselves is limited unless we have the regular critical feedback from intimates, and unless we can observe ourselves relating to others. Conversely, our relationships are likewise limited without substantial self-knowledge. Self-knowledge and personal relationships are food for the other's growth. Close personal bonds will promote self-knowledge. Enhanced self-knowledge will promote deeper personal relationships, which will enhance self-knowledge, etc.

9

Equity in Relationships

Most people assume close personal relationships must be fair or equitable; that is, each party to the relationship must contribute and receive *roughly* the same. Exactly what people mean by "the same" and how they determine equity varies. Some people claim successful partners swap benefits tit for tat ("We did what you wanted yesterday; today we will do what I want"). Most, however, acknowledge that each individual's contributions may vary in kind and in degree. That is, one person may contribute (or receive) either physical goods (e.g. expensive presents, a fancy house, economic security) or psychological goods (e.g. peace of mind, heightened self-esteem, personal security). Although these exchanges do not involve any common standard of comparison, we can still judge if the exchanged goods are approximately equal. For instance, Joyce might assume financial burdens while acquiring a heightened sense of self-esteem; Clive might gain peace of mind while losing some independence. Despite the difficulties of comparing disparate goods, Joyce and Clive could judge that each of them benefits and forfeits roughly the same.

The equity thesis can be interpreted descriptively or normatively. Some people maintain the descriptive claim that inequitable personal relationships will fail, or that if they survive, the partners will be discontent. Others embrace the normative claim that inequitable relationships are flawed even when they endure. Put differently, the former claim successful close relationships *are* equitable, while the latter claim close relationships *ought* to be equitable, even if they are not. I will begin by discussing the descriptive thesis that relationships must be equitable to survive and prosper. Later in the chapter I discuss the normative claim.

Descriptive Equity: Only Equitable Relationships Survive

Numerous socio-psychological studies apparently support the descriptive claim. Following is a typical statement of these findings: "This study extends our confidence that considerations of equity are important, even in deeply committed relationships . . . [as much as in] casual and business relationships" (Utne et al. 1984). Some psychologists reject the equity thesis in its strong form, but even many of these conclude that: "Difficulties, problems, or ineptness in conducting relationships equitably, can lead to the disruption or even the dissolution of the relationship" (Duck 1983: 110).

A few psychologists dispute this widely held belief that close relationships must be equitable. In a series of studies Margaret Clark found that although people expect equity in exchange relationships (what I call impersonal relationships), they do not expect equity in "communal" relationships (what I call close personal relationships) (Clark 1985).

Within exchange relationships participants are expected to benefit those who benefit them. The relationship will continue only as long as each reciprocally benefits the other. For instance, an employer and employee exchange money for labor. As long as each receives what she considers fair, the relationship will likely continue. Or Jan and Dean will continue to carpool as long as both share the costs equally.

Within communal relationships, however, people are expected to respond to each other's needs – not reciprocate benefits. More strongly, they are expected to *not* reciprocate benefits. Participants in communal relationships who try to return benefits will likely thereby harm their relationships (Clark 1979). Suppose Sue's close friend, Ron, is a bit depressed. To cheer him up, she buys him the latest Michael Crichton novel. She does not expect him to pay for it or to reciprocate with a similar gift. After all, she gave him a gift; she did not engage in an exchange.

But reciprocate he does. He buys her the latest book by Stephen Jay Gould. Although Sue loves the book and would have been thrilled had he given her the book as a gift, she is upset. He purchased the book not so much as a gift, but as part of an exchange. Perhaps he misperceived the purpose of her gift. But if they had a full-fledged communal (close personal) relationship, he would not have misunderstood her gesture: he would know she gave him the book to cheer him up, not as a circuitous way of obtaining a copy of Gould's latest book. Hence, she would likely infer that Ron does not want a communal relationship with her; he wants to keep the relationship distant, formal, impersonal.

Of course if theirs were an impersonal relationship, both she and Ron would expect benefits to be reciprocated. Not only would each expect benefits to be reciprocated, each would be offended if they were not. Thus, behavior which is the norm in an exchange relationship would be intolerable in a communal relationship, and vice versa. That is why we must be cognizant of the type of relationships we have and want; otherwise, we may act inappropriately – reciprocating benefits when we should not, and not reciprocating benefits when we should. In short, Clark's studies showed that although equity is the hallmark of exchange relationships, it is an anathema to communal relationships. Intimates do not seek equity.

Some psychologists would insist, however, that concern for equity pervades close relationships, although this concern takes different forms in impersonal and personal relationships. Whereas non-intimates expect immediate reciprocity, intimates expect reciprocity, but not immediately. On this view, intimates will keep tabs of each other's contributions to and benefits from the relationship. They want to ensure that the relationship is ultimately equitable, even if it is not equitable at all times (Hatfield and Traupmann 1981).

This suggestion is tenable, however, only if intimates keep track of each other's contributions to and benefits of the relationship. For if they don't have some mental record of contributions and benefits, they have no way to determine if the relationship is equitable. Clark claims, however, that participants in communal relationships do not keep track of each other's contributions; in fact, they try to mask them (Clark 1984; 1985). Thus, neither person has a basis for saying that a relationship is equitable; according to Clark, equity is simply not a conscious concern.

Of course, if asked, intimates might have some vague subconscious sense of each other's contribution to the relationship. But that does not show that the relationship is based on any desire for equity, or, for that matter, that they are even concerned about equity. People motivated by and concerned about equity would make efforts to take note of their contributions and benefits, more efforts than Clark says they do make.

I am not particularly well equipped to assess the methodological soundness of her studies, although they appear to be well designed and executed. Nonetheless, I can offer philosophical arguments supporting Clark's findings. Those studies which indicate that equity is important for interpersonal relationships are correlative: people claim to be satisfied in relationships they deem equitable. Although that may well be true, it does not show people are satisfied because they think relationships are equitable. It may well be that they consider relationships equitable because they are satisfied. I suspect many people in close relationships never consciously consider if the relationship is equitable, although if asked they will infer it is equitable since they are satisfied. On the other hand, people dissatisfied with their relationships quite naturally look for the cause of the dissatisfaction. In the current ideological environment, being exploited by their intimates seems a plausible candidate.

Doubtless some of the correlation discovered by social scientists may be explained in this way. Some, but not all. Perceived inequity may well lead intimates to be dissatisfied with their relationships. Nonetheless, there are two very different explanations of why this is so. According to the first, each of us enters personal relationships to attain benefits from one another. Nonetheless, we recognize we are likely to get what we want only if we give the other what she wants. So we establish an exchange relationship. If, at some point, the exchange is no longer equitable, then, since the relationship is no longer a good bargain, we will likely leave it.

Most psychologists think this is the best explanation of people's dissatisfaction; indeed, many think it is the only explanation. Not so. To understand why, we must remember that many people seek a personal relationship because they want an intimate relationship, not because they want a beneficial exchange. That is, they want a relationship in which each person responds to her intimate's needs and promotes her intimate's interests. In such a relationship intimates have no need to keep score – each expects the other to care for her. Nonetheless, since both believe intimates respond to each other's needs, once in the relationship they will plausibly expect something approximating equity. Equity, though, will be the expected result of most intimate relationships; it will not be their purpose.

Let me explain. Intimates believe partners do not intentionally take advantage of one another; rather, they spontaneously satisfy one other's needs, etc. Moreover, they also plausibly assume that any two people will have roughly equivalent needs and roughly equivalent abilities to satisfy other's needs. Given these plausible assumptions, intimates will expect that both partners in a close personal relationship will contribute and benefit *roughly* the same. But this is an expectation about what results from an intimate relationship, not about the relationship's goal or purpose. Given this expectation, what would you conclude if you were in a notably inequitable relationship? Probably not that you are getting a bad bargain – indeed, that would understate your reaction. Probably you would conclude your partner does not love you, or that she loves you only marginally.

"But surely it makes no difference," someone might say, "whether I interpret my intimate's failure to respond to my needs as a lack of love or as an inequitable exchange. In both I am carrying the load and I do not like it; in both my supposed intimate is having a free ride." However, this is not a distinction without a difference. Rather it is a pivotal distinction that isolates a significant practical difference between these types of relationship. Consider two cases in which Patti believes Jeff has treated her inequitably. In the first they have an exchange relationship; in the second, a communal one. The nature of their relationship will determine: (1) how Patti determines she is being mistreated, (2) her reaction to being treated inequitably, and (3) what, if anything, Jeff can do to restore the relationship.

Suppose Jeff borrowed money from Patti, i.e. they have an exchange relationship. If he missed a payment, she would notice it immediately; after all, in exchange relationships we typically have clear and rigid expectations of how the other will behave. His failure to make the payment need not be insidious; perhaps he is just absent-minded. The explanation for the failure, however, is irrelevant. He must restore equity by making the missed payment and by paying some compensation or penalty. Once he does so (assuming he is not *too* delinquent), the exchange relationship will continue intact – at least as long as he continues to make timely payments (or makes appropriate recompense for missed payments).

If Patti and Jeff had a close personal relationship, however, matters would be different. Since intimates do not keep tabs on their contributions and benefits, then Patti would not immediately notice an inequity – likely not until Jeff had been taking advantage of her for some time. Consequently, her recognition that the relationship is inequitable suggests the problem has been brewing for some time.

Second, Patti will likely be more upset by this inequity than she would be if they had an exchange relationship. All of us enter exchange relationships to benefit ourselves. We assume others do likewise. It seems reasonable to think the motive *for* the relationship also operates *within* the relationship. Hence, most of us anticipate that others will have some inclination to take advantage of us in an exchange relationship. That is why we frequently erect external barriers to prevent such abuses. Laws require us to meet our contractual obligations. The threat of legal sanctions gives us an additional reason to live up to our agreements.

Within a communal relationship, however, we respond to our intimates' needs – not because we fear reprisals if we don't, but because we care for them and they for us. That is, our deepest-disposing traits are to respond to our intimates' needs, regardless of the personal payoff. Thus, if Jeff fails to contribute to his presumably communal relationship with Patti, she will probably conclude that Jeff does not really love her, at least not as much as she loves him. Once she reaches this conclusion, Jeff cannot restore the relationship simply by rebalancing the scales. He must convince her that he still loves her. That can be difficult. Restoration and compensation may well be insufficient; sincere assertion of his love may not suffice.

On the other hand, if Patti is convinced that Jeff does love her, then he would not need to rebalance the scales. For example, Jeff might reassert his love for her, explain that he was insensitive because he was preoccupied with problems at the office, and convince her that he would be more vigilant in the future. Regardless of the details, if she is convinced that he loves her, he would not need to compensate her for his inequitable behavior. Indeed she would not expect it. Compensation is inappropriate within close personal relationships. If she forgives him for his negligence and selfishness, then all is well. But, of course, forgiveness is not a genuine option within a pure exchange relationship. A mortgager does not ask a loan company to forgive her; the only way to continue the relationship is to pay up. Period.

Nonetheless, Jeff might temporarily contribute more to the relationship. But if he did, he would not be trying to rebalance the scales. Trying to act equitably after Patti had forgiven him would be to doubt her forgiveness. Rather, by taking an extra share of the load, he symbolically reasserts his love for her, his commitment to the relationship. In short, there are significant practical differences between exchange and communal relationships. We expect intimates to care for each other; we expect parties in exchange relationships to reciprocate benefits. This is no small difference between personal and impersonal relationships. It *does* matter how we perceive and conceptualize our relationships.

Normative Equity: Justice in Personal Relationships

Others have argued that equity in personal relationships is morally required. In this view, inequitable relationships are not merely unsatisfying (though usually they are); rather, they are unjust. People who take advantage of their intimates have acted unjustly or immorally, they have wronged or violated the rights of their intimates (Friedman 1993: 127–32). At one level this claim seems eminently reasonable, even indisputable. If Jeff lets Patti carry a full-time job, do all the housework, completely care for the children, while he spends his evenings watching television and his weekends golfing, then Jeff has obviously wronged Patti. What more can be said? As it turns out, a great deal.

Doubtless one partner's behavior in a "personal" relationship may be so exploitative that we can only conclude that she has acted unjustly. On this point most people will agree. That does not show, however, that close relationships are best evaluated by standards of justice or by an appeal to rights. Rather, we should conclude that such relationships can properly be evaluated by criteria of justice only because they are no longer close or fully personal. If you may recall, a close personal relationship is defined (in part) as one in which each party promotes the interests of the other. If one person regularly ignores the interests of the other, the relationship is not, properly speaking, close.

This should not be interpreted as a victory by definition, though it may appear that way. It seems I have defined "close relationships" so that they cannot properly be evaluated by considerations of justice. Not so. In the first chapter I identified the central features of "close relationships," and tried to show how these reflect considered ordinary usage. Now it turns out that a relationship, so defined, does not exist if one person regularly mistreats the other. This isn't victory by definition.

Nonetheless, the victory is premature. Many people assume inequitable relationships exist and think they are, in some significant sense, personal. This cannot be banished by definition. To defend my claim that grossly inequitable relationships are not really close, I must remind the reader of the two criteria of close relationships. A close personal relationship is one in which (1) each party relates to the other as a unique individual, and (2) each has the other as one of her interests. The relationship in question (Jeff's and Patti's) likely satisfies the first criteria; that is, the relationship is personal since it is based on the unique embodiment and style of the other. It may also have the trappings of close relationships: Patti and Jeff may spend time together and say fond things to each other. However, in an abusive relationship, these trappings are the hallmark of mere familiarity, not intimacy. Why? Because the relationship does not satisfy the second criterion of close personal relationship: Jeff does not have Patti as one of his ends.

Suppose, though, that Jeff mistreated Patti even though he had her as one of his ends. What should she do? Should she demand justice? I think not. After all, he does care for her; that is, he is behaviorally disposed to promote her interests. Therefore, he must have mistreated her only because he could not identify her needs or did not know how to satisfy them. In these circumstances, the best way to strengthen their relationship is not for Patti to insist on justice, but to help him see and understand her needs and interests.

Inferior (i.e. non-close) forms of personal relationships *can* be judged on grounds of justice; indeed, they should be. But that does not show that close relationships should be so judged. Of course, in one sense they can be. Patti can simply say: "Jeff is treating me unjustly." Moreover, if we define "justice" so that Jeff's failure to fulfill Patti's needs is unjust, then, of course, he has acted unjustly. This usage, however, distorts the notion of justice. To be just is to give people their due (Aristotle 1985). Principles of justice establish minimal guidelines to evaluate impersonal relationships, interactions between strangers, especially those who reside within the same political community. Philosophers have typically distinguished between three types of justice. (1) Distributive justice requires that we give others their fair share or deserved portion of the social good. (2) Retributive justice requires that we distribute rewards and punishments according to criteria of desert. (3) Compensatory justice requires that we provide appropriate compensation to those we harm.

My earlier arguments, however, showed that these notions are inappropriate in close personal relationships. Close friends do not give or expect what is their due, they do not reward or punish their intimates, nor do they expect compensation for interpersonal wrongs.

143

Nor do intimates claim their rights. Yet rights, according to most theorists, are intimately connected to the notion of justice. Rights guarantee or protect what people are due. Thus, if I own my house, then it can be said that I have a property right to that house. That means, among other things, that I can, within limits, use that house as I see fit. I might in certain circumstances give someone permission to live in it. If, however, she were to use it without permission, she has violated my rights. Of course I can waive (choose not to exercise) or relinquish (give up) my rights, but I must do so explicitly. No one can legitimately use my house without my express permission.

Although rights talk plays a valuable role in impersonal, political contexts, talk of rights is both too stringent and too lenient to provide what we desire and expect from our intimates. Rights are too stringent because friends have a license to treat us in ways we would not tolerate from strangers. Close friends may borrow from us without asking; in fact, we expect them to do so. A close friend, for instance, may enter my office in the evening to borrow a book; I would feel free to do likewise. Or a friend might expect me to help her cope with her personal trauma, even though the cost to me is substantial; I would expect the same from her. Or a depressed friend might become angry at me in ways or in circumstances I would not permit from a stranger. Thus, talk of rights fails to capture the nature of our relationship. A friend who interrupts me to talk about her problem does not violate my right to privacy. A close friend who borrows a book without asking has not violated my right to property. Both have done what I would have expected from good friends.

Perhaps the reader is not comfortable with the particular illustrations provided. Perhaps, you do not want *anyone* taking your books without permission. Or perhaps you do not want *anyone* to get angry with you – even if they are friends. These examples, though, are just that: examples. My point is merely that there are some things which intimates can do without explicit permission – actions which, if performed by a stranger, would constitute a violation of your rights.

On the other hand, we also have higher expectations of our intimates than of strangers, expectations rights cannot provide. If I have a right, it is merely a claim to some minimal level of decent treatment. I do not have a right that others care. We expect strangers to respect our rights and to fulfill their obligations. We expect them, for example, not to steal our property (or to steal anyone else's, for that matter). However, we do not want abstract respect from our friends; we want personal affirmation. We do not want friends to be kind to us out of a sense of duty (to respect our rights); we want them to be kind to us because they love us. Spouses should not sleep with each other out of a sense of obligation; nor should close friends spend time with each other merely out of a sense of duty.[1]

Imagine how repugnant it would be to have a spouse or friend who assumed she should be with us simply because we had a right to her presence. For example, "Don't worry, honey, I will fulfill my conjugal duties to you." Or "Sure we will talk this evening; I realize I am obliged to do so." Such behavior makes a mockery of the relationship. We do not want our friends motivated by a sense of justice, but by the desire to promote our interests.

Of course sometimes our desire to promote our intimate's interests may lead us to do something we do not, for other reasons, particularly want to do at that moment. That is part of what it means to say that I am disposed to care for my intimates: I habitually promote their interests. For instance, Patti may not want to listen to Jeff's problems right *now*. Nonetheless, she may do so because she loves him. That is rather different, however, from listening to him merely because she is obliged to do so. Minimally, duty should not be the driving force in a close relationship; if it is, the relationship is in serious trouble. That is why close relationships cannot be completely or adequately judged by considerations of justice.

Nonetheless, some philosophers have argued that participants should be fully aware that considerations of justice are operative in the background of personal relationships, even if they are neither invoked nor explicitly considered.

> Though marriage is certainly more than rights and correlative duties, and though one will not expect to hear claims of rights in a happily functioning marriage, nevertheless the strength and security of the marriage commitment in the modern world depends in part on there being an array of legalistic rights and duties that the partners *know* [emphasis mine] they can fall back on, if their mutual affection ever fades (Waldron 1993: 373–4).

Waldron is obviously correct in one sense, that people might appeal to considerations of justice when relationships are seriously inequitable. But that does not show that those considerations are operative in well-functioning relationships; still less does it show that they should be.

In fact, to think about, appeal to, or even conceive of our personal relationships in terms of rights is to misconstrue them, and will likely subvert them. By introducing considerations of justice we will probably undermine the very thing we most want within those relationships, namely a sense that we are loved and cared for because of who we are. If we begin to construe our personal relationships in terms of justice or rights, we will see our partners' interests as limitations on us (as we do in impersonal relationships) rather than as interests we wish to promote (as we should in personal relationships). Rights talk governs interactions between strangers, between two people who do not care for each other and who may even be in overt conflict. Patti's right to property limits Jeff's ability to use that property, even if he wants or needs it. Jeff's right to life limits Patti's options; Patti cannot swing her new bat in an area occupied by Jeff's head. In short, rights tell us what we cannot do to each other. They thereby emphasize (or create) distance between us. Consequently, if we begin to think about or conceptualize our relationships in terms of rights, we begin to ask: "What *must* I do for my intimate?" rather than "What *can* I do for her?" Thoughts of justice or rights will limit the love and care we want in personal relationships.

None of this should be taken to suggest that people in personal relationships never, in fact, think it terms of rights, justice, or equity. Certainly we do. Given Western civilizations's preoccupation with rights it would be surprising were it otherwise. What I am suggesting is that we would be better off if we didn't; if, instead, intimates conceptualized and dealt with their differences as two people who care about each other rather than as two people who treat each other justly. For, if two people do care about each other they will treat each other well. When they don't, they can repair their relationship best by emphasizing their mutual care, rather than their individual rights.

Consider a situation in which intimates have an apparent clash of interests. Marie and Tom must decide which car to purchase, where to take their vacation, or where to live. If they conceptualize and judge their relationship by standards of justice or rights, each of them will likely become preoccupied with his or her rights and responsibilities. If there is no obvious solution to their "conflict," they may compromise. But compromises over important issues rarely satisfy either person. Both of them will feel they sacrificed to the relationship. Neither will be satisfied by the compromise.

Suppose they conceived of their apparent clash of interests as intimates do. That is, Tom wants to promote Marie's interests as well as his own; Marie wants to promote Tom's as well as her own. If they conceive of their differences in light of their mutual care, there is no straightforward way to identify a conflict of interest between them. Of course this does not eradicate their differences. The shift in perspective does not make disagreements vanish the way some dime store novels suggest. It does, however, change the way they understand those differences, the parameters within which they make a decision. For instance, Tom may recognize that his interest in Marie is more important than his interest in buying a new Prelude. Or Marie may decide that her interest in Tom is greater than her interest in visiting Orlando.

Although this maneuver may well not result in a quick solution, it will encourage them to consider alternative solutions that might satisfy them both, rather than settling for a compromise that satisfies neither. If they find a real solution, both will advance their own and their intimate's interests. In short, considerations of justice, although they may in some sense lie in the background of personal relationships, are best ignored by parties within them.

To borrow an apt analogy from Hardwig:

> Rights are like the net underneath the tightrope act. The net keeps people and their lives from being ruined if they fall off the wire. But the act is ruined if the net actually comes into play. Maybe it would be foolish to get up on the wire if we did not know there was a net beneath us, and yet the act would be even better if we could have enough confidence in ourselves and each other to do it without thinking of the net at all (1984: 453).

A Complication

No matter how the situation is described, sometimes people in intimate relationships feel their partners have taken advantage of them. This often creates problems unique to close relationships. In pure exchange relationships, participants generally know precisely what is expected of them; therefore, inequity is relatively easy to spot and relatively difficult to fantasize. If a person does not fulfill her end of the bargain, it will be fairly apparent. It is equally apparent if she has contributed her expected share. However, as I noted earlier, intimates typically do not notice inequity since they do not consciously keep tabs on one another's contributions and benefits.

On the other hand, intimates may also find it easier to fantasize inequity since each party is often unaware of the other's contributions or sacrifices. Let me explain each in turn. Suppose Kristie wants to see a movie Jason is not particularly keen to see. He wants to go shopping. Nonetheless, he wants to be with Kristie and, within limits, to do what she wants to do. So he goes to the movie: he waives his immediate desire in order to help Kristie promote her desire. Although he does not resent going, he has temporarily subordinated one of his self-directed interests to satisfy one of hers However, since one of his central interests is to promote her interests, he has not abandoned his self-interests. Rather he has promoted one of his interests (to promote hers) over another (to go shopping).

Subordinating one's desires is commonplace in close personal relationships. Because each of us desires to be together and to make the other happy, we will occasionally subordinate some purely self-directed desires. There is nothing surprising, unusual, or objectionable here. Each of us has multiple desires and interests – we are not unidimensional. Usually we cannot satisfy all those interests at the same time. Most choices require us to elevate some interests over others. If I choose to work on a paper rather than to have a beer with colleagues, one interest is subordinated to another. Likewise if I choose to go walking in the woods rather than watch a movie. In these cases, though, both interests are self-directed interests.

We often face similar choices in close personal relationships. Sometimes we elevate the interests in our intimate and subordinate some purely self-directed interests. That is part of what it means to have a close relationship: one of our highest interests is in promoting the interests of our intimates. However, because some subordination is a common occurrence in close relationships, it is more difficult to spot inequity; after all, one does not abandon one's interests when promoting one's intimate's interests.

On the other hand, inequity can also be imagined where it does not exist. To pursue the earlier example, suppose Jason never sees Kristie subordinate her self-directed interests. He might eventually become bothered by what appears to be the one-sided nature of the relationship. Nothing surprising here. He subordinated one of his immediate interests and he knows it. He does not see Kristie similarly subordinate her interests. He feels unloved or mistreated.

What Jason can all too easily forget is that Kristie may well be similarly subordinating her interests in ways he does not recognize. She may go shopping with him when, in fact, she would rather go bowling with Tom. Because she cares for Jason, she subordinates her interest in bowling. But, like Jason, she may see only her own "sacrifices." For instance, when he goes to the movie with her, she may assume he really wants to go independently of his interest in her. Hence, she never sees him subordinate his interests to her; she may thus begin to feel abused or unloved. The relationship is in trouble: both are aware of their own contributions to the relationship, each is oblivious to the other's contributions.

The problem here is not that either of the intimates is insensitive or blind. The problem arises – very understandably – from the desire of each to care for the other. Friends and lovers do not standardly announce that they are subordinating their interests to the relationship. It is easy to see why. If Jason really wants to make Kristie happy by going to the movie with her, he knows she will not enjoy herself if she thinks he does not really want to go. So he feigns an interest in the movies; or, perhaps more accurately, he feigns an interest greater than he, in fact, has. Correspondingly, if Kristie decides to go shopping with Jason to make him happy, she acts as if she has an independent desire to go; or, more precisely, she acts as if she has a greater desire than she, in fact, has.

Each plausibly assumes that such subordination of one's self-directed interests must be hidden, at least at the time of the subordination. Otherwise, the intimate will not enjoy the activity – and hence, the subordination will not achieve its aim. Although restricted versions of this claim are probably true, in unqualified form it is false. And, if intimates are not careful, this understandable and well-meaning activity can easily lead both parties to assume they are unduly sacrificing their personal interests to help sustain the relationship.

The situation here is still more complex when we recognize that each intimate may not only subordinate her interests on a single occasion, but will, at least occasionally, alter her interests so she will want to do what her intimate wants to do. To continue the previous example, suppose Jason is not especially fond of movies. Nonetheless, he realizes Kristie is. Because Kristie is one of his ends, and her happiness makes him happy, he cultivates an interest in movies, and suppresses his interest in shopping. Eventually he *wants* to go to the movies and is no longer especially interested in shopping. In one

149

important sense, he has not sacrificed his interests. Rather, he has tried to harmonize two interests which were previously in tension. This helps explain why the distinction between egoism and altruism often blurs in personal relationships (LaFollette 1988).

This is exactly what we would expect in close personal relationships. Because each person loves the other, she will, to some degree, modify her preferences so that she will want to do what her intimate wishes. Of course this process will not eradicate the need for singular subordination of her interests, but it will eliminate the need for some of it.

The danger, though, is that this process might eventually lead one participant (or both) to believe she has subordinated too much to the relationship. Thus, at some point Jason might conclude he has given up more than Kristie has. But if that happens, he will not be concerned with any particular subordination. Rather he will feel he has altered too many of his self-directed preferences, while she has altered few. He will thus understandably infer that she does not love him as much as he had supposed. He may subsequently resent Kristie; that resentment may be deep and, thus, difficult to eradicate.

Sexism

Social and political structures may create expectations that one person will regularly subordinate her interests to a relationship, while no such expectation is placed on her partners. Such has been the expectation placed on women. They have been expected to adopt their husbands' interests while their husbands were not expected to adopt their interests. The natural tendency of intimates – discussed in the last section – was perverted in ways which gave men considerable power over women. That was intolerable. It still is.

These historical abuses of women must be rejected by throwing off the yoke of sexism, which has bound male–female relationships. But that is easier said than done. We are products of a pervasively sexist culture. Sexism permeates our society; it pervades our attitudes. It haunts and – if allowed to run wild – devours our heterosexual relationships. Among other things, it exploits the natural tendency for intimates to subordinate some self-directed interests to promote the interests of others. To stop such exploitation, we must individually and collectively shed sexism and its control over us.

If the sexist culture had merely erected legal obstacles to equality, that would be relatively easy. Legal obstacles, being obvious, can be attacked. The women's movement has made considerable effort to remove the most onerous legal barriers to equality. They have had considerable success, albeit less than many people might suppose (Faludi 1991). However, the primary engines of sexism are not legal barriers, but veiled, sub-conscious forces. The dominant culture promulgates sexist stereotypes which pervade television, movies, books, and music. These embody well-defined gender roles that infuse the relationships children see at home, at school, and when visiting their friends. They establish expectations to which all of us are subject, images to which all of us respond – to some degree or another. They shape our desires, interests and perspectives, thereby making informed, unbiased choice difficult, if not impossible.

For instance, men are encouraged to be determined, strong, and perhaps even aggressive. They are taught to be interested in math and science, to crave success, to be competitive. Men are discouraged from developing interests or personality traits which are deemed "feminine," e.g. an interest in children or a tendency to cry. Conversely, women are taught to fear math, to enjoy literature and art. They are encouraged to be giving, supportive, soft, maternal, and, if need be, subservient.

Of course not every man and woman is shaped in precisely these ways or to this extent. But even children reared in relatively liberated, non-sexist homes are shaped, at least in part, by these dominant cultural stereotypes. The effects of such shaping cannot be obliterated. Those of us reared in a pervasively sexist culture will never be entirely free from those early influences. Even those of us sensitive to the insights of feminism will still hear sexist voices from the past. They inevitably modulate our interpersonal interactions, even as we seek to free ourselves from their influence.

Consider. Trust is important in intimate relationships. Trust involves, among other things, trusting that your partner will not intentionally harm you or your interests. Such trust requires vulnerability: I cannot trust you unless I am willing to be vulnerable with you – unless I am willing to put myself in a position where you can harm my interests. The influences of our sexist culture make trust difficult for most men. Men can "trust" bankers and colleagues: we are good at institutionalized, impersonal trust. However, most men's fear of being really vulnerable, of personally trusting another, has often made close relationships difficult. The cardinal sin for men is to be weak, vulnerable. We are supposed to be made of iron, Spartans all. We were told we must know what to do or, short of that, to act as if we did – after all, men must be "kings in their castles." We may occasionally be weak with our spouses; that is acceptable. But such weakness must be contained; most assuredly it must not be public. In short, men dominated by these standard images of masculinity cannot establish relationships as close as those who are willing to be vulnerable.

Even those men who are relatively free of these images, those who are willing to be emotional, to cry, to be vulnerable, are not free of our sexist upbringing. They often find – at the most inopportune times – that their fathers' urgings "to be strong" dominate the more informed voices that tell them to be vulnerable, to be human beings. Sexism harms men as well as women. It makes genuine, intimate, and fulfilling heterosexual relationships exceedingly difficult – as if they were not difficult enough on their own.

If both men and women wish to minimize detrimental effects of social conditioning, both must be especially attuned to the influence our upbringing exerts over us. Then we must contain those influences. That is easier said than done. For, *ex hypothesi*, the sexist culture shaped not only our first-order desires, for example the desire to be a successful professional or to play football, but also our second-order desires and abilities: our values and our ability to reason. These second-order desires govern how we evaluate and subsequently modify our first-order desires. They thereby influence the contours of the people we become.

If we wish to free ourselves from these culturally induced desires, we must first identify them. That is difficult since they are amorphous, indefinite. To the extent that we can identify them, we can do so only after careful and sustained self-examination. Consequently, we cannot easily excise them or restrain their undesirable effects. We cannot immediately destroy the culture's power, nor can we eradicate its influence. But we must try.

In trying, however, we should not throw the proverbial baby out with the bath water. For although this natural tendency of close relationships has been perverted by our sexist culture, the solution is not to abandon that tendency, but to constrain its inappropriate influence. For intimates must occasionally subordinate some of their interests – that is an essential element of any relationship in which each person has the other as one of her interests. Perhaps the best way to fight these sexist influences is by encouraging men to subordinate some of their interests to the interests of their female partners.

Even if we successfully shun sexism, though, the aforementioned problem can still appear in individual relationships. And *that* problem can be eliminated only if intimates discuss the ways each thinks he or she has subordinated interests to the relationship – ways the other may not have noticed. Once again, we see the importance of honesty in intimate relationships.

We have now seen that intimates should care for each other, they should try to satisfy one another's needs. Or, in common parlance, intimates should love each other. But exactly what it means to love one another is not always evident. Certainly comments throughout the past few chapters give some indication about what that means. But in the following chapter I shall explore some of the questions in more detail.

NOTE

1 In this section I draw heavily on Hardwig (1984).

10

The Art of Loving

In earlier chapters, I explored several significant features of close personal relationships, most especially intimacy, trust, honesty, and equity. In later chapters I discuss jealousy and commitment. However, there are other features of and questions about close relationships which merit discussion, although they do not fit neatly under the rubric of any of these topics. These features concern the day-to-day conduct of our relationships. First, how can we become more adept at loving our intimates? Second, in what sense and to what degree should we be independent of or dependent on our intimates? Third, how should we react to the faults of someone we love (and they to ours)? Should we accept our intimates "warts and all," or should we try to change them? If so, how? In particular, should we ever treat intimates paternalistically? Grappling with these nitty-gritty questions will give us a better understanding of the character of personal relationships.

Learning to Love

How do (can) we learn to love others? Is there a simple recipe for love? Some social psychologists seem to think so. They say or imply that love is a set of behaviors we can learn and then reproduce in our own relationships. Steve Duck, for example, claims that ". . . people who have no friends are not social and personal failures. They are probably just not performing the *behaviors* of friendship in a perfectly polished manner. It isn't that they possess some magic anti-charm; it is not a fixed attribute, but something they can learn to change" [emphasis mine] (Duck 1983: 11).

As stated, this is not wholly objectionable. Some of us do not know how to care for another, and caring is something we can, to some degree, learn. Nonetheless, his emphasis on "performing behaviors" foretells the precise nature of his view. Duck does not just baldly assert that such skills can be taught. He offers examples to illustrate his contention:

> Therapists, social workers, doctors and dentists nowadays receive instructions on ways to establish rapport with patients and how to develop a reassuring and constructive "bedside manner." We also know insurance or car staff are trained in how to relate to possible customers, that airline cabin crew and the police alike receive instruction on relating to the public, and that managers are now encouraged to spend time building up good personal relationships with employees (Duck 1991: 5).

However, the ability of an airline steward to get along with her passengers is one thing; her ability to establish deep and enduring intimate relationships is something entirely different. Of course some stewards might be able to import skills from the airplane to their personal lives; however, it is a mistake to assume most people can. And even when these skills are imported into their personal lives, we should not infer that these are primarily friendship skills.

Let me explain. Airline stewards, car sales people, and insurance agents are taught how to interact with clients in a pleasant and superficially friendly manner. For instance, they are taught to be friendly, to understand their customers' needs. Doctors are taught to be reassuring and calm, to be concerned about their patients' medical complaints. Teachers are taught to be sensitive, to meet their students' educational demands.

I am pleased professionals are taught these skills – although I wish the instruction were more successful. They can make social intercourse more pleasant, and they may empower professionals to perform their jobs better. And, if the instruction is of the appropriate sort, it may inculcate skills which, if imported into the professionals' private lives, would foster intimate relationships. For instance, insurance agents are trained to look people in the eye while talking to them. Presumably that makes clients feel at ease with the agents, and thus, more likely to buy a policy from them. The same skill might generally encourage others to trust and confide in them, thereby increasing the chance that these agents will develop and sustain personal relationships.

However, the airline, insurance, and medical industries do not teach stewards, agents, and doctors these social skills to promote their personal lives. Rather, these industries want their employees/students to be more effective representatives of the industry. Managers plausibly assume well-trained insurance agents will sell more policies, that friendly stewards will encourage passengers to fly their airlines in the future, and that sensitive doctors will heal more patients. Consequently, we should not be surprised to learn these skills are insufficient for close personal relationships – after all, that is not why these skills were inculcated. Close relationships are not business exchanges writ small.

We listen to our friends not because we wish to make a sale, but because we care. We smile at our friends not to encourage them to fly our airline, but because we are glad to see them or because we wish to cheer them. That is why these "social skills" are not only insufficient for friendship, they are frequently inimical to them. On more than a few occasions I have been put off by the gregarious salesman who feigns a personal interest in me in order to make a sale. I am similarly annoyed at the politician who pretends to care for me so he can obtain my vote. I suspect you react similarly to feigned friendliness. Superficial amiability will not promote intimacy; usually it bars it.

There is all the difference in the world between mimicry and behavior which embodies a person's character. An ignorant person who memorizes a series of difficult mathematical equations is not transformed into a brilliant mathematician. A mathematician does more than recite equations; she understands why they are true. She could solve equations she has never seen. An individual who can follow explicit recipes is not transformed into a world-class chef. Chefs don't just follow recipes; they produce their own recipes. Chefs understand how flavors meld together. In short, making mathematical calculations and devising great meals are not isolated behaviors people perform. Rather they are part of a way of life betokening behavioral patterns, deep-disposing traits.

Why should we assume it is otherwise for people in close relationships? Indeed we should assume this is more so for intimates; after all, relationships are more complex than recipes. To this extent, loving others is more an art than a skill (Fromm 1957). It requires sensitivity, insight, and cultivated judgement. It is not a hodgepodge of actions but springs from an integrated personality.

None of this implies that friendship skills cannot be learned. Obviously they can be. Those among us who are friendly were not born that way (although perhaps some people do have genetic traits which incline them to be friendly). Friendly people have skills conducive to intimacy: listening attentively, expressing concern, or showing affection. They did learn these skills, but not in a skills seminar run by their company. If they have these skills, they acquired them by experience and careful instruction, not by rote (Aristotle 1985). These skills are not isolated behaviors, easily mimicked by others. Rather, they are habits embodying an individual's deeper-disposing traits. They are part of who she is, her self.

People listen to their intimates not because they acquired some specified set of behaviors to parrot, but because they care for each other. The range and tone of care is framed by the kind of person we are. If we are basically selfish people, preoccupied with our own interests and problems, then we will not be able to really care; concern for ourselves will always get in the way. That is why we care for others to the extent that we are good (virtuous) people. And virtue is acquired (if at all) over a lifetime, not during an intensive weekend conference on social skills. Thus, unless we are at least somewhat morally good, we cannot establish close personal relationships. This is a thesis I have advanced several times in this book, for instance when discussing reasons for love and the value of personal relationships. I have tried to make this thesis plausible by showing how it is integrally connected with our broader understanding of personal relationships. I will pull all the strands of this argument together in the book's final chapter.

Personal Independence

People in close relationships must be sensitive to one another's interests and needs. If you and I are close friends, each of us will occasionally suspend or subordinate our immediate interests to promote the interests of the other. I may have a personal desire to go skiing but, instead, go to visit your sick aunt. You may have a self-directed desire to read a new novel but, instead, play a game of checkers with me. That is part of what it means for us to love one another. We do not have a single-minded desire to promote our own self-directed interests. We must also have a strong interest in promoting the interests of each other.

However, neither of us should completely sacrifice our self-directed interests and needs to the other. Put differently, we should be neither too dependent on nor too independent of one other.

Each should have her own interests, favored activities, friends, etc. Yet intimates, particularly those who are married, not infrequently suppose they and their partners should not have any life substantially independent of the other. They assume both their existences should be wrapped up in the marriage. Clearly this extreme dependence is detrimental to both parties; I shall discuss one form of excessive dependence in the following chapter.

Here I discuss the opposite tendency, the tendency to assume that we are largely or even completely independent of one other. People who hold this view tend to see intimate relationships, including marriage, as simply one form of trade or exchange. Each of the parties maintains her complete independence; they simply agree to trade ideas, affections, or money, as long as it seems profitable to each.

However, this is a dangerous stance to take toward close relationships. It fails to describe what happens in successful close relationships. Furthermore, it offers imprudent advice to anyone wanting close relationships. If adopted, this stance would seriously constrain, if not bar us, from establishing or maintaining loving relationships.

That this is a mistaken account of close relationships should now be apparent. A close personal relationship is one in which each person has the other as one of her interests. Consequently, if Jane has Sarah as one of her ends – as one of her interests – then what happens to Sarah will make a difference to Jane. Jane will care what Sarah believes, how she feels, what she is thinking, and what she is doing. Sarah's interests are not something Jane can ignore.

That is exactly what the empirical research reveals (Clark 1985; 1979). As noted in the previous chapter, Clark claims people in communal relationships do not see themselves as completely independent of each other. Rather, each takes an interest in the other's interests. In fact, those in close relationships fail to clearly demarcate between their interests and the interests of their intimates. If two people spend time together, listen to each other, share with each other, and care for each other, then they simply cannot be independent in the way the view I am discussing supposes. Their lives are intermingled; they are not parallel occurrences that just happen to be going in a similar direction. That is a significant part of what it means for us to love and care for another.

Our Response to the Perceived Faults of an Intimate

All of us are bothered or annoyed by at least some characteristics of our intimates. Sometimes these annoyances are minor. We may, for instance, be bothered by some of our intimates' mannerisms. Other times, though, we may be seriously concerned about what we take to be an important trait or a serious defect. For instance, we may think our intimate is compulsive or a workaholic. Probably we would prefer that our intimates not have these traits; perhaps we simply wish the traits did not bother us. However, they do bother us. So if we are to think carefully about what it means to love our intimates, we need to determine how to react to them. Should our desire to be sensitive to our intimates lead us to accept these traits, even if we think they are deficient in important ways? Even if we find them substantially aggravating?

Of course we must remember that we may be mistaken when judging that an intimate is flawed. What we consider a character flaw may be nothing more than a trait we do not like or appreciate, especially if it clashes with our personality. Suppose, for example, that Jane is patient and careful, while Sarah is spontaneous. Sarah may well perceive Jane's patience as undue caution; Jane may perceive Sarah's spontaneity as impetuousness. Perhaps Sarah thinks Jane stifles her (Sarah's) spontaneity while Jane thinks Sarah makes her (Jane) careless. However, although Jane has trouble relating to someone with Jane's traits (and vice versa), neither should conclude that most people find those traits annoying or objectionable. Thus, we should be cautious before claiming that our intimates are flawed. We should be open to differences in character.

The checkered nature of character traits

This is especially apparent once we realize that even highly prized traits may be detrimental in some circumstances, while questionable traits may be advantageous in others. For instance, patience and care are generally deemed admirable traits. Like all deep traits, they pervade a person's lifestyle. However, in circumstances which require that I act quickly and decisively, patience may hinder speedy action. By the same token, a generous person may find it difficult to react appropriately to an acquaintance who regularly takes advantage of her. The same is true of morally neutral traits like excitability. Sometimes I enjoy the company of a highly energetic, excitable person: it lifts me up when I am depressed. Nonetheless, I would find it exhausting or distracting to spend a great deal of time with her.

Conversely, persons with morally questionable traits may, in some circumstances, be able to accomplish great moral feats. Oskar Schindler, who rescued large numbers of Jews at great personal risk, could achieve this laudable goal only because he had certain vices. "The very qualities that most of us would find morally problematic in Schindler – his hedonism, his avarice, his ability to maintain convivial but purely instrumental relations with others – were precisely the qualities which put him in a position to save thousands of Jew's . . ." (Flanagan 1991: 8).

In short, character traits are rarely wholly positive or negative. Thus, in at least in some circumstances, intimates will likely perceive each other's traits as flawed. It is not even uncommon that traits which initially attracted intimates to each other may end up annoying them. How should we respond? There are two rather different answers. Proponents of each claim theirs is consistent with, if not required by, genuine love for their intimates. As with most issues we have discussed, there is some insight in both perspectives. The difficulty comes in extracting that insight from the fluff and hyperbole.

Two views

The first view is that we should uncritically accept our intimates, faults and all. We should neither attempt nor desire to change them. Rather we should accommodate to their flaws – and they to ours. This view appears to spring from my proffered account of close relationships. In personal relationships intimates care for each other, as uniquely embodied people. That is, if Jane wants a personal relationship with Sarah, she wants a relationship with *Sarah*, with her specific embodiment and style. She must love Sarah *as she is*. Thus, it would seem Jane should not wish to change or modify Sarah. Otherwise, it appears Jane not so much loves Sarah, but the person Sarah could become (Fromm 1957: 28).

The second view claims that Jane's loving Sarah as she is is not inconsistent with her also wanting Sarah to grow and improve. According to this view, a central element of love is wanting to promote the other's interests, wanting the best for her. What is best for people is to recognize their potential, "to be all they can be." Thus, it is not only permissible to desire our intimates to change, it is a central element of all close personal relationships.

The first view clearly isolates an important truth about close relationships. Desiring to change someone appears to be at odds with accepting her as she is. If I say I like a house *as is* and then completely refurbish it – or even express a strong desire to do so – I thereby show that I do not like it as it is, regardless of what I say. If I say I like a car *as is* and then substantially modify it, I thereby show that I am lying or mistaken.

To this extent there is something right about Fromm's claim. If Jane says she loves *Sarah*, though she would like Sarah to change her hair, occupation, hobbies, and basic character, then we can be confident that Jane does not love Sarah after all. At most she loves the person she thinks Sarah can become. If this is the danger of which Fromm warns us, we must heed his warning. And it appears many people have not done so; more than a few of us desire or attempt to bring about wholesale changes in our spouses and close friends. That is inappropriate. This shows that we not so much love these people as the people we want to make them. That is the insight in the first view.

Nonetheless, Fromm's admonition is too strong. He claims it is inappropriate to desire or expect *any* changes in one's intimates. Presumably he would find it inappropriate to seek not only wholesale reconstruction of our intimates, but minor repairs as well. Not only should my intimates not desire or seek to alter my fundamental character and interests, neither should they encourage me to control my temper or to become more patient. If this is Fromm's advice, his counsel is both imprudent and impossible. Imprudent because intimates should promote the growth and well-being of friends and spouses; impossible because intimates inevitably do change one other, in at least some respects.

Think for a moment about the earlier examples. If I buy a house I claim to "love," and then proceed to raze it and build another in its place, then you can be quite certain I do not love it. However it would not be in the least inappropriate or contradictory for me to paint the house, particularly when the reason for doing so is to preserve the house I love. Part of what it means to love something as it is to desire that it should stay in good repair.

161

Analogously, if we can care for our intimates, we will want for them to remain "in good repair." Of course, this desire takes on added dimensions for persons. After all, they have their own interests; they are not merely objects I own. Moreover, they change in ways houses and cars do not. To keep a house or a car in good repair is to keep it in the same condition as it was when new. We do not expect a car to improve with age; at most we try to slow its deterioration. Persons, however, change constantly, and if they do not improve, they deteriorate. A fully functioning human should learn and grow from experience. If a ten-year-old acts as she did when she was four, we think she is psychologically and emotionally stunted. If an eighteen-year-old has changed little since she was ten (except in body size), we assume she is maladjusted. If a thirty-eight-year-old is indistinguishable from her eighteen-year-old self, we think she is immature – even if she was considered mature at eighteen. Properly functioning humans continually grow.

Consequently, if we truly love our intimates we will want them to continually grow. To settle for or desire stagnation – to want our intimates to remain the same – would indicate our lack of love for them. Of course, we might have selfish reasons why we do not want our intimates to change. We may like our intimates (and they like us) now; we may fear that if they change, we will not like them, or they us. However, this is a selfish reason to stymie change. Indeed, I fear that something like this undergirds rigid love; we try to maintain our attachment to a particular person by acting as if she never changed.

Perhaps I have been a bit unfair to Fromm. Fromm recognizes humans change; he thinks they should grow. What he denies is that we should try to direct or control the change of another. Instead, we should encourage one other to "unfold as they are" (1957). It is not evident to me what Fromm – or laypersons who speak in these ways – mean by this. Apparently they think each of us is a fixed determinate self – even if that self has not yet fully blossomed. They speak as if all we need do is realize or actualize our true inner natures. Seemingly they conceive of persons as seeds or kernels which should be allowed to sprout and grow without interference. Others provide sunshine, earth, and water; but the seed has a determinate nature which should be permitted to flower without interference.

If this *is* what Fromm means (and I see no other plausible way to read him) then he embraces a mistaken view of persons. He adopts some brand of Cartesianism whereby people are well defined at birth (if not before). The job of parents, educators, and intimates is not to create, mold, or even influence us; rather it is simply to provide nourishment which helps us unfold.

I have already argued that dualism is untenable. Distinct and well-defined selves do not exist prior to socialization and development. Selves are made by social influences – and by our actions. For instance, I am a spouse, a father, and a philosophy professor who is generally content with his lot. I see no reason to believe, however, that at birth there were husband, father, and philosopher "seeds" that, with the proper nourishment, would sprout and grow to fruition. The particular array of parental, educational, and peer influences encouraged the dispositions and interests that inclined me in certain directions. My choices and actions, themselves influenced by those dispositions and interests, brought me here. I have *no* doubt that had I been brought up in a different environment my life would be very different. Or that had I been brought up in the same environment with slightly different opportunities, I would likewise be very different. My environment did not merely nourish my blossoming self. It shaped me; in some important sense, it made me who I am.

No doubt I inherited genetic tendencies that constrained my options. I have large fingers which preclude expertise in jobs requiring fine motor skills. I am too large to be a jockey. My particular mental capabilities and incapacities preclude my interest or success in some fields. These genetic characteristics set boundaries within which I developed. However, there was no particular way I had to develop. The *I*, the self, emerged from the social environment in which I was reared – and in which I now reside. I did not unfold from some predetermined form.

Consequently, Fromm's idea of standing back and just letting our intimates unfold, if interpreted in any strong sense, is both impossible and imprudent. It is impossible because we are constituted by our social setting – especially our interpersonal relationships. It is imprudent because our closest friends should help guide our development. If intimates do not influence one other, it is probably because they are not really close. There is no way to be close with someone and then just "let them be." Intimates share ideas, reactions, and activities with their partners; we listen to them and we tell them what we think. We care about and respect them, and they us. Thus, each of us will inevitably modify some of our views or behavior because of the other's influence. That is not something we choose to do; it is an inevitable feature of caring about others and having them care about us.

There may be one way to partially rescue Fromm. Although everything I know of Fromm indicates he embraced a dualist account of self, we could reformulate his claim that "we should let others unfold" so that it identifies a significant truth about personal relationships. By the time we are old enough to develop close personal relationships, we have some determinant traits and interests. These are not fixed or unchangeable; nonetheless, they usually resist change. Attempts to change them may be painful, disruptive, or counter-productive (Feinberg 1980: 148–51).

Consequently, unless the trait we wish our intimates to change is especially injurious or immoral, it may not be worth the effort. Attempts to change might well end in failure. Or, since the trait is presumably so deep, even if we succeed in removing it, we might thereby introduce other equally detrimental traits. To use an earlier example, if Sarah encourages Jane to become less cautious (Sarah's desired result), Jane might subsequently become reckless. Or perhaps she might develop some different, but equally annoying, trait. Therefore, it is likely imprudent to force or encourage an intimate to attempt a time-consuming and possibly unsuccessful character change, unless the trait is immoral or especially detrimental.

Earlier I suggested that our genetic make-up sets parameters within which we can develop. In a similar manner, our early upbringing sets further parameters within which any changes take place. That is, as time progresses each of us develops certain talents and interests which will circumscribe potential changes. Rather than try to eradicate an irritating trait, perhaps a person should merely modify that trait to eliminate its most annoying effects.

Thus, we can see the element of practical wisdom in Fromm's advice: intimates should not strive to wholly reconstruct each other. Nonetheless, the advice is problematic inasmuch as it implies that we should never encourage or help our intimates to change and grow. It is highly objectionable if it leads intimates to blithely accept especially harmful or immoral traits in each other.

Paternalism

Of course urging an intimate to change, especially if she does not want to, inevitably involves elements of paternalism. In some views – for example the justice view discussed in the previous chapter – paternalism is absolutely prohibited. In any view, paternalism within intimate relationships is always risky.

Paternalism is especially problematic in heterosexual romantic relationships, especially given the sexist culture in which we were all reared. Men should be wary of treating their spouses paternalistically, lest they thereby reinforce the dominant sexist culture. However, there are some cases in which paternalism might well be justified. For instance, suppose a man's spouse or significant other always wants him to make all the decisions. If he continues to make all the decisions, then he will be treating her paternalistically. And, if he tries to change her, he will be treating her paternalistically.

The problem, though, is that if she always accedes to his interests and preferences, then that undermines the possibility of their having a genuinely close relationship. Intimates take the other's interests as their own. But in this case she has no identifiable interests which he can assume. Thus, the man should not permit his partner to be so dependent on him. That is what love and care require.

Of course this should not be taken as an across-the-board endorsement of paternalism. For as I noted, unconstrained paternalism of men toward their female partners is a sexist rut we must avoid. The only circumstances in which it is permissible are dramatic situations like those just described. In other, seemingly parallel, circumstances, paternalism is clearly out of order. For instance, relatively liberated people may legitimately leave remnants of their sexist upbringing in place. After all, we cannot plausibly eliminate all of them in a single generation. Moreover, some effects might be alterable only by making efforts which "cost" more than they are worth.

Consider Ralph, a twenty-year-old man who is preparing for a career in mathematics. His father was a mathematician who imbued him with a love for math; perhaps his father thought math was an especially manly profession. It is a shame the father shoved Ralph in this direction. With different parents, Ralph might have become a nurse, an accountant, an elementary school teacher, or a lawyer. But the fact is, he loves math. Hence, it would be ludicrous for him to try to alter his desires because he recognizes that, had his parents been liberated, he might have chosen differently. Of course if the parents had wanted him to become a criminal he should try to change (although I suspect he would have trouble doing so). But as long as he now desires a worthwhile and personally satisfying line of work, there is nothing wrong with his pursuing that career. Likewise, there would be nothing wrong if Ralph decided he wanted to be a nurse. It's up to Ralph.

The problem becomes stickier, though, if we imagine a similar situation which many women face. Imagine a twenty-year-old woman completing her training to be an elementary school teacher. Although there is absolutely nothing wrong with her chosen career – it is a noble profession indeed – she likely developed her interest in teaching young children because of the gender roles into which she was inculcated. Perhaps she would have selected the same career had she been reared in a non-sexist culture; perhaps not. We will never know. Although she might have had different interests and desires, she is now the person whose first-order interests (including the desire to be an elementary school teacher) were shaped by her sexist upbringing. Under such circumstances she may decide that it would be counterproductive to try to develop different career interests. She might determine that she could not alter those interests. Or perhaps she might reason that she could alter those interests only by changing "who she is," that is, she could diminish her desire to teach elementary school only by diminishing her interests in young children. That she does not want to do.

The woman does nothing wrong if she continues her preparation for teaching elementary school. Even though she (and Ralph) realize they might have pursued different careers had their upbringing been different, each decides that the cost of trying to alter their interests is either impossible, unnecessary, or imprudent.

If we are partners with a woman facing such a dilemma, it would be foolish *and* paternalistic to try to change her desires, even though these desires were largely formed by her sexist upbringing. (Of course if *she* wishes to change them, then her partner should support her in whatever way possible.) For, although the culture shaped her first-order desire to be a teacher, her current second-order judgement (which, admittedly, was also partly shaped by the sexist culture) is that her first-order desire need not be changed. If, under the circumstances, her male partner were to force her to change her career plans, it would be unacceptably paternalistic.

Indeed, I think this is but one more casualty of our sexist culture. In a completely non-sexist culture, intimates might well be justified in acting paternalistically toward their partners – at least in some cases. After all, we assume our intimates *really do* wish to promote our best interests; likely, too, they know what those interests are. But, given the tendency of males to dominate their female partners, paternalism should be avoided in all but the most extreme cases – like the first case I discussed.

11

Sex and Jealousy

Whenever two people have a close relationship, one or both of them may occasionally become jealous. Jealousy can occur in any type of relationship, although it is more frequent and typically more potent between lovers. Hence, I shall begin by discussing jealousy among lovers. Later I will show how that account is also applicable to other close personal relationships.

Identifying Jealousy

Frank and Joan are lovers. Joan begins to notice, though, that Frank seems especially pleased when one of her friends, Lucy, comes to visit. He warmly greets Lucy at the door, listens raptly while she talks, and gazes soulfully into her eyes. In these circumstances, we would not be surprised to find that Joan is jealous. That is not to say that she would necessarily be jealous. She may not notice Frank's attentiveness to Lucy. Perhaps she doesn't interpret Frank's behavior as indicating any special interest in Lucy, since he is equally friendly and gracious toward most people. Possibly they have an "open marriage," and each expects the other to be attracted to, and even to become sexually involved with, others.

Nonetheless, it is the type of situation which makes people jealous. But not all forms of jealousy are created equal. Some forms are virtually unavoidable and morally innocuous, while others are morally destructive and should be avoided like the proverbial plague. Yet most accounts fail to adequately distinguish them; those that do distinguish them often treat them as differing only in degree. I think that is a mistake. Although these two types of jealousy have some significant features in common, in other respects they are profoundly different, perhaps so different as to warrant calling only the latter "jealousy."

To identify these differences I will take a closer look at the case just described. Joan is jealous because Lucy is getting something she (Joan) wants, Frank's attention. This suggests a general description of jealousy which, although not entirely adequate, will suffice to begin the discussion: person A is jealous if C is getting affection or favored treatment from a third person B – favored treatment that A wants (Farrell 1980; 1988).

This account isolates a crucial difference between jealousy and envy: jealousy standardly involves three people, while envy involves two. Joan is *envious* of Lucy if Joan wants an object or trait Lucy has – for instance money, a new car, green eyes, a warm personality, etc. The focus or object of envy is always an object or trait. However, Joan is *jealous* if Lucy is getting something she (Joan) wants, for example Richard's affection. The focus or object of jealousy is paradigmatically a third person (Farrell 1988: 248–9).

This points to another difference between jealousy and envy. If Joan envies Lucy she wants what Lucy has. It may be, however, that what Lucy has, for example a new car, can be had by more than one person. Perhaps Joan not only wants the car for herself, but also wants Lucy not to have it. But not necessarily. She could well be indifferent about what Lucy has. What bothers her is only that Lucy has it while she (Joan) does not.

Not so with jealousy. By definition, what the jealous person wants, for example to be favored by another, is not something both parties can have. Both Joan and Lucy might be friends or even lovers with Frank; but they cannot both be favored in the ways and at the times. That is why the jealous person not only wants the favored treatment for herself; she also wants no one else to receive it.

This initial account, though, is deficient since, among other things, it treats the desire to be favored as a unitary and all-encompassing desire. But this desire need not be unitary or all-encompassing. The desire to be favored usually has a focus, often relatively narrow. Thus, to say that Joan is jealous of Lucy is not to say she expects to be favored by Frank in every respect. Although some people may desire such favoritism, that is not the norm. Indeed, to expect our partners to favor us in all respects, all of the time, is misguided. No one person can satisfy all of anyone's needs.

Most people do not want to be favored in all respects. Although

Joan might wish to be Frank's favored sexual partner and personal confidante, she may have no interest in being Frank's favored hunting or bowling partner. Not only is she not bothered if someone else is his favored bowling partner, she would probably be glad. Hence, we must refine our account: person A is jealous if C is getting some *specific type* of favored treatment from a third party B – favored treatment which A wants. Thus, Joan might be jealous if Lucy were Frank's favored sex partner, but not be jealous in the least if Lucy were Frank's favored hunting partner.

Finally, to favor someone, I need not assume they are "the best," even in those respects I favor them. Simply because Betty favors Belinda as a friend does not mean she thinks Belinda is the very best friend she could possibly have. Betty *might* think this, but there is no reason why she must.

To assume her intimate must be "the best" is to commit two errors. First, it ignores the volitional and historical elements of personal relationships. As I explained in chapter 3, we typically initiate relationships because we find ourselves attracted to someone – or simply because we choose to befriend them. After we relate to them, we may come to care for them, to favor them. Thus, we favor one another partly because of our shared experiences and activities – not because we think the other best.

Second, to assume our partners are the best in every regard is a dangerous fantasy. We need not think our intimates are ideal lovers, thinkers, conversationalists, or parents. We can love them without thinking they are best at anything – let alone everything. Love, as I argued earlier, is constrained – but not dictated – by the traits of the other. We have some choice in whom we love. And it is best if we exercise that choice fully cognizant of each other's deficiencies. Otherwise we are setting ourselves up for disappointment.

This account is still incomplete; it suggests that Joan is jealous because she thinks or fears that Lucy is *receiving* something she (Joan) wants (say, sexual pleasure) from Frank. It might well be, however, that she is jealous because Lucy is *giving* Frank something that Joan wants to give him, e.g. consolation or companionship or pleasure. Intimates not only want to receive from each other; they want to give. Most of us want to be the person who consoles or pleasures our partner. It seems intimates adopt some variation of the Biblical injunction that "it is more blessed to give than to receive."

This can be accommodated by slightly modifying the original account. Jealousy occurs whenever one party is bothered because someone else is being favored. Normally people are inclined to think of this favored status as something we receive. Sometimes, though, the favored status is being the provider of some good or pleasure to a third party.

One further qualification is necessary. Joan is not automatically jealous simply because someone else receives the favored treatment she desires. It might be that Joan wants Frank's affection, realizes Lucy is receiving it instead, yet is still not jealous. Why? Because she may not be bothered by or upset about Lucy's favored status. Jealousy isn't merely the desire to be favored; it is to be *bothered* by someone else's being favored (Farrell 1988: 256–7). Although Farrell's account is on the right track I think it must be further qualified. Of course different people may be differently bothered, and, as we shall see, these differences underlie the distinction between two types of jealousy.

Evaluating jealousy

Our culture has conflicting views of jealousy. On the one hand many people assume jealousy is not only unavoidable but even laudable. In this view, unless your partner is jealous if she thinks you are with someone else, then she does not really care for you. Sometimes this lore is expressed like this: "Don't worry about her jealousy; after all, it just shows she loves you." On the other hand, our culture also embraces the advice of Shakespeare: ". . . jealousy . . . is the green-eyed monster which doth mock the meat it feeds on . . ." (*Othello*, Act II, Scene 3).

As it turns out there is something right about both views. One form of what is ordinarily called "jealousy" is virtually unavoidable and morally innocent, while the other is avoidable and morally odious. It is unfortunate that both are called "jealousy." It suggests, among other things, that they both fall along the same continuum: that jealousy in the second sense is just an excess of an unavoidable response. Not so. For, although these two senses of "jealousy" are alike in some respects (both stem from the desire to be favored) this desire is based on such radically different beliefs – and functions in such radically different ways – that it is misleading to call them both "jealousy." Let me explain.

George might strongly desire Millie's affections, yet not be substantially bothered by the realization that she loves Jonathan instead. Perhaps he thinks Millie should make her own decisions. That is, although he might wish that things were otherwise, nonetheless he might not be bothered *in the relevant sense*.

What, though, do I mean by "being bothered in the relevant sense?" Suppose, for a moment, that George really loves Millie and wants very much to be with her. Yet he realizes she loves Jonathan. We might even suppose that he realizes Jonathan will be better for her. Unless the claim that George loves and wants to be with Millie is exceptionally weak, then *of course* George will be bothered that Millie is with Jonathan. After all, he does love her; she is very important to him. He will likely be depressed, mope, and cry. But if he is jealous, he is not jealous in the sense which most people find worrisome.

This attenuated sense of jealousy is virtually unavoidable. Any time we love and want to be with another, then if that desire is (or we fear it will be) thwarted, we will, of course, be bothered. Since being bothered in these ways and under these circumstances is a natural and unavoidable accompaniment of unreciprocated caring, it is relatively uninteresting; certainly it is morally innocuous. Doubtless this underlies the folk wisdom: if someone claims to love you dearly but does not seem bothered *in the least* by the prospect of losing your love, then you can perhaps infer that she does not really love you. This minimal sense of being bothered I will call jealousy$_1$; probably we shouldn't call it jealousy at all.

However, even if we continue to call being minimally bothered "jealousy," there is a considerable difference between this reaction and being bothered "in the relevant sense" – what I will call jealousy$_2$. Jealousy$_2$ is not just an unavoidable result of the loss of favored status. Rather it is a certain kind of understanding of and reaction to that loss or feared loss. Someone who is jealous$_2$ is not merely upset that he has lost his favored status; he is convinced that he should not have lost that status. Thus, if George is jealous$_2$ of Millie, he thinks Millie *should* still be with him, that it is somehow improper or wrong for her to be with Jonathan.

George's belief that it is wrong for her to be with Jonathan is more than the belief that she has acted imprudently. He might honestly believe she would be happier or more fulfilled with him (George) than with Jonathan, without thinking her decision is wrong. However, if he is jealous$_2$, then he thinks her choice is wrong, period. George perceives Millie as *his* in some sense. She is a thing which he (should) control. If Jonathan "has" Millie, it is only because he stole her. *That* is why George is jealous$_2$.

This type of reaction to a loss of one favored status explains why jealousy$_2$ is often thought to imply possessiveness. The jealous$_2$ party thinks that his former (or desired) partner is, in some sense, his to do with as he pleases. That explains the ordinary conviction that jealousy$_2$ is morally objectionable. But not even all instances of jealousy$_2$ should be evaluated the same. For instance, if I am upset by your leaving and think, in some small measure, that it was wrong for you to do so, then my jealousy$_2$ may be *relatively* innocuous. However, if jealousy$_2$ becomes transformed into its more virulent forms, so that when you are friendly with another man I become incensed, then I have acted in a morally outrageous manner.

Although jealousy$_2$ is morally objectionable, we should not infer that all desires to be favored in personal relationships are objectionable. We cannot have genuine personal relationships unless we are so favored. If no one preferred spending time with me, then I would have no close relationships. So the only way to eliminate jealousy$_1$ is to cease genuine personal relationships. However, since personal relationships are valuable, we should abandon neither them nor the minimal sense of favoring required to maintain them. In short, jealousy$_1$ is psychologically unavoidable and morally unobjectionable. Nonetheless, our desire to be favored by intimates should not be unbound, nor should our reaction to the loss of favored status be unbound. If you break off our relationship, I may legitimately be bothered by your decision – that is, I may understandably become jealous$_1$; however, I should not become outraged by your decision – that is, I should not become jealous$_2$ – jealous in the morally objectionable sense.

Jealousy and adultery

It might be thought that my account overlooks the moral legitimacy of jealousy$_2$ if one's spouse has an affair. But we must be careful to distinguish two forms of upset or outrage that a betrayed spouse might feel. If I have an affair even though I had agreed to be monogamous, then my spouse has good reason to be upset. After all, I have broken a promise, deceived her, and made light of our relationship. Under the circumstances, it would not be at all surprising were she *bothered* by my infidelity; indeed, it would be surprising were she not.

But perhaps she is not jealous$_2$. Although she feels betrayed, she need not think I am *hers* to do with as she pleases. She may simply think that I have acted badly when I broke a most solemn vow. Of course, her sense of betrayal may be mingled with some jealousy (of either stripe). However, we should not confuse jealousy with anger at being betrayed. Nor should we evaluate them similarly. People are understandably hurt and angry when intimates deceive and betray them. But this in no way indicates that they believe they own or possess their significant others.

Finally, it is important to recognize that what differentiates jealousy$_2$ from anger at being betrayed (or from jealousy$_1$ for that matter) is not some event inside a person's mind, but her behavior. People who are hurt and betrayed act one way, while those who are jealous$_2$ act differently. If I cry and am upset by your betrayal, then I am probably not so much jealous$_2$ as distressed. If, instead, I verbally attack you for "giving it away" then I am jealous$_2$. Of course, there is no *single* set of behavior which invariably indicates jealousy rather than hurt. My only point is that most of us can usually distinguish jealousy from hurt – and it has nothing to do with what is residing "in the mind" of the person who was betrayed.

Sex and Jealousy

In many long-term relationships sex is the primary focus of jealousy. (Through the remainder of this chapter I will not use subscripts. "Jealousy" will imply both senses of the term.) That is, we are more often jealous if the respect in which we are not being favored involves sex. For instance, Jo and Fred may have numerous friends, including opposite sex friends. Jo talks politics with Russell; Fred plays tennis with Cathy. Neither feels the slightest twinge of jealousy as long as each is confident the other is not sexually involved with (or interested in being sexually involved with) anyone else.

If, however, either thinks the other is (or is interested in becoming or has not explicitly disavowed an interest in becoming) sexually involved with a third party, then trouble is brewing. Although Fred might think Jo has been faithful, he might well become insanely jealous once he learns Russell is sexually attracted to Jo – and she has not explicitly rejected his overtures. Why? Fred would not be jealous if he thought Russell wanted to play rummy with Jo – or that Jo was likewise interested in playing rummy with Russell. Yet he would likely be deeply disturbed if he thought she was seriously interested in a sexual encounter with Russell.

Why does Frank put such importance on sex? More generally, why do most of us expect sexual fidelity, but not archery or communication fidelity? Why do we fear loss of our favored status as a sex partner in ways and to degrees that we do not (generally) fear loss of our favored status as a bowling partner? Is it reasonable to put such a premium on sex relative to other activities?

At first glance there is something peculiar here. Often the same people who become insanely jealous if they think their partner is sexually involved with another will decry any suggestion that sex is the most important element in a marriage or a long-term relationship. That is odd. If people do not think sex is the most important element of their relationship, then why would they be so disturbed were they to lose their favored sexual status; after all, they would not flinch if they were no longer favored hiking partners, squash partners or conversationalists.

What, then, is the explanation of this apparent paradox? Apparently most people think that even if having sex is not all that important in a long-term relationship, there is nonetheless some special link between sex and love. Perhaps sex has a unique symbolic function: it indicates or signals that the other is especially favored – not just as a sexual partner, but as a significant other. If so, then being sexually favored could be of special importance to a long-term relationship, even if sexual activity is not.

The belief that sex has such a symbolic function might well explain why sex is often the focus of jealousy. If Fred thinks sex indicates the presence of or desire for some special favored status, then if Jo sleeps with Russell, Fred will infer that she loves (or is desirous of loving) Russell. Fred's favored status is thereby threatened. Therefore, to ascertain whether it is reasonable that sex is the primary focus of jealousy, we must discern whether it is reasonable to think sex has this special symbolic function: that is, whether sex and love are intricately connected. I shall quickly canvass three explanations for this presumed link between sex and love.

The biological explanation

Some people suggest there is a biological correlation between sex and love. Thus, sex has some special symbolic function since humans are biologically predisposed to prefer sexual relationships with those they love. As it stands, though, it is difficult to ascertain how we might establish this claim. We don't have any study of human beings outside of culture. And, since cultures can inculcate a view so deeply that we come to see culture's expectations as if they were biologically necessary (Mill 1978: 5), then we should be wary of the claim that sex and love are biologically linked.

Furthermore, a survey of animal behavior would not clarify matters since some animals mate for life while others do not. Moreover, even if most animals did (or did not) mate for life, we could not infer with any confidence about the natural condition of humans. Since humans have evolved differently from other animals, then our biological propensities may well differ from those of even our nearest biological ancestors. Consequently, we cannot claim that humans do or do not have a natural tendency to link sex and love. Nor would it be easy to ascertain that sex had some natural symbolic function; indeed, it would be difficult to know what that would mean.

The cultural explanation

We can, however, point to certain biological facts about humans which, although they do not necessitate linking love and sex, might, nonetheless, explain why many cultures have encouraged mating for life. Many animals are born sufficiently well developed that they can fend for themselves almost immediately. Other young animals may require some parental care but are dependent on adults for a relatively short period of time. But not humans. Virtually all human children below the age of four could not survive on their own; most six- or seven-year-olds would fare little better. They simply would not have the wherewithal to survive if left without the care of an adult. Human infants are dependent on parent care far longer than any other mammal, even adjusting for the relative length of the life span.

Why? Because human infants are born prematurely to accommodate the size of the human brain. The human skull is large relative to total body size. If birth were delayed until the infant could survive on its own, the baby would simply be unable to pass through the mother's pelvis. Consequently, the fetus must be expelled from the womb before it can survive on its own.

Relatedly, much behavior of lower animals is "hardwired" (and thus the infant requires relatively little instruction from its parents). Conversely, human infants are relatively "softwired," that is, they rely less on instinct than most animals. Together these biological facts require that human infants receive extensive and prolonged care if they are to survive. Until relatively recently, the mother had to provide milk. Thus, although she could work in nearby fields, she could not be too far away from the nursing child.

To accommodate the infant's need and the mother's relative immobility, adults usually lived together. One person might venture some distance from home to gather or produce food, while another worked near the home and cared for the children. Who would hunt for the food? Often the children's father. Who would care for the children? Often the children's mother. Eventually social institutions were established to promote the "nuclear" family. Once established, these institutions perpetuated the family. Family units were further strengthened by two factors: there were no adequate methods of birth control, and there were potent economic-biological reasons for families to have numerous children. Consequently, the mother was often tied to the home for years.

In short, the needs of human infants likely established an expectation that heterosexual relationships would be monogamous and permanent. Since most of us were brought up thinking these units were natural, it is not surprising that most of us, to some degree or another, think sex and love are linked.

However, even if this is a plausible explanation of how we came to link love and sex, it does not provide compelling reasons for continuing to link sex and love. The cultural and biological conditions which spawned the need for multiple parents have not disappeared, but they are far less compelling than they once were. Changed economic conditions make it easier for either parent to support their children; sometimes neither is financially dependent on the other. Thus, the biological, cultural, and economic conditions which encouraged mating for life – and thus linked sex and love – can now be satisfied in alternative ways. Hence, although this argument might well explain our tendency to associate love and sex – and give some reasons to continue to do so – it does not explain the strong assumption which our culture propounds.

The psychological explanation

Those who wish to psychologically explain the link between sex and love do not completely dismiss the previous arguments. Rather, they claim the biological and cultural explanations can show, at most, that we have reasons to link sex with love if we have, or intend to have, children. If, however, we have no intention of having children – especially if we have taken measures to virtually eliminate the risk of pregnancy – then the concern for rearing children offers no reason for monogamy. Thus, the biological and cultural explanations for associating sex and love are inapplicable to childless relationships. In contrast, the psychological explanation is supposed to show that there are reasons for linking sex and love, even when the possibility of pregnancy never arises (for example, if both parties are sterile).

Here's the explanation: touch, according to all psychological theories, is a biologically natural way of showing intimacy, closeness, and caring. It is the primary sensation experienced by fetuses. It is also the first way adults care for infants. Parents quickly learn that snuggling and caressing a child is the best way to comfort her, to make her feel better. Of course the parents enjoy snuggling the child. Adults, too, need tactile stimulation. Indeed, when we don't get it from someone else, we may acquire a pet, or engage in "self-touching" – crossing our legs or arms, rubbing our hands together, etc. (Marsh 1988: 92).

In short, touch is the first and most fundamental form of intimacy – a form of intimacy we inherited from our evolutionary past. Monkeys and apes groom each other as part of a ritual whereby they both indicate and promote bonding within the group. Sexual interaction, whether it involves intercourse or not, is primarily tactile and, therefore, is often seen as a special form of intimacy.

Additionally, sex often creates conditions of vulnerability and trust – conditions which make intimacy more likely. For instance, sexual interaction is most satisfying when the partners are to some significant degree, not self-conscious. Stopping during sex and noting, "Oh, my, I am having sex, isn't this fun?" detracts from the tactile experience, and thus, diminishes the intensity of the sexual encounter. Sex is best when we are absorbed in the sexual experience and are not particularly aware of *our* having the experience.

However, when we are not self-conscious, we are less able to control our verbal and bodily behavior, we have less control over how others perceive us. We cannot tailor how we look or what we say. The intellectual barriers we usually construct to keep others at bay are dropped. Thus, sex involves not only physical nakedness, but psychological nakedness as well. During sex we are physically and psychologically vulnerable. And most of us do not wish to be vulnerable with someone we do not trust. Since we are unlikely to completely trust someone with whom we are not close, then we will be less likely to pursue sex – or at least unselfconscious sex – with someone we do not love.

These observations do not in any way establish that love and sex *must* be associated, or even that we would be better off if we had sex only with someone we love. They do, however, suggest that the general conviction that sex and love should be linked has some plausibility. Thus, to return to the original point, it is understandable why someone might be jealous if her partner has sex with another. She would plausibly infer (or fear) that she might lost the intimacy she wants.

Jealousy Among Friends

Although jealousy is more frequent and more potent between lovers, "companion friends are given to jealousy in precisely the same way as lovers" (Thomas 1989: 125). Jealousy has the same structure in both types of relationship: one person A fears that some person C will received favored treatment from B – favored treatment A wants. Among companion friends, the favored treatment which A wants usually is B's company and time – much as is the case with lovers. That explains the similarities in jealousy among friends and among lovers. However, companion friends typically do not want to be favored sexually. Hence, the focus of the jealousy among companion friends is often narrower and, thus, less potent. But that is not to say that jealousy among friends cannot be powerful.

Indeed, jealousy among companion friends – like that among lovers

– may range from the relatively innocuous to the morally odious. That is, John can be jealous$_1$ of Jeff in the minimal sense that he wants a personal relationship with Jeff and will naturally be bothered if that relationship is put in jeopardy. Or John might be jealous$_2$ of Jeff in the stronger sense that he thinks Jeff is – or ought to be – subject to his (John's) wishes – that Jeff is, in some sense, his. The first form is innocent since it is a natural outgrowth of close relationships; the second is odious since it demonstrates John's attempt to possess Jeff. Jealousy$_2$ among companion friends is thus every bit as objectionable as jealousy$_2$ among lovers – no more, no less.

I should also mention a variation on jealousy among companion friends. Suppose Leon and Bertha are dance partners (or skating partners). If, after three years of dancing (skating) together, Bertha expresses an interest in dancing (skating) with Larry instead, then Leon may become jealous. Leon wants to be favored by Bertha, at least on the dance floor (skating rink). But if Leon and Bertha are nothing more than dance (skating) partners, then the nature of the jealousy differs from cases discussed earlier.

For instance, Leon's jealousy may simply reflect the belief that his chances of going to the nationals have diminished. Or perhaps he and Bertha had agreed to stay together for at least five years, and she has, effectively, broken that contract. In the former case he may be seriously disappointed; in the latter case, angry. In both cases he is reacting to the loss of his favored status. But the loss is different from the loss of being favored as an intimate. In the former case he had no reason to expect they would continue to be dancing (skating) partners, and hence, his jealousy, though understandable, is not justified. In the latter case his reaction may be justified, but not so much because of his loss of favored status as because Bertha broke her promise. Of course – as is often the case among dancing (or skating) partners – Leon and Bertha may not merely be dancing (skating) partners, but have a personal relationship as well. Thus, Leon could be jealous for both professional and personal reasons.

Conclusion

At the base of jealousy lies the belief that especially close relationships – whether between companion friends or lovers – should be long-term. Often that has been understood as implying that intimates – whether lovers or companion friends – should have some kind of commitment. That is, most people assume intimates must commit themselves to preserve the relationship for a long time, perhaps come what may. In the following chapter I shall discuss the place of commitment in close personal relationships.

12

Commitment

The idea that people should be committed to their intimates is most readily associated with marriage. People standardly enter marriage with an explicit, legally sanctioned commitment to love one another "in sickness, in health; for richer, for poorer . . . till death do us part." Given the staggering rise in divorce rates, it might appear that such a commitment is little more than a well-intentioned, but meaningless, verbal spasm. Most people don't think so; they think marital commitment is practically important and morally desirable (Martin 1993: 63).

People are committed not only to their spouses, but also to their friends and families. Being committed to our intimates, however, need not imply that we will never give up on these relationships – although that is integral to some people's conception of commitment. It does, however, minimally imply that we will not abandon the relationship as soon as it falters. Most of us think it is especially laudable to stick by our friends and family – as well as our spouses – even if our relationships with them cease to be personally beneficial. Indeed, the idea that we would quickly abandon a relationship with our spouse, parents, children, or close friends simply because it was no longer a "good deal" is an anathema.

Why Commitment?

However, the idea that people should commit themselves to their intimates has recently come under considerable scrutiny. Critics think interpersonal commitment is unreasonable, unnecessary, incompatible with genuine love, or just plain silly. It is easy to see why: given the high divorce rates it looks as if marital commitment is at best ineffective and quite possibly silly. Moreover, some people doubt whether we should commit ourselves to stick by intimates if our relationships with them are no longer beneficial to us.

Although these are sensible questions, they are not questions simply about the value of commitment, but about the value of personal relationships. Recall the distinction between personal and impersonal (exchange) relationships. Exchange relationships are an indirect way of satisfying our self-directed interests: we enter an exchange relationship to gain some good or benefit we cannot (or cannot easily) attain on our own; we expect the other to behave similarly. Consequently, we will bail out of an exchange relationship which no longer satisfies our self-directed interests; we expect others to do likewise.

In contrast, although close personal relationships are often beneficial, they are not good deals – they are not deals at all. Intimates adopt one another's interests as their own. Thus, if either participant in a relationship were to leave (or seriously consider leaving) a presumably close relationship as soon as it no longer satisfied her purely self-directed interests, we would have good reason to think that relationship had not been genuinely personal, but was, instead, a trade relationship masquerading as a personal one. In short, we should not be surprised when a close personal relationship fails to promote the self-directed interests of each participant; after all, that was not their aim.

To this extent, commitment is not something added to a personal relationship, but is a thread woven into the fabric of all close relationships. We do not enter an intimate relationship and then choose to be committed. To have a close relationship just is to be committed, at least in some minimal sense. This minimal commitment, which is a constituent of all close relationships, has personal depth as well as temporal length. Most people think of commitment as simply agreeing to stay together for a long time. Doubtless this is a dimension of commitment. But it is not the only dimension – or the most important one. "Commitment to a person . . . has as its particular focus the unique concatenation of wants, desires, identity, history, and so on, of a particular person" (Friedman 1993: 190–1). Or, as Friedman puts it later, "Commitment to a particular person involves some readiness to be attentive to her, to take her seriously, and to act on her behalf" (1993: 194). Thus, to be committed to a particular person is to single her out for special treatment, to take a special interest in her interests.

Put differently, the primary emphasis of commitment is commitment to the person *now*, not in some distant future. It is all too easy to make a commitment to do something in the indefinite *then*. It is more difficult, more demanding, and more meaningful, to do something *now*. A commitment to have a certain depth of relationship (a relationship in which we spend time and energy with and for each other) will be more likely to insure that the relationship will have temporal length. As Dewey would say in general terms: "To reach an end we must take our mind off from it and attend the act which is next to be performed" (1988: 27). As we focus on our intimates now, our lives become intermingled: we create conditions which make it more likely that our relationship will persist.

Nonetheless, this does not yet explain the sort of commitment people envision when they speak of a life-long or a long-term commitment. Typically they envision some sort of explicit commitment, like that made in a marriage ceremony. Those who think we should explicitly commit ourselves to one another think (1) long-term relationships are especially valuable and (2) that close relationships are more likely to endure if the partners explicitly commit themselves. Thus, to determine if an explicit commitment is desirable, we must determine whether long-term relationships are, in fact, especially valuable, and whether an explicit commitment does, in fact, make it more likely that a relationship will endure.

The Value of Long-term Relationships

Not everyone thinks long-term relationships are especially beneficial: consider the view espoused in the popular literature by Alvin Toffler (1970: 86–99). According to Toffler we must relinquish the notion that most relationships should be long-term. We must recognize the inevitability of – and indeed the desirability of – disposable, serial relationships. He predicts we will change relationships far more frequently than people did in the past, and, more relevant to the current discussion, that we will be better for it. "Rather than entangling ourselves with the whole man, we plug into a module of his personality" (Toffler 1970: 88). We will have "limited involvement" with people around us; we will focus on those aspects of others which we find interesting or rewarding. We will continue to relate to them until either of us decides it is no longer prudent to do so. Then we will move on to our next relationship. Is there anything wrong with disposable relationships? What, if anything, can they not provide as well as a long-term relationship?

Some would claim we don't need to answer these questions – that long-term relationships are intrinsically valuable, certainly more so than intermittent ones. Building on the argument in chapter 5, I claim that although long-term relationships are intrinsically valuable, that does not mean their value is disconnected from other values. Rather, we deem some values "intrinsic" primarily because they both promote and are promoted by a whole network of other values. By specifying how long-term relationships are especially able to promote all the significant values of close relationships, I will lend further credence to that argument.

I earlier argued that close relationships are valuable, in part, because they promote self-knowledge. Long-term relationships are especially apt to promote self-knowledge, and thus are especially valuable. The power of long-term relationships to enhance self-knowledge is expressed succinctly in the lines of a song by Harry Chapin (1974):

> Old friends, mean much more to me
> Than the new friends do;
> They can see where you are,
> And they know where you've been.

Old friends have a perspective which enables them to see things a "new friend" cannot see. That is not to say that some new friends cannot know us better than some long-time friends do. They may. Someone who met us relatively recently may be more perceptive, less biased, or have spent a great deal of time with us. Nonetheless, there is a perspective which the new friend cannot have: a grasp of how we evolved, of how we came to be who we are. Although we can always tell a new friend about our formative years, that is not the same as if she had witnessed them. A person who has observed our development will be better positioned to understand our interests, desires, aversions, personality, and plans. By understanding the direction of our development, she is better situated to anticipate the trajectory of our future development. And, of course, inasmuch as a close friend knows us well, she is better positioned to heighten our self-knowledge. We gain a better understanding of who we are and why we act as we do, if those who know us well provide candid and critical feedback.

"Old friends" are also especially able to heighten our self-esteem. We often tailor our behavior and words to give "new friends" a good impression. Thus, when they say they like us, we have no reason to believe they like us as we are; after all, they have seen only the self we have projected. Not so with old friends. They have witnessed our full range of emotions and behavior: they have seen us depressed and happy, kind and insensitive, generous and mean, patient and impetuous, caring and spiteful. Perhaps we once put on airs for them, but no more. We now have nothing to hide; they know precisely what we are like. Yet they care for us just the same. They think we are valuable despite our worst flaws. That should heighten our self-esteem. But not so much as to make us haughty: for old friends also are especially aware of our flaws.

Finally, long-term friends are especially well-equipped to satisfy each other's needs, to increase each other's happiness, and to help each grow and mature. After all, they know each other well. Thus, each is more likely to know what the other needs and wants, to know the other's faults and strengths. This knowledge empowers them to enhance one another's happiness, to satisfy their needs, to help them control their faults, and to encourage them to accentuate their strengths. Of special interest to the current discussion, they can help one another become morally better persons. As I shall argue in the next chapter, that is one of the most valuable features of close relationships, and especially long-term ones.

The Force of Commitment

Even if I have correctly identified the significant benefits of long-term relationships, that still does not explain why we should explicitly commit ourselves to maintain our relationships come what may. Such commitment might well seem unnecessary. If we are suitably committed to having a deep relationship, we are more likely to have an enduring relationship. So why not simply work on our immediate relationship, and let the long-term take care of itself? If the relationship succeeds, fine; if not, fine. In important respects, this is sound advice. But it is advice a dualist is likely to ignore. Dualists construe commitment as an inner experience or state which only the person in question can directly detect. Moreover, it is a state which the person may or may not express, a state on which she may or may not act. Thus, a dualist will be more inclined to make verbal commitments which are unconnected to how she behaves. Here, as elsewhere, adherence to a defective view of the self, has detrimental effects.

For a genuine commitment is not an inner experience to which only the agent in question is privy. Rather, commitment is part of who we are, it is reflected in how we behave. That is why an activity view of the self provides a better understanding of commitment. Someone who embraces an activity view of the self is less likely to make verbal commitments detached from her behavior. And if, on some occasion, she were to make such an empty pledge, she presumably would admit its vacuity if others demonstrate that it is inconsistent with her behavior.

Thus, although some explicit commitments (those a dualist might be prone to make) are mere formalities – intended to satisfy parents, friends, church, or the law – they need not be. There are important reasons why we should, at least in some circumstances, explicitly commit ourselves to our intimates. And an activity view of the self helps identify these reasons. An explicit commitment can be one form of embodied behavior which deepens and sustains a relationship. If Jim makes a public commitment to Tammy, he declares to the world and to her his intention to stay in the relationship, if not "till hell freezes over," at least beyond the point where it no longer immediately and directly benefits him. If his public declaration is compatible with his behavior toward Tammy, then it is simply one vivid way Jim can reveal his intention to work through problems and sustain the relationship. But, again, we must be careful not to construe his intention as some inner experience which only Jim can discern. Rather, his intention is nothing more than one of his deeper-disposing traits, a trait embodied in his behavior. That is why knowing his intentions enables others to reasonably predict how he will behave in the future.

Put differently, an explicit commitment (if genuine) is not a report, but a performative which is a constituent of a person's behavior. This visible, embodied commitment will make her more comfortable with him, less inclined to put on a face for him. Assuming the commitment is reciprocal, he will likewise be more comfortable and more honest with her. Since each will likely be more open and honest with the other, the relationship is more likely to survive.

Investment

An explicit public commitment is one way people invest in their relationships. It is a form of investment which naturally leads intimates to make still further investments in their close relationships. Intimates standardly invest in each other and in their relationships: they give intimates things of value (personal and monetary) and do things of value for and with them. Many of these investments are not straight-forwardly recoverable if the relationship falters. Consequently, the more intimates irretrievably invest in a relationship, the less likely they are to abandon it when troubles arise.

There is a sense, of course, in which all activities and all relationships involve some investment. Whenever I act – or interact – I invest at least my time; and time is not straightforwardly retrievable. However, when the action is strictly for personal gain, or the interaction is purely impersonal, then I invest something now simply in the hope of reaping a larger return later. Our investments in personal relationships, how-ever, are quantitatively and qualitatively greater than these minimal investments which constitute *all* action; personal investments have a depth and range which bring our lives together. When I spend time with a close friend, I am not merely investing my time in the hopes of securing a larger payoff later; I am not using my intimate as an indirect means to promoting my own interests. Rather I am investing time *in her*. If I share intimate details of my life with a close friend, I am giving myself *to her*. These investments are not retrievable; indeed, I never consider retrieving them.

When I invest myself in a close relationship, I behaviorally commit myself to that relationship: I have shown just how much the relation-ship means to me. I am saying, in effect: "I will bet all these invest-ments that our relationship will endure." Or, in more common language, I have put my investments where my mouth is. Thus, you have a vivid indication of the strength of my commitment. I have not idly claimed to "love, honor and cherish." Rather, I have issued an embodied, self-fulfilling prophecy. My investments now make it more difficult for me to extract myself from the relationship later.

Thus, making investments is a form of commitment with psycho-logical and moral bite. Their presence indicates a sincere interest in maintaining the relationship; their absence, a lack of commitment. If Jim and Tammy are in a relationship yet Jim is reluctant to invest in it, then Tammy can plausibly infer that Jim is not committed to the relationship, perhaps not even in the minimal sense that all people in personal relationships are committed to one another. If he were really committed to her and to their relationship, he would invest in it.

Marriage

A special form of commitment in our society is the commitment to another in marriage. Here one publicly pledges to stay with another, usually for life. Why is this pledge thought to be especially significant – so significant as to be established and protected by law? Is this a mere prejudice or blind adherence to social custom? Or are there reasons for socially and legally promoting and protecting marriage?

Once a life-long marriage was a goal of virtually everyone. Recently, though, it has come under fire, both in theory (from numerous critics) and in practice (from the decline of the nuclear family). Nonetheless, the idea of life-long marriage continues to be an important part of our culture, even if the role it plays is less important than previously thought. Are there reasons which might undergird the practice of marriage?

Clearly marriages differ from other close friendships in one significant respect: children are standardly born and reared within the former, but not the latter. The primary responsibility of caring for a child typically falls to the child's parents – those who are causally responsible for bringing the child into the world. Although one of the parents could provide that care, it is certainly easier if they share parental duties. Moreover, it would be unfair to require only one of the parents to provide financial and parental care. Finally, it is often traumatic for children to be separated from either parent. Thus, it is better, all things being equal, if the adults who parented the child stay together – for their own sakes, as well as for the sake of the child.

Furthermore, and partly because they often rear children, married couples typically live together. Thus, they must decide where to live, what sort of house to buy or rent, if, when, and where they will move, etc. All these decisions involve, at least in our culture, substantial financial ramifications for each of the parties. Many people will be unwilling to undertake these financial obligations if they think the relationship is transitory. That is, most people will be reluctant to move to a different town or assume a hefty mortgage if the future of their relationships is in doubt. Conversely, most people will make these important decisions more easily and more confidently if they are convinced their partners will work to maintain the relationships, even in the face of difficulties. Hence, there are potent reasons for thinking a genuine commitment to marriage may benefit both children and adults.

Companion friends

Friends, as well as lovers, can commit themselves to one another. Often this commitment is not stated explicitly; still less often is it stated publicly. Yet we are prone to think that good friends should stand by one another – even when one partner has mistreated the other, even when one partner has changed radically. There is unquestionably much to be said for sticking by one's friends through "hell or high water." Perhaps, though, the decision to support one's friends, even if they have changed radically, is more an indication of steadfastness than love. Or, perhaps more accurately, steadfastness indicates a rigid love rather than a historical love. To help explain why, let's look at the limits of commitment.

The Limits of Commitment

As I previously argued, life-long relationships are highly valuable. Some forms of commitment are derivatively valuable since they promote long-term relationships. Moreover, most of us desire long-term relationships: we like thinking someone will be there for us whenever we need her. All this seems relatively incontestable. However, many people transform the desire for long-term relationships into a desire for unconditional love; they transform the belief that long-term relationships are especially valuable into the belief that unconditional love is especially valuable. Religious leaders, philosophers, lovers, and poets have all extolled the virtues of unconditional love. Many follow Shakespeare in claiming that real love *must* be unconditional: "Love is not love which alters when it alteration finds." Genuine love, in this view, must be constant – despite even fundamental changes in the beloved.

It is difficult to deny the abstract appeal of unconditional love: it seems to provide emotional security from the winds of circumstance. But security comes at a cost. The nature of this cost comes into focus once we realize that unconditional love is rigid, not historical. A rigid love attaches unwaveringly to a particular individual, a particular organism. To say that Bridget loves Bernie rigidly (extensionally) is just to say she loves the organism referred to as "Bernie." Her love is rigidly tied to this organism, no matter how it behaves. Thus, it is not surprising that she loves Bernie come what may.

Consequently, a rigid love provides great security. But here we begin to see the cost of that security. As Amélie Rorty argues, if you love me no matter what (if you love me rigidly), then your love in no way depends on what I say or do (1993: 399–412). And if you love me no matter *what* I do, there is a sense in which you do not really love *me* at all. Or perhaps it would be more accurate to say that if Bridget loves Bernie no matter how he changes, then she does not love Bernie in a historical way.

However, that is no small admission. Historical love is based on reasons – and those reasons must refer to the beloved's traits – to who she really is. But if Bridget loves Bernie rigidly, she loves him no matter what his traits. To that extent, she does not love him for who he is. Or, more to the point, Bridget does not really love *him*. Perhaps, though, she does *rigidly* love him.

This explains why unconditional love, however desirable it might be in some respects, fails to satisfy many of the values of love (first cited in chapter 5). For instance, if you love me no matter how badly I behave, then my self-esteem will not be heightened from knowing that you love me. Your loving me will heighten my self-esteem only if I know you love me for who I am. Hence, unconditional love will not promote self-esteem. Neither is it likely to help me grow, mature, or develop. And, since these are the some of the most important values long-term relationships are thought to promote, then a rigid love, even if it persists "till death us do part," won't satisfy these significant values. This suggests a paradox: one of the reasons for wanting unconditional love is to gain the benefits of long-term relationships, yet long-term relationships yield these desirable benefits only if they are based on a historical love. A rigid love thus fails to achieve the very goals which initially motivated it.

Commitment and the Self

These deficiencies of rigid love give us still one more reason to favor the activity view of self set out in chapter 4. Close personal relationships – including long-term relationships – are most valuable if they are based on a historical love. And a historical love requires an activity view of the self. Once again we see that a proper understanding of the nature of the self has significant ramifications for our understanding of personal relationships, and that the nature of personal relationships can inform our understanding of the self (Parfit 1973: 144–6).

We can put this understanding to work in the current debate about commitment. Commitment to a historical love cannot be unconditional. But it can still be valuable. However, it would serve a different purpose than in a relationship based on rigid love. Here's how. It is a fundamental fact about persons that they change. What I am today, though a continuation of my earlier selves, is nonetheless different from these selves. The self who willed that certain things would happen, the self that made certain promises, is no more. Here's a personal example. As I mentioned earlier, I was once a strict literalist fundamentalist. Although I am no longer religious, neither am I particularly hostile to religion – I realize it has made numerous positive contributions to me and to the world. However, *that* self would have wished that it had died, rather than become *this* self. That is a radical change – but not, I suspect, all that unusual. Even lesser changes will nonetheless dramatically alter the shape of a historical relationship.

If we recognize the pervasiveness of change, then we can immediately see the difficulty which arises for unconditional, life-long commitment. Experience suggests that rigid love is perhaps not *all* that rigid. People are prone to abandon their relationships if the object of their love changes dramatically. The pervasiveness of change creates serious problems even for those interested in rigid love, albeit in a somewhat indirect manner. For even if Tammy decides to love Jim rigidly, her commitment to Jim *now* may be foreign to *her* in ten years: she may be noticeably different from the self who committed herself to him. It is not enough that the *object* of love must be rigid, the agent of a rigid love must be fixed as well. And, although we may be psychologically capable of overlooking changes in the beloved – especially if the beloved's characteristics were not the basis of our love – we will have more difficulty ignoring changes in ourselves. Furthermore, since

Tammy may change in ways Jim dislikes, then unless he also loves her rigidly, he may lose interest in her.

On the other hand, suppose Tammy and Jim know they will both change. What should they do if they want to have a long-term relationship? They should not merely verbally commit themselves to love forever. Rather they should act in ways which enhance the chances that they will love forever; they should invest in their relationship. Moreover, they should attend to the ways each of them changes. If they do, their chances of maintaining a long *and vital* relationship is considerably enhanced.

Conclusion

Selves are not unchangeable entities which decide now exactly what they will do into the indefinite future. That is why verbally announcing my intention to be your friend indefinitely is, if disconnected from my behavior, an empty gesture. Rather, the self is dynamic and constantly changing. Bare psychic intentions (utterance to ourselves about what we plan to do) about the indefinite future are, in and of themselves, inefficacious. Genuine intentions are embodied; these can make that future more likely. This is true not merely for personal relationships but in all our endeavors. For instance, I will not lose weight if I merely say to myself "I must lose weight." I will begin to lose weight only if I act in ways which are likely to lead me to lose weight, e.g. eating smaller meals, cutting back on my consumption of fat, etc. (Dewey 1988: 5).

This conclusion should not be surprising. Most of us know that the only relationships which persist (and are worth preserving) are those in which people behaviorally commit themselves to one another. That is, they act in ways which ensure they will regularly communicate with one another. On the other hand, many who engage in mere formal verbal commitments are not likely to have enduring relationships.

Since the traditional dualistic view of the self indicates that formal commitments are not only reasonable but sufficient, whereas an activity view of the self suggests that commitment is determined more by what we do than by what we say, then we have one more reason to favor the activity view of the self.

13

Morality and Personal Relationships

Throughout this book, I have made frequent reference to a wide range of moral issues: honesty, jealousy, sexual fidelity, commitment, paternalism, caring, etc. This suggests there is an intricate connection between morality and personal relationships. There is. Of course personal relationships do not always promote moral values, nor do people find all relationships salutary. Some friendships, marriages, and kin relationships are anything but healthy or valuable. We all know (and perhaps are in) some relationships which hinder personal growth, undermine moral values, and diminish both parties' happiness – in short, relationships which systematically undermine the values they should promote.

Arguably such relationships are not close in any robust sense of the term. Nonetheless, I think many of them are personal. They are personal inasmuch as each person loves the other as a specific, unique individual. However, they are not close inasmuch as the parties cannot or will not take the interests of the others as their own. I suspect many of these marginal relationships fail because they are founded on a rigid love. Rigid love, if you may recall, is tied to a particular organism, not to that particular person with specific, embodied characteristics. Since this form of love is indifferent to the beloved's particular characteristics, the lover is likely less sensitive to the beloved's interests, needs, and desires.

The presence of detrimental relationships, however, does not undermine the claim that personal relationships are intricately connected with morality. Throughout the book I have offered numerous examples which indicate the pervasiveness and breadth of this connection. Here I want to bring these disparate suggestions together to defend an Aristotelian-type two-pronged thesis: that (1) close personal relationships are likely to be formed and persist only among morally

194

good people, and that (2) close personal relationships are prerequisites for the development of morally good people.

Many people, I suspect, will think these claims are mistaken. Some will object to them on empirical grounds: they will claim that some corrupt people have close personal relationships, while some good people do not. Although I think this occurs far less often than the objectors might think, neither Aristotle's nor my account asserts that it is *impossible* for immoral people to be close friends – especially if the term "immoral" is construed weakly enough. Nor need either account claim it is impossible for those without close relationships to be morally good. What both accounts do suggest is that people who are moral are considerably more likely to have close personal relationships, and that the personal relationships of immoral people are in jeopardy.

Some philosophers reject my thesis on purely theoretical grounds. In their view, not only are morality and personal relationships not intricately connected, they are often diametrically opposed. It is not difficult to see why. Morality, as typically conceived, requires impartiality. The principle of impartiality (or the equal consideration of interests) specifies that we must treat all humans (creatures?) alike unless there is some general and morally relevant difference between them which justifies a difference in treatment. This principle is central to traditional ethical theory. According to J. L. Mackie, it is "in some sense beyond dispute" (1977: 83). The principle of impartiality does permit treating different people differently, but any difference in treatment must be justified by general features of the circumstances, so that others in like circumstances should act similarly (Singer 1971; Frankena 1973; Hare 1963). Specifically, impartiality forbids any deviation in one's moral duties because of one's "variable inclinations" (Gewirth 1978: 24) or "generic differences between persons" (Mackie 1977: 97). Put differently, "the class of persons alleged to be an exception to the rule cannot be a unit class" (Singer 1971: 87). Thus, a teacher should give equal grades to students who perform equally; unequal grades are justified only if there is some general and relevant reason which justifies that difference. For example, it is legitimate to give a better grade to a student who does superior work; it is illegitimate to give her a better grade because she is pretty, wears pink, or is named "Molly."

On the other hand, personal relationships are partial to the core: the subject of attention is *always* "a unit class" – ". . . its particular focus [is] the unique concatenation of wants, desires, identity, history, and so on, of a particular person" (Friedman 1993: 190–1). That is why personal relationships (which have partiality at their core) clash with morality, typically conceived (which has impartiality at its core). How, if at all, can this conflict be resolved? (1) Is there some way to show that the conflict is more apparent than real? (2) If not, does morality supersede the demands of personal relationships? (3) Or do the demands of personal relationships supersede those of morality? If not, (4) can we have an adequate morality without the principle of impartiality? (Rachels 1988). I shall briefly canvass each response.

Three Responses

The conflict is only apparent

A common – and once the standard – move is to claim that morality and personal relationships do not really conflict. Those who embrace this view claim the partiality of personal relationships is explained and justified by impartial moral principles. Those who take this tack point out that the principle of equal consideration of interests is not a substantive moral principle: it does not specify exactly how anyone is to be treated. As a formal principle it requires only that we treat people the same unless there is some general and relevant reason which justifies a difference in treatment.

Those who embrace this view further claim that the general and relevant reason why I should treat Eva (my wife) better than I treat Phyllis (a stranger) is simply that she is my wife. That is, I should treat my wife – whoever she turns out to be – better than I treat strangers. Thus, were Phyllis my wife and Eva a stranger, then I should treat Phyllis better than I treat Eva. I should also treat my friends, children, and kin better than I treat strangers. Likewise you should treat your friends, children, and kin better than you treat strangers – including strangers who happen to be my intimates. The moral rule which justifies partiality toward intimates is itself impartial; it does not make any reference to specific individuals. The rule impersonally allows (requires?) *everyone* to treat intimates better than they treat strangers. Consequently, the demands of morality and of personal relationships do not conflict, appearances to the contrary.

Is this a satisfactory resolution? "Being an intimate" *is* a general characteristic; it does not make reference to any specific individual. But not all general characteristics are morally relevant. After all, a racist's principles are general. She claims all white people should be treated better than all non-white people. "It would even apply to me," she might say, "if I were non-white. The fact that I happen to be white does not show the principle is unacceptable." The problem, of course, is that although skin color is undoubtedly a general characteristic, it is not morally relevant (Wasserstrom 1971). Skin color is a biological characteristic unrelated to personal characteristics (e.g. character) that are morally relevant. It is difficult to even imagine a plausible reason one could give for thinking skin color is morally relevant.

On the other hand, it is easy to see why someone might think intimacy is morally relevant. "Being an intimate" appears to be not only a general characteristic, but also morally relevant. Intimate relationships generally promote honesty, caring, loyalty, self-knowledge, patience, empathy – significant values by anyone's lights. Indeed, intimate relationships – which are partial to the core – may be uniquely able to promote these values. Hence, so the argument goes, partiality toward intimates is morally legitimate; after all, it is justified by impartial moral principles. The apparent conflict evaporates.

In this view, close personal relationships are akin to the relationships between professionals and their clients. *My* doctor should pay special attention to my medical needs and *your* doctor should pay special attention to yours. Why? That is the best way for each of us to receive sound medical care. If each doctor tried to care equally for the needs of all people, then likely none of us would receive adequate care. That is why we not only permit but expect physicians to be partial. A physician's partiality toward her patients is thus justified by impartial principles. Similarly, close personal relationships are the best way to promote certain important values. That is why we not only permit but expect intimates to be partial toward one another. Impartial moral principles permit partiality between intimates.

There is considerable insight in this maneuver; but it is inadequate as it stands. Many people would deny that intimacy is, as this view implies, only derivatively valuable. Moreover, even if this maneuver could resolve the apparent tension between morality and personal relationships a parallel problem emerges when thinking about how we should treat specific intimates. The previous arguments explain that, since intimacy is a general and morally relevant characteristic, it is legitimate to treat intimates better than we treat strangers. But that explanation implies that we should treat all intimates the same unless there is some general and relevant reason that justifies our treating them differently. Yet most of us assume it is legitimate to treat different friends (and different kin) differently. However, there is no feasible way to provide impartial (i.e. general and relevant) reasons which would justify *these* differences in treatment.

Morality trumps personal interests

Those who embrace the second option likewise think that (1) moral principles must be impartial, and that (2) impartial moral principles can justify some partiality toward intimates. That is, they think we have special duties to family and friends; and these partial duties are themselves justified by impartial moral principles. However, unlike proponents of the previous view, they think morality and personal relationships do sometimes conflict – and that, when they do, the demands of morality are more compelling. Since close relationships are derivatively justified, when the demands of personal relationships conflict with the impartial moral principles which justify them, then the demands of morality are always more weighty. "Universal love is a higher ideal than family loyalty, and . . . the obligation within families can be properly understood only as particular instances of obligations to all mankind" (Rachels 1988: 46).

What this means in concrete terms is that we are not morally justified in treating intimates as preferentially as most of us are wont to do. Impartial moral principles likely justify parents' giving preferential care to their children, much as they justify people in institutional roles (police officers, judges, doctors, or lifeguards) treating people under their care preferentially. That is the best system for giving children maximum care and preparing them for life as adults. But, Rachels argues, we cannot justifiably give so much preferential care that we ignore the needs of other well-off children.

For instance, although physicians should give preferential care to their patients, they are not justified in ignoring a bleeding person by the side of the road. Likewise, we cannot heap trivial benefits on our children or friends, while completely ignoring the needs of strangers. Partial personal relationships of some stripe are extremely valuable – and are thus justified by impartial moral principles. However, close relationships which are morally justified cannot be *fundamentally* partial since their partiality is justified derivatively. The scope for legitimate impartiality is limited.

This view will likely strike most readers as wrong. In unqualified form I think it is wrong. Wrong, but not nonsense. It includes significant insights we should not ignore. Impartiality is vital to our understanding of morality: "something deeply important, that we should be reluctant to give up. It is useful, for example, in explaining why egoism, racism, and sexism are morally odious, and if we abandon this conception we lose our most natural and persuasive means of combatting these doctrines" (Rachels 1988: 48).

Moreover, although it is appealing to be able to lavish attention on those for whom we care, such attention seems at least tacky, and probably cosmically unfair, given that other people, through no fault of their own, are so poorly off. These other people's lives could be improved if we would spread our attention beyond our close friends and family. For instance, it seems unfair that Sarah can legitimately buy her child alligator shoes or her husband a $100,000 sports car while people living next door starve. Luck plays an inordinately large role in determining people's lot in life, and morality should attempt to diminish, if not eradicate, these undesirable effects of morally irrelevant luck (Rawls 1971: 101ff). That, most assuredly, is a significant insight of the impartialist view.

However, we should not wholeheartedly embrace impartialism. In its unqualified form this view does not merely indicate that we cannot have the depth and range of personal relationships we might want, it arguably entails that we cannot have close personal relationships at all. Here's why. Personal relationships are partial to the core: they are *always* focused on one single person – that is why we consider them so valuable. Rachels's view, however, rejects fundamentally partial relationships. His view suggests parents should care for children – and that we should act kindly toward our friends and spouses – not because we love them, but because morality demands it.

If that is a consequence of his view, then his view is untenable. It would undermine what is most precious about personal relationships, that intimates care for one another and want to spend time with each other, because of who they are, because of their specific personality traits. Knowing we are loved for who we are will, among other things, heighten our self-esteem. It will also increase the opportunities for personal and moral growth. If, however, others befriend us simply because morality requires it, then we lose these benefits of close personal relationships.

Perhaps, though, there is a way to salvage both an impartial morality *and* genuinely partial personal relationships. Doing so, however, requires showing how impartial moral principles might *justify* personal relationships, even though the *motives* for acting within the relationships would be fully partial. I think we can show this, and thereby preserve – albeit in somewhat attenuated form – the best of impartialism and personal relationships. But a full description and defense of that view must be delayed until I canvass the third option.

Non-moral values occasionally trump moral requirements

Several prominent philosophers, most notably Thomas Nagel (1979; 1986), Michael Stocker (1990), Bernard Williams (1981) and Susan Wolf (1982) have argued not only that impartial moral theories are incompatible with the partiality of personal relationships, but also that non-moral concerns sometimes (frequently? always?) trump moral concerns.

Though the arguments each offers for these views differ, each concludes there are two radically different perspectives from which a person can determine how she should behave. She should determine how any rational agent should act, or she should determine how she – with her particular interests and relationships – should act. These philosophers claim the second perspective is often the most compelling: that close relationships and personal projects often take precedence over the demands of an impartial morality.

Williams offers the following case to illustrate his point. Suppose two people are drowning and a rescuer can save only one of them. It so happens that one is the rescuer's wife. Should the rescuer be impartial between these potential victims and decide whom to save by some impartial means, for example by flipping a coin? No. He should straightforwardly save his wife. That choice, Williams claims, requires no further justification.

Williams point, I take it, is not that the impartialist cannot provide the right prescription in this case (although in some cases Williams thinks just that). Rather he claims the impartialist will give the wrong reasons even if she gives the right answers.

The consideration that it was his wife is certainly, for instance, an explanation which should silence comment. But something more ambitious than this is usually intended [in someone's saying that he was justified in his action], essentially involving the idea that moral principle can legitimate his preference, yielding the conclusion that in situations of this kind it is at least all right (morally permissible) to save one's wife. . . . But this construction provides the agent with one question too many: it might have been hoped by some (for instance, his wife) that his motivating thought, fully spelled out, would be the thought that it was his wife, not that it was his wife and that in situations of this kind it is permissible to save one's wife (1981: 18).

Williams claims that when close personal relationships are at stake, it is inappropriate to guide (or even think we should guide) our actions by impartial moral standards. Our personal projects, including our commitments to friends and family, will occasionally trump moral standards. Without such relationships and projects, Williams asserts, "there will not be enough substance or conviction in a man's life to compel allegiance to life itself" (18). Put differently, if life is to be meaningful, we cannot guide our lives by principles which subvert close relationships or personal projects. And that, he asserts, is exactly what impartial moral principles do.

Certainly Williams's view strikes a responsive chord in most of us: we sometimes think personal interests should take precedence over the needs of strangers. Yet we can also see the intellectual and moral appeal of Rachels's view. Our personal interests and relationships should not always take precedence over the demands of morality – for example, should Williams save his wife from drowning rather than defuse a nuclear bomb which is about to devastate New York? (Even those who might think it obvious that he should save his wife would presumably recognize this is a question with undisputed moral dimensions.) Hence, it would be ideal if we could find some way to show that a proper understanding of both morality and personal relationships are not necessarily at odds, but actually mutually supportive.

The Fourth Response: the Interplay of Morality and Personal Relationships

Ideal, but difficult. For, as I mentioned earlier, they do appear to be at odds. Sometimes when moral concern for strangers conflicts with concern for those we love we assume concern for our intimates should take precedence. Yet giving unbridled preference to our intimates appears to conflict with the principle of impartiality, and that principle lies at the heart of our ordinary moral understanding. Perhaps, though, these views are not as far apart as we first supposed, not even for the advocates of each. Rachels, for example, acknowledges the importance of personal relationships; indeed, he sees them as ineliminable elements of the moral scheme. However, he thinks concern for our intimates should not blind us to the legitimate needs of strangers. Specifically, he decries the callousness we sometimes show when we become preoccupied with our intimates or with our projects.

And, although Williams claims concern for our intimates should take precedence over impartial moral demands, he relies on some form of impartialism to explain his misgivings with impartialism. Let me explain. Williams claims a man can save his wife rather than a stranger, even if impartialist principles suggest otherwise. Yet his commentary on the case indicates that he believes something stronger than this, that it would be positively *wrong* for the man to save a stranger rather than his wife – and it would be wrong regardless of his reasons for doing so.

Suppose my "personal project" were to be impartial. Therefore, I decide whom to save using some impartial means, perhaps flipping a coin. I suspect Williams would think it would be wrong for me to save the stranger instead of my wife, even if that were what my personal project required. That is, he thinks *any* person should save his spouse instead of a stranger. And this belief reflects some impartial principle. Of course, as Williams notes, it would be most infelicitous were the man to announce this principle (even to himself) while rescuing his wife. But that only shows that the principle does not – and should not – consciously motivate his actions. It in no way shows that impartialist principles do not *justify* the action. Indeed, as I suggested earlier, distinguishing between the motive and justification for an action may help us reconcile these seemingly opposed positions.

Why an accommodation is difficult

But an accommodation will not be easy. For there are elements of traditional morality which make it more likely to conflict with personal relationships. Specifically, widely held views of morality: (1) construe moral rules legalistically and, therefore, (2) give limited scope to moral judgement. Moreover, they (3) have a narrow understanding of moral motivation and are, therefore, (4) unconcerned about how people can develop the appropriate moral motivation.

Immanuel Kant, as traditionally interpreted, embodies just such a view of morality. Kant apparently embraces a legalistic view of morality according to which moral rules uniquely determine what we ought to do – at least they uniquely determine what Kant deems our "perfect duties" (1981: 30–3). Legalistic views naturally leave little room for moral judgement: moral agents need judge only how to apply the exceptionless moral rules. Moreover, those who embrace such views are relatively unconcerned about how to make people behave morally. Kant claims, for instance, that an act is devoid of moral worth if we are motivated by self-interest or inclination (1981: 7–12). Put differently, an action has moral worth only if we are motivated exclusively by the desire to do our duty. He has no suggestions about how to inculcate the desire to do our duty. Indeed, he couldn't. It is not hard to see why: any suggestion would inevitably make reference to other motives (self-interest, inclination, love, etc.) and, on his view, it would be morally inappropriate to develop moral motives for non-moral reasons or by non-moral means.

In a series of influential articles (1993; 1985; 1983), Barbara Herman challenges this standard interpretation of Kant. However, even if Herman is correct, many people do interpret Kant in these ways; moreover, whether Kantian or not, it is a view many people do hold. Even William Frankena, who more than 20 years ago recognized the potential appeal of "virtue ethics," nonetheless describes the first job of morality as determining our "moral obligations" – where his examples of obligations are described in terms of specific actions we should perform (1973: 10–11).

However, this Kantian view of morality fails to give specific guidance about how we should behave in real-life situations. Moreover, this account makes it nigh impossible to understand or inculcate moral dispositions. To help understand these defects of a legalistic morality, I will borrow an example from an earlier paper. Suppose I have a friend who, some months ago, experienced a profound personal tragedy. How should I relate to her? Should I be a non-judgemental listener, sensitive to her continuing pain? Should I offer advice, even if it is not requested? Or should I simply ignore, or at least play down, the trauma to help her "get on with her life"?

Clearly it is desirable – though doubtless annoying – to have friends play these (and other) diverse roles. If everyone were a sensitive listener, she could get mired in her trauma. If everyone offered her unsolicited advice, she could lose her self-respect. If everyone refused to discuss the trauma, she might never be able to satisfactorily resolve it. A mixture of reactions is not simply permissible, it may well be crucial for her recovery. One response will not help her (LaFollette 1991: 148–9).

Hence no general rule will tell me what I should do. I must judge what I, with my particular temperament and abilities, can best do to respond to her sensitively, given her needs and the character of our relationship. If I have inculcated sensitivity and kindness, I may act appropriately. Yet there is no precise description of what "acting appropriately" would be.

But on a traditional Kantian account of morality, abstract rules – not concrete moral judgement – should direct my action. In this view, the only role for judgement is to apply exceptionless moral principles – much like a referee. The rules of the football game may be variously interpreted and, even if the rule is unambiguous, its application in a particular case may be uncertain. Therefore, someone must apply those rules: that is the referee's task. Likewise for ethics in the traditional view. Ethical rules are exceptionless; but agents must apply them to individual circumstances. That is the (only) proper role of moral judgement.

However, this analogy gives inadequate scope to judgement. In football there are clearly delineated rules all referees must follow. Moral agents, however, do not merely apply rules, certainly not in the case under discussion. It *might* be tempting to say that all her friends are following a rule, perhaps one like: "Be loving to your intimates." However, this is not a rule, at least not one comparable to the rules of football. It is vague. (A comparably vague, and thus totally useless, rule in football might be: "Play fairly.") This rule has no content. Any attempt to give it precise content will either fail, yield an unacceptable rule, or reduce to some more precise rule. Consequently, since this case describes moral choices people frequently do face, then this Kantian account of moral judgement will be inadequate to the task.

Relatedly, this standard view is relatively indifferent about what motivates people to be moral and how they can become moral. Admittedly some traditional theorists are quite concerned about moral education and morality. For instance, J. S. Mill, who is often portrayed as endorsing a rule conception of morality, recognizes the importance of judgement and the need for moral education:

> As the means of making the nearest approach to this ideal, utility would enjoin, first, that laws and social arrangements should place the happiness . . . of every individual, as nearly as possible in harmony with the interest of the whole; and secondly, that education and opinion, which have so vast a power over human character, should so use that power as to establish in the mind of every individual an indissoluble association between his own happiness and the good of the whole; . . . so that not only he may be unable to conceive the possibility of happiness to himself, consistently with conduct opposed to the general good, but also that a direct impulse to promote the general good may be in every individual one of the habitual motives of action (1979: 17).

In fact, a growing number of philosophers are concerned about moral development (Flanagan 1991; Thomas 1991). Embedded in a richer understanding of moral development and moral psychology we will find an account of morality that both supports and is informed by personal relationships.

Moral habits

The key to understanding the interplay of morality and personal relationships is understanding that morality is, at its core, not a continuous series of choices, but a network of habits. By "habits" I do not mean some mere behavioral repetition, like biting one's nails. I follow Dewey in seeing habits as working adaptations of the organism with its environment. Habits are "that kind of human activity which is influenced by prior activity, which contains within itself a certain order of systemization of minor elements of action; which is projective, dynamic in quality, ready for overt manifestation; and which is operative in some subdued subordinate form even when not obviously dominating activity" (Dewey 1988: 39).

Most human activity is habitual. It couldn't be otherwise. We couldn't walk or write or drive or think if we had to consciously determine to take the next step, write the next word, apply the brakes, or add two numbers. Morality joins thinking, emotions, and work as habits. "Habit means special sensitiveness of accessibility to certain classes of stimuli, standing predilections and aversions, rather than bare recurrence of specific acts. It means will" (41).

For instance, thinking is generally thought to be the paradigm of a conscious, self-directed activity. Dewey and I would beg to differ: thinking is also a habit, albeit a complex one. A thoughtful person does not *decide* to think about an important issue, nor does she typically have to decide *how* to think about it. Her education and training make her sensitive to certain types of problems; they instill a disposition to think about those problems in a certain way. Emotions are also habits. Certain kinds of situations (or people) typically incite anger or desire or fear. I do not have to decide to become angry if someone attacks my child. I do so, and I do so habitually.

However, I wish to emphasize again: habits are not mere repetitions of behavior. Habits – at least those of interest here – are very fine-grained: they prompt different responses to different situations. For instance, the habit of thinking does not require that we think about all problems in exactly the same way. The habit can be sufficiently complex and supple so that we make suitable adjustments in the *way* we think about a problem, depending on the nature of that problem.

Morality – like thinking – is not some mysterious and inexplicable practice of abstract rational contemplation, but a complex habit. To treat morality as primarily the conscious adherence to a set of rules inevitably spells its failure. If in each and every case we had to consciously decide to be moral, we would be even less moral than we are. Moral education (whether by others or by ourselves) is successful if we become habitually sensitive to the needs and interests of others. That is, if we are moral we do not have to decide to consider the interests of others, we just will consider their interests. And, since moral habits, like habits of thought, can be very complex, very fine-grained, they empower us to respond sensitively to others in a variety of circumstances.

Once we appreciate the habitual nature of morality, the weakness of Kant's views (as traditionally understood) becomes apparent. We are not – nor could we be – moral if, on each and every occasion, we had to (1) decide what was morally relevant, (2) decide to fully consider all that is morally relevant, and (3) decide to act upon the results of our deliberations. Rather, if we are moral we do habitually what we should do (Aristotle 1985: 34). A truly moral person is not forced to act morally; rather it is something she does by inclination – it is part of her; that is, it is one of her habits, one of her deeper-disposing traits.

Of course to acknowledge that morality is a habit does not mean we need never deliberate, nor does it imply that we need never act against our current habits (although the ability to abandon or modify a current habit is, itself, a different type of habit, a meta-habit if you will). As Kant rightly points out, morality sometimes demands that we act against our inclinations. Modifying our habits so that we are inclined to do what we ought is a crucial element of morality. Unfortunately, many of us do not have the strength – or the sufficiently ingrained meta-habits – to do that. My point here is simply that *most* behavior – including moral behavior – is habitual. Thus, if we do not have deeply ingrained and finely textured moral habits, then we will behave immorally.

Inculcating moral habits

Once we see that morality is a habit, we are better equipped to understand two ways in which morality and personal relationships are supportive: (1) close personal relationships give us the knowledge and the motivation to develop impartial moral habits; and (2) intimacy flourishes in an environment which impartially recognizes the needs and interests of all. Understanding these connections will not dissolve the tensions between impartial moral demands and close personal relationships, but it will certainly make them more amenable to resolution.

For instance, close personal relationships can empower us to act morally, they are grist for the moral mill. Ethical theorists disagree about the extent of our concern for others, but all agree we should morally consider, even promote, the interests of others. But how do we learn how to promote others' interests? How do we become motivated to promote those interests? These are questions Kant does not ask; indeed, he couldn't. But they are questions we should ask.

Suppose, for example, you are standing next to someone who has an epileptic seizure, but you have never heard of epilepsy, let alone witnessed a seizure. Or suppose you are stranded on an elevator with someone having a heart attack, but you don't know people have hearts, let alone that they can malfunction. In short, try to imagine that you were in one of these circumstances when you were seven years old. You would do nothing. Or if you tried, it would likely do more harm than good; any success would surely be serendipitous.

It is difficult to imagine how we could develop the knowledge necessary to act morally had we not been in personal relationships. No one knows how to do mathematics or to play football without acquaintance with the discipline or the game. So why should we think we could know how to promote the interests of others if we had no close acquaintance with others? Someone reared by uncaring parents, who never established close personal ties with her peers, will be unlikely to know how to look after or promote the interests of intimates or strangers. We cannot promote interests we cannot identify, and the way we learn to identify the interests of others is by interacting with them. Most of us learned from our parents how to recognize the needs of others. Our parents comforted us when we were hurt; they laughed with us when we were happy. Eventually, we learned to identify their and our siblings' interests.

Equally importantly, that is likely how we learned to be concerned about the interests of others. Indeed, unless we had personal relationships, it is difficult to know how we would be motivated to care for others. Though I expect we may have *some* biologically inherited sympathetic tendencies, these wither unless others care for us, and we for them. If we are not motivated to promote the needs of our families or friends, how can we be motivated to promote the needs of strangers?

On the other hand, if we develop empathy toward our friends, we will have some inclination to generalize it to others. In close relationships we become so vividly aware of our intimates' needs that we are willing to help them, even when it is difficult to do so. Since empathy tends to be non-specific, by learning to respond to the interests of friends we learn to respond to the interests of acquaintances and even strangers.

My point is not simply that a person must have some exposure to loving, personal relationships in order to know how to care and to be motivated to care. There is also a strong correlation between the *extent* of our involvement in close relationships and the extent of our ability and motivation to care for strangers. That is, if we have had numerous close relationships, our moral horizons will be wider than if we had only one. We will learn how to respond to different intimates' needs, in a variety of circumstances. We will learn what causes them pain. And we will learn how to ease their pain. Generally, we will learn the myriad ways we can promote the interests of others.

That is not to say that those who develop close relationships always come to care for strangers. My point is simply that a person needs some exposure to personal relationships to acquire the knowledge and motivation to be moral. Put differently, a person cannot be just or moral in a vacuum; she can become just only within an environment which countenances personal relationships.

On the other hand, an environment which recognizes the needs of strangers (i.e. an impartialist's morality) will be one in which intimacy is more likely to flourish. A society concerned about the needs and interests of everyone, including strangers, is one in which empathy, caring, and honesty, etc. are prized. And a society which prizes these behaviors will be one which thereby equips its citizens for close personal relationships.

We can see this clearly if we try to think about attempted personal relationships between non-moral people. Their relationships will be at risk. Morally wicked people cannot be close friends. I recognize this claim is rather controversial; many people would consider it patently false. I think, though, that is because they do not fully appreciate what it means to have a close relationship. Let me rehearse a number of arguments from throughout the book to support this claim.

First, in a close personal relationship each party must have, as one of her interests, an interest in the other. Thus, if Al and Frank are close personal friends, then one of Al's interests must be to promote Frank's interests, and one of Frank's interests is to promote Al's. Put differently, neither Frank nor Al can be entirely egoistic. Each must be concerned with something besides himself, i.e. his friend. But can a morally wicked person have such concerns? I don't see how. Moral wickedness is paradigmatically a complete disregard for the interests of others. (Of course not all evil in the world stems from morally wicked people. Arguably most evil stems from the ignorance and inattention of morally decent people. My point here, though, is not about the primary sources of evil, but about the troubles wicked people will have in establishing and maintaining close relationships.)

All this seems too easy. Surely even crooks and gangsters – whom we typically consider morally wicked – can have close friends. We do think this, but perhaps we shouldn't. If (and this is a big if) these people do have close relationships – if they really do care for other people – then, although they are doubtless immoral in some respects (as are we all) we should conclude that they are not completely wicked. They are good inasmuch as they really care about others. In fact, I suspect this is the right way to think about most criminals; the world is not neatly divided into "the good guys" and "the bad guys." We all have flaws and foibles. Even the worst person has good features and the most saintly person is riddled with faults.

However, let us think, for a moment, about two people who are paradigmatically evil, yet appear to be friends. Do these people have genuine friendships? My answer is a guarded "No." There are other plausible explanations for their seeming friendly behavior. Suppose Al and Frank are kingpins in organized crime. By all outward appearances they are the best of friends. They say they care for each other; they are friends. I would suggest, however, that they are friendly merely because they are afraid not to be. What makes them act amicably toward each other is not that each wishes the other well (one of the criteria of friendship). Rather it is that each thinks he can best promote his own interests by maintaining an air of friendship with the other.

But that air can be polluted suddenly if either thinks the other is in some way jeopardizing "the family business." Chronicles of gangland days in the United States are replete with cases where one boss would kill his best friend or even members of his family because they had violated some code. In these cases Frank and Al do not have a friendship; rather they have a role relationship supported by an unwritten code of conduct. What keeps the "relationship" together is not mutual well-wishing, but a fear of what will happen if either breaks that code. And that, most surely, is not at the center of close personal relationships.

We can understand the failure of these relationships in general terms by citing each person's exclusive attention to his own interests. There are, however, more fine-grained explanations. Close relationships, as I have argued throughout the book, are possible only inasmuch as each party trusts the other (chapter 8). Each must trust the other will not hurt or abuse her; each must trust the other to care for her. But trust cannot survive, let alone flourish, in an environment of distrust and hate.

Intimates must also be honest with one another; dishonesty will chip away at the foundations of the relationship (chapter 9). Yet people cannot be honest in the ways they need to be if they are immersed in a sub-culture built on dishonesty and deceit. Dishonesty, like all traits, is not something we can turn on and off. If we are dishonest with large numbers of people at work, we will be similarly inclined at home. Assuming Frank and Al are not stupid, they know that. That is why each will be cautious of the other; each will always be suspicious that the other is lying. And, to connect concerns about honesty with the previously mentioned concern about trust, we cannot really be honest with others unless we trust them. Mistrust constrains honesty.

In short, the possibility of genuine personal relationships is limited, if not eliminated, in an unjust environment. More especially, a person is unlikely to have close relationships unless she is moral. Anyone unconcerned with the welfare of other people, that is anyone who is amoral or immoral, will enter a relationship for her own benefit. Thus the relationship will not be personal in the relevant sense.

Consequently, personal relationships and morality are not at odds in the ways many philosophers have supposed. Rather, they are mutually supportive. Experience and involvement in close relationships will enhance our interest in and sympathy for the plight of others. Conversely, concern about the plight of the stranger will help us develop the traits necessary for close personal relationships.

Of course not everyone who has friends is concerned for strangers and not everyone who is concerned about strangers will be a good friend – though I suspect each will at least be capable of doing so. Nonetheless, these concerns could not exist in isolation. They are mutually supportive; they are not in constant conflict. Conflicts do arise. They arise in the same way that any moral conflicts arise; for instance, duties to two friends may conflict as may duties to two strangers. But such conflicts do not show that morality is impossible; they only show that it is sometimes difficult to achieve. But then, we already knew that.

Bibliography

American Psychiatric Association 1980: *Diagnostic and Statistical Manual of Mental Disorders* (3rd edn). Washington, DC: APA.

Argyle, M. 1972: *The Psychology of Interpersonal Behavior*. New York: Penguin.

Argyle, M. and Henderson, M. 1985: *The Anatomy of Relationships*. New York: Penguin.

Aristotle 1985: *Nicomachean Ethics*, Terrence Irwin (tr.). Indianapolis, IN: Hackett Publishing.

Arnold, M. and Gasson, J. 1968: Feeling and emotions as dynamic factors in personality integration. In M. Arnold and J. Gasson (eds), *The Nature of Emotion*. New York: Penguin.

Badhwar, N. 1993: Introduction. In N. Badhwar (ed.), *Friendship: A Philosophical Reader*. Ithaca, NY: Cornell University Press, 1–36.

—— 1987: Friends as ends in themselves. *Philosophy and Phenomenological Research*, **48**, 1–24.

—— 1985: Friendship, justice, and supererogation. *American Philosophical Quarterly*, **22**, 123–31.

Baier, A. 1988: Trusting ex-friends. In G. Graham and H. LaFollette (eds), *Person to Person*. Philadelphia: Temple University Press.

—— 1986: Trust and anti-trust. *Ethics*, **96**, 231–60.

Barber, B. 1983: *The Logic and Limits of Trust*. New Brunswick, NJ: Rutgers University Press.

Baron, M. 1991. Impartiality and friendship. *Ethics*, **101**, 836–57.

—— 1984a: On the alleged moral repugnance of acting from duty. *Journal of Philosophy*, **81**, 197–220.

—— 1984b: *The Moral Status of Loyalty*. Dubuque, IA: Kendell/Hunt.

Baumeister, R. 1996: *Identity: Cultural Change and the Struggle for Self*. Oxford: Oxford University Press.

Baxter, L. A. and Wilmot, W. W. 1985: Taboo topics in close personal relationships. *Journal of Social and Personal Relationships*, **2**, 253–69.

—— 1984: Secret tests: social strategies for acquiring information about the state of a relationship. *Human Communication Research*, **11**, 171–201.

Bedford, E. 1964: Emotion. In D. Gufstafson (ed.), *Essays in Philosophical Psychology*. New York: Doubleday.

Bell, R. 1981: *Worlds of Friendship*. Newbury Park, CA: Sage.

Berenson, F. M. 1981: *Understanding Persons*. Bloomington, IN: Harvester.

Bernstein, M. 1985: Love, particularity, and selfhood. *Southern Journal of Philosophy*, **23**, 287–93.

Bersheid, E. and Walster, E. 1969: *Interpersonal Attraction*. Reading, MA: Addison-Wesley.

Blum, L. 1980: *Friendship, Altruism, and Morality*. New York: Routledge.

Bok, S. 1978: *Lying*. New York: Vintage.

Brentano, F. 1960: Psychology from an empirical standpoint. In R. Chisholm (ed.), *Realism and the Background of Phenomenology*. New York: The Free Press, 39–61.

Bringle, R. 1991: The psychological aspects of jealousy: a transactional model. In P. Salovey (ed.), *The Psychology of Jealousy and Envy*. New York: Guilford Press, 103–30.

Bruner, J. and Postman, L. 1949: On the perception of incongruity: a paradigm. *Journal of Personality*, **18**, 206–23.

Bryson, J. 1991: Modes of response to jealousy evoking situations. In P. Salovey (ed.), *The Psychology of Jealousy and Envy*. New York: Guilford Press, 178–207.

Cacioppo, J., Berntsen, G. and Klein, D. 1992: What is an emotion? In M. Clark (ed.), *Emotion and Social Behavior*. Newbury Park, CA: Sage.

Carlson, N. 1988: *Discovering Psychology*. Boston: Allyn and Bacon.

Cherlune, G. J. 1976: *Self-Disclosure*. San Francisco, CA: Jossey-Bass.

Churchland, P. 1979: *Scientific Realism and the Plasticity of Mind*. Cambridge: Cambridge University Press.

Clark, M. (ed.) 1992: *Emotion and Social Behavior*. Newbury Park, CA: Sage.

—— 1985: Perceptions of exploitation in communal and exchange relationships. *Journal of Social and Personal Relationships*, **2**, 403–18.

—— 1984: Record-keeping in two types of relationships. *Journal of Personality and Social Psychology*, **47**, 549–57.

—— 1979: Interpersonal attraction in exchange and communal relationships. *Journal of Personality and Social Psychology*, **37**, 12–24.

Conway, M. and Ross, M. 1984: Getting what you want by revising what you had. *Journal of Personality and Social Psychology*, **47**, 738–48.

Cooper, J. 1980: Aristotle on friendship. In A. Rorty (ed.), *Aristotle's Ethics*. Berkeley: University of California Press.

Davidson, D. 1963: Actions, reasons, and causes. *The Journal of Philosophy*, **LX**, 685–700.

Dennett, D. 1978: *Brainstorms: Philosophical Essays on Mind and Psychology*. Cambridge, MA: MIT Press.

—— 1969: *Content and Consciousness*. New York: Routledge.

Derlega, V. J. and Chaiken, A. L. 1976: *Shared Intimacy*. Englewood Cliffs, NJ: Prentice-Hall.

Descartes, R. 1972: The passions of the soul. In E. Haldane and G. R. T. Ross (tr.), *The Philosophical Works of Descartes*, vol. 1. Cambridge: Cambridge University Press.

Dewey, J. 1988: *Human Nature and Conduct*. Carbondale, IL: Southern Illinois University Press.

—— 1929: *The Quest for Certainty*. New York: Modern Library.

Dilman, I. 1987: *Love and Human Separateness*. Oxford: Blackwell.

Duck, S. 1991: *Understanding Relationships*. New York: Guilford Press.

Duck, S. 1986: *Human Relationships: An Introduction to Social Psychology*. Newbury Park, CA: Sage.

—— (ed.) 1984: *Personal Relationships*, vol. 5: *Repairing Personal Relationships*. San Diego, CA: Academic.

—— 1983: *Friends for Life*. New York: St. Martin's.

—— (ed.) 1982: *Personal Relationships*, vol. 4: *Dissolving Personal Relationships*. San Diego, CA: Academic.

—— 1977: *The Study of Acquaintance*. New York: Saxon.

Duck, S. and Gilmour, R. (eds) 1981a: *Personal Relationships*, vol. 1: *Studying Personal Relationships*. San Diego, CA: Academic.

—— (eds) 1981b: *Personal Relationships*, vol. 2: *Developing Personal Relationships*. San Diego, CA: Academic.

—— (eds) 1981c: *Personal Relationships*, vol. 3: *Personal Relationships in Disorder*. San Diego, CA: Academic.

Dummet, M. 1978: *Truth and Other Enigmas*. Cambridge, MA: Harvard University Press.

Ellis, C. and Weinstein, E. 1986: Jealousy and the social psychology of emotional experience. *Journal of Social and Personal Relationships*, **3**, 337–57.

Elliston, F. 1984: In defense of promiscuity. In R. Baker and F. Elliston (eds), *Philosophy and Sex*. Buffalo, NY: Prometheus.

Elster, J. (ed.) 1985: *The Multiple Self*. Cambridge: Cambridge University Press.

Fadiman, J. and Frager, R. 1994: *Personality and Personal Growth*. New York: Harper Collins.

Faludi, S. 1991: *Backlash*. New York: Crown Publishers.

Farrell, D. 1988: Jealousy and envy. In G. Graham and H. LaFollette (eds), *Person to Person*. Philadelphia: Temple University Press.

—— 1980: Jealousy. *Philosophical Review*, **89**, 527–59.

Feinberg, J. 1980: The child's right to an open future. In W. Aiken and H. LaFollette (eds), *Whose Child? Children's Rights, Parental Authority, and State Power*. Totowa, NJ: Rowman and Allenheld.

Flanagan, O. 1991: *Varieties of Moral Personality*. Cambridge, MA: Harvard University Press.

Frankena, W. 1973: *Ethics*. Englewood Cliffs, NJ: Prentice-Hall.

Freud, S. 1989: *The Freud Reader*. P Gay (ed.). New York: W. W. Norton.

Fried, C. 1970: *An Anatomy of Value*. Cambridge, MA: Harvard University Press.

Friedman, M. 1993: *What Are Friends For?* Ithaca, NY: Cornell University Press.

—— 1991: Practice of partiality. *Ethics*, **101**, 818–35.

—— 1986: Justice among friends. American Philosophical Association, Eastern division.

Fromm, E. 1957: *The Art of Loving*. New York: Allen & Unwin.

Gewirth, A. 1978: *Reason and Morality*. Chicago: University of Chicago Press.

Gilligan, C. 1982: *In a Different Voice: Psychological Theory and Women's Development*. Cambridge, MA: Harvard University Press.

Gordon, R. 1987: *The Structure of Emotion*. Cambridge: Cambridge University Press.

—— 1980: Fear. *Philosophical Review*, **89**, 560–78.

—— 1974: The aboutness of emotion. *American Philosophical Quarterly*, **11**, 27–36.

Graham, G. 1988: Love, marriage, and commitment. In G. Graham and H. LaFollette (eds), *Person to Person*. Philadelphia: Temple University Press.

Graham, G. and LaFollette, H. (eds) 1988: *Person to Person*. Philadelphia: Temple University Press.

Greenspan, P. 1988: *Emotions and Reasons: An Inquiry into Emotional Justification*. New York: Routledge.

Hardwig, J. 1988: Towards an ethics of personal relationships. In G. Graham and H. LaFollette (eds), *Person to Person*. Philadelphia: Temple University Press.

—— 1984: Should women think in terms of rights. *Ethics*, **94**, 441–55.

—— 1981: *Moral Thinking*. Oxford: Oxford University Press.

Hare, R. M. 1963: *Freedom and Reason*. Oxford: Oxford University Press.

Hatfield, E. and Traupmann, J. 1981: Intimate relationships and equity theory. In S. Duck and R. Gilmour (eds), *Personal Relationships*, vol. 1: *Studying Personal Relationships*. San Diego, CA: Academic.

Heider, F. 1958: *The Psychology of Interpersonal Attraction*. New York: Wiley.

Hendrick, C. and Hendrick, S. 1982: *Liking, Loving, and Relating*. Belmont, CA: Wadsworth Publishing.

Hendrick, C., Hendrick, S., Foote, F. and Slapion-Foote, M. 1984: Do men and women love differently? *Journal of Social and Personal Relationships*, **1**, 177–95.

Herman, B. 1993: *The Practice of Moral Judgement*. Cambridge, MA: Harvard University Press.

—— 1985: The practice of moral judgement. *Journal of Philosophy*, **82**, 414–36.

—— 1983: Impartiality and integrity. *The Monist*, **66**, 233–50.

—— 1981: On the value of acting from the motive of duty. *Philosophical Review*, **90**, 359–92.

Hinde, R. 1981: The bases of a science of interpersonal relationships. In S. Duck and R. Gilmour (eds), *Personal Relationships*, vol. 1: *Studying Personal Relationships*. San Diego, CA: Academic.

—— 1979: *Toward Understanding Relationships*. San Diego, CA: Academic.

Hunter, J. F. M. 1980: *Thinking about Sex and Love*. New York: St. Martin's Press.

Isenberg, A. 1980: Natural pride and natural shame. In A. Rorty (ed.), *Explaining Emotions*. Berkeley: University of California Press.

Johnson, M. 1982: Social and cognitive features of dissolving commitment to relationships. In S. Duck (ed.), *Personal Relationships*, vol. 4: *Dissolving Personal Relationships*. San Diego, CA: Academic.

Jones, E. and Gordon, E. 1972: Timing of self-disclosure and its effects on personal attraction. *Journal of Personality and Social Psychology*, **24**, 358–65.

Jourard, S. 1964: *The Transparent Self*. New York: Van Nostrand.

Kant, I. 1981: *Grounding for the Metaphysics of Morals*, J. W. Ellington (tr.). Indianapolis, IN: Hackett Publishing.

Kelley, H. 1979: *Personal Relationships: Their Structures and Processes*. Hillsdale, NJ: Lawrence Erlbaum.

Kierkegaard, S. 1962: *Works of Love*. New York: Harper & Row.

Kraut, R. 1986: Love de re. In P. French, T. Uehling Jr and H. Wettstein (eds), *Midwest Studies in Philosophy*. Minneapolis: University of Minnesota Press.

Kuhn, T. 1962: *The Structure of Scientific Revolutions*. Chicago: University of Chicago Press.

LaFollette, H. 1991: The truth in ethical relativism. *Social Philosophy*.

LaFollette, H. 1988: The truth in psychological egoism. In J. Feinberg (ed.), *Reason and Responsibility*. Belmont, CA: Wadsworth Publishing,

——1982: Applied philosophy misapplied. In N. Rescher et al. (eds), *The Applied Turn in Contemporary Philosophy*. Bowling Green, OH: Bowling Green State University Press.

LaFollette, H. and Graham, G. 1986: Honesty and intimacy. *Journal of Social and Personal Relationships*, **3**, 3–18.

Laing, R. D., Phillipson, H. and Lee, A. R. 1966: *Interpersonal Perception*. New York: Tavistock.

Lazarus, R. 1991: *Emotion and Adaptation*. Oxford: Oxford University Press.

Levinger, G. and Raush, H. L. 1977: *Close Relationships: Perspectives on the Meaning of Intimacy*. Amherst: University of Massachusetts Press.

Luhmanm, N. 1979: *Trust and Power*. New York: Wiley.

Lyons, W. 1980. *Emotion*. Cambridge: Cambridge University Press.

Mackie, J. L. 1977: *Ethics: Inventing Right and Wrong*. New York: Penguin.

Marsh, P. 1988: *Eye to Eye*. Topsfield, MA: Salem House.

Martin, M. 1993: Love's constancy. *Philosophy*, **68**: 63–77.

Maslow, A. 1973: *The Farther Reaches of Human Nature*. New York: Penguin.

——1968: *Towards a Psychology of Being*. New York: Van Nostrand.

——1966: *The Pscyhology of Science: A Reconnaissance*. New York: Harper & Row.

Mayeroff, M. 1971: *On Caring*. New York: Perennial Library.

Meilander, G. 1981: *Friendship: A Study in Theological Ethics*. Notre Dame, IN: University of Notre Dame Press.

Mercer, P. 1972: *Sympathy and Ethics*. Oxford: Oxford University Press.

Metts, S. et al. 1991: Redefining relationships. *Journal of Social and Personal Relationships*, vol. 6, no. 2.

Meyers, D. T. and Kittay, E. F. 1988: *Women and Moral Theory*. Totowa, NJ: Rowman and Allenheld.

Mill, J. S. 1979: *Utilitarianism*, G. Sher (ed.). Indianapolis, IN: Hackett Publishing.

——1978: *On Liberty*, E. Rapaport (ed.). Indianapolis, IN: Hackett Publishing.

Miller, G. (ed.) 1976: *Explorations in Interpersonal Communication*. Newbury Park, CA: Sage.

Miller, J. B. 1976: *Toward a New Psychology of Women*. Boston: Beacon.

Miller, R. and Leary, M. 1992: Social success and interaction: functions of emotion. In M. Clark (ed.), *Emotion and Social Behavior*. Newbury Park, CA: Sage, 202–21.

Mischel, T. (ed.) 1974: *Understanding Persons*. Oxford: Blackwell.

Montagu, A. (ed.) 1975: *The Practice of Love*. Englewood Cliffs, NJ: Prentice-Hall.

Montefiore, A. (ed.) 1973: *Philosophy and Personal Relations*. New York: Routledge & Kegan Paul.

Morgan, D. 1986: Personal relationships as an interface between social networks and social cognitions. *Journal of Social and Personal Relationships*, **3**, 403–22.

Nagel, T. 1991: *Equality and Partiality*. Oxford: Oxford University Press.

——1986: *The View from Nowhere*. Oxford: Oxford University Press.

——1979: *Mortal Questions*. Cambridge: Cambridge University Press.

Neu, J. 1977: *Emotion, Thought, and Therapy*. New York: Routledge & Kegan Paul.

Oatley, K. 1992: *Best Laid Schemes: The Psychology of Emotions*. Cambridge: Cambridge University Press.

Parfit, D. 1984: *Reasons and Persons*. Oxford: Oxford University Press.

—— 1973: Later selves and moral principles. In A. Montefiore (ed.), *Philosophy and Personal Relationships*. London: Routledge & Kegan Paul, 137–69.

Parrott, W. G. 1991: The emotional experiences of envy and jealousy. In P. Salovey (ed.), *The Psychology of Jealousy and Envy*. New York: Guilford Press, 3–30.

Pateman, C. 1980: The disorder of women: women, love, and the sense of justice. *Ethics*, **91**, 20–34.

Quine, W. 1960: *Word and Object*. Cambridge, MA: MIT Press.

—— 1953: Two dogmas of empiricism. In his *From a Logical Point of View*. New York: Harper & Row.

Rachels, J. 1988: Morality, parents, and children. In G. Graham and H. LaFollette (eds), *Person to Person*. Philadelphia: Temple University Press.

Rawls, J. 1971: *A Theory of Justice*. Cambridge, MA: Harvard University Press.

Raymond, J. 1986: *A Passion for Friends*. Boston: Beacon.

Reisenzein, R. 1983: The Schachter theory of emotion: two decades later. *Psychological Bulletin*, **2**, 239–64.

Rorty, A. 1993: The historicity of psychological attitudes: love is not love which alters not when it alteration finds. In N. Badhwar (ed.), *Friendship: A Philosophical Reader*. Ithaca, NY: Cornell University Press.

—— (ed.) 1980a: *Explaining Emotion*. Berkeley: University of California Press.

—— 1980b: Explaining emotion. In A. Rorty (ed.), *Explaining Emotions*. Berkeley: University of California Press.

Rorty, R. 1982: *Consequences of Pragmatism*. Minneapolis: University of Minnesota Press.

—— 1979: *Philosophy and the Mirror of Nature*. Princeton, NJ: Princeton University Press.

Ross, M. 1989: Relation of implicit theories in the constitution of personal histories. *Psychological Review*, **96**, 341–57.

Russell, B. 1981: *The Problems of Philosophy*. Oxford: Oxford University Press.

Ryle, G. 1966: *The Concept of Mind*. New York: Barnes & Noble.

Sabini, J. and Silver, M. 1982: *The Moralities of Everyday Life*. Oxford: Oxford University Press.

Sartre, J. P. 1971: *Sketch for a Theory of Emotions*. New York: Methuen.

Schachter, S. and Singer, J. 1962: Cognitive, social, and psychological determinants of emotional states. *Psychological Review*, **89**, 527–59.

Schoeman, F. 1985: Aristotle on the good of friendship. *Australasian Journal of Philosophy*, **63**, 269–82.

Scruton, R. 1986: *Sexual Desire: A Moral Philosophy of the Erotic*. New York: Free Press.

Sherman, N. 1989: *The Fabric of Character: Aristotle's Theory of Virtue*. Oxford: Clarendon Press.

Shoemaker, S. and Swinburne, R. 1984: *Personal Identity*. Oxford: Blackwell.

Singer, M. 1971: *Generalization in Ethics*. New York: Athenium.

Skinner, B. F. 1974: *About Behaviorism*. New York: Free Press.

—— 1953: *Science and Human Behavior*. New York: Macmillan.

Slote, M. 1982: Morality not a system of imperatives. *American Philosophical Quarterly*, **19**, 331–40.

Solomon, R. 1981: *Love: Emotion, Myth, and Metaphor*. New York: Doubleday.

Solomon, R. 1976: *The Passions: The Myth and Nature of Human Emotion.* New York: Doubleday.

Sommers, C. H. 1986: Filial morality. *Journal of Philosophy,* **83**, 439–56.

Steinberg, R. J. 1986: A triangular theory of love. *Psychological Review,* **93**, 119–35.

Stocker, M. 1990: *Plural and Conflicting Values.* Oxford: Clarendon Press.

—— 1981: Values and purposes: the limits of teleology and the ends of friendship. *Journal of Philosophy,* **78**, 747–65.

—— 1976: The schizophrenia of modern ethical theories. *Journal of Philosophy,* **73**, 453–66.

Taylor, G. 1980: Pride. In A. Rorty (ed.), *Explaining Emotions.* Berkeley: University of California Press.

Telfer, E. 1971: Friendship. *Proceedings of the Aristotelian Society,* 223–41.

Thalberg, I. 1977: *Perception, Emotion, and Action: A Component Approach.* Oxford: Blackwell.

Thibaut, J. and Kelley, H. 1959: *The Social Psychology of Groups.* New York: Wiley.

Thomas, L. 1989: *On Living Morally.* Philadelphia: Temple University Press.

—— 1988: Friends and lovers. In G. Graham and H. LaFollette (eds), *Person to Person,* Philadelphia: Temple University Press.

—— 1986: Friendship. *Synthese.*

—— 1985: Love and morality: the possibility of altruism. In J. Fetzer (ed.), *Sociobiology and Epistemology.* New York: D. Reidel, 115–29.

Titmuss, R. M. 1970: *The Gift of Relationship.* New York: Allen & Unwin.

Toffler, A. 1970: *Future Shock.* New York: Random House.

Tooley, M. 1972: Abortion and infanticide. *Philosophy and Public Affairs,* **2**, 37–59.

Tov-Rauch, L. 1980: Jealousy, attention and loss. In A. Rorty (ed.), *Explaining Emotions.* Berkeley: University of California Press.

Utne, M., Hatfield, E., Traupmann, J. and Greenberger, D. 1984: Equity, marital satisfaction, and stability. *Journal of Social and Personal Relationships,* **1**, 323–32.

Van de Vate, D. 1981: *Romantic Love: A Philosophical Inquiry.* State College: Pennsylvania State University Press.

Vannoy, R. 1980: *Sex Without Love: A Philosophical Exploration.* Buffalo, NY: Prometheus.

Waldron, J. 1993: When justice replaces affection: the need for rights. In his *Liberal Rights: Collected Papers 1981–1991.* Cambridge: Cambridge University Press.

Walster, E., Walster, G. and Berscheid, E. 1978: *Equity Theory and Research.* Boston: Allyn & Bacon.

Wasserstrom, R. 1977: Racism, sexism, and preferential treatment. *UCLA Law Review,* **24**, 581–622.

Watson, D. and Tharp, R. 1972: *Self-Directed Behavior: Self-Modification for Personal Adjustment.* Monterey, CA: Brooks/Cole.

White, A. 1970: *Truth.* New York: Anchor Books.

Wilkes, K. V. 1978: *Physicalism.* New York: Routledge & Kegan Paul.

Williams, B. 1981: Persons, character, and morality. In his *Moral Luck.* Cambridge: Cambridge University Press.

Wilson, T. D. and Klaaren, K. J. 1992: Expectations whirl me around: the role of affective expectation in affective experience. In M. Clark (ed.), *Emotion and Social Behavior.* Newbury Park, CA: Sage, 1–31.

Winch, R. 1958: *Mate Selection: A Study of Complimentary Needs.* New York: Harper & Row.

Wittgenstein, L. 1958: *Philosophical Investigations*, G. E. M. Anscombe (tr.). New York: Macmillan.

Wojtyla, K. 1981: *Love and Responsibility.* New York: Farrar, Straus & Giroux.

Wolf, S. 1982: Moral saints. *Journal of Philosophy*, **79**, 419–39.

Wright, G. H. von 1963: *The Varieties of Goodness.* New York: Routledge & Kegan Paul.

Wright, P. 1988: The nature and value of personal relationships. In G. Graham and H. LaFollette (eds), *Person to Person*, Philadelphia: Temple University Press.

—— 1984: Self-referent motivation and the intrinsic quality of friendship. *Journal of Social and Personal Relationships*, **1**, 115–30.

—— 1978: Toward a theory of friendship based on a conception of the self. *Human Communication Research*, **4**, 196–207.

Index

Printed in the USA
CPSIA information can be obtained
at www.ICGtesting.com
JSHW022146281223
54437JS00001B/31

9 780631 196853